JAGC-Off

Other works written by Jonathan P. Tomes:

Servicemember's Legal Guide, 5th ed., Harrisburg, PA: Stackpole Books, 2005.

Lawful Orders, Overland Park, KS: Veterans Press, 1998.

HIPAA Hysteria, Overland Park, KS: Veterans Press, forthcoming.

The Compliance Guide to HIPAA and the DHHS Regulations, 4th ed., Overland Park, KS: Veterans Press, 2010.

HIPAA Documents Resource Center CD, 4th ed., Overland Park, KS: Veterans Press, 2010.

Electronic Health Records: A Practical Compliance Guide, 2d ed., Overland Park, KS: Veterans Press, 2010.

Medical Records Retention Guide, 3d ed., Overland Park, KS: Veterans Press, forthcoming.

Basic HIPAA Training Video with Workbook, 2d ed., Overland Park, KS: Veterans Press, 2010.

JAGC-Off

A Politically Incorrect Memoir of the Real Judge Advocate General's Corps

A Novel By

Jonathan P. Tomes

VETERANS PRESS INC

This novel is a work of fiction. Any resemblance of any character to any person living or dead is purely coincidental.

Cover design: Jonathan P. Tomes
Print/bind: Network Business Products, Inc., Grandview, MO
Editing & internal design: Alice M. McCart

Published by
Veterans Press, Inc.
7111 W. 98th Terrace, Suite 140
Overland Park, KS 66212
Phone 913.341.8783
Fax 913.385.7997
Email jon@veteranspress.com
Website www.veteranspress.com

Printed in the United States of America

First Edition

First Printing

19 18 17 16 15 14 13 12 11 10 10 9 8 7 6 5 4 3 2 1

ISBN 1-880483-26-2 ISBN 978-1-880483-26-8

Dedication

To COL Michael I. Spak (USA, Retired).

For Reg,
Best wishes &
thanks for your
service!
Jon

Acknowledgments

Many people contributed to this novel, including, in no particular order, Colonel (Retired) Michael I. Spak, Colonel (Retired) James A. Wosepka, Colonel (Retired) James D. Mogridge, my law partner, Richard D. Dvorak, a former Marine, and Ike Money and Walter (Joe) Marm, who taught me how to be a soldier so that I could later be a JAGC-Off.

1

Give Me That Old Time Military Justice

"Black Belt—a white belt who never quit."
—Karate saying by unknown martial arts master

Ok, as a former Judge Advocate General's Corps officer, I've got a confession to make. I often watched the TV series JAG. Although it is not horribly accurate—no Navy JAG is going to tell the captain of an aircraft carrier what to do because a Navy captain of a combat ship or boat or whatever it is they insist you call it is the closest thing to God in the Armed Forces. And as in one episode, the Judge Advocate General (so-called even though he is actually an admiral in the Navy) is not going to defend the third-highest ranking Al Qaida terrorist. But the show is entertaining and very watchable, although I'm the real JAGC-Off, not some wimpy naval aviator. Where's his Combat Infantry Badge for standing up to the Viet Cong and North Vietnamese Army regulars as an Infantry platoon leader? Did he hold his ground when Judge Savage threw his gavel at him for objecting too strongly to the judge's ruling (see, I'm talking like a lawyer already)? No, all he did was land his jet on a pitching aircraft carrier deck at night.

Military justice, whether a contradiction in terms or not, initially seemed fairly simple to me. I entered active duty just one year before it got a whole lot more complicated with the adoption of the Manual for Courts-Martial, 1969 (Revised), which actually gave a military defendant some rights. My first exposure to military justice was during the first hour that I spent in my first actual unit. I had completed Infantry Officer Basic and Airborne School and was assigned to the 4th Battalion, 30th Infantry, the lone Infantry unit in school support of the Artillery School at Fort Sill, Oklahoma. Fort Sill was south of Oklahoma City and next to Lawton, which had the well-deserved distinction of being ranked as the worst city in the nation at that time. The Army had a policy that new second lieutenants had to have six months of troop duty before the Army could send them to Vietnam. Given the life expectancy of an Infantry lieutenant, no one except the most rabid, gung-ho, West Point graduate objected to this policy even if it landed him at Fort Sill.

Bad as Fort Sill was, I expected that it was better than the 'Nam. I later learned that the most miserable day out on the ranges firing mortars so that the Artillery School students could perform crater analysis was better than any day in Vietnam except your DEROS date (the Date you were Eligible to Return to OCONUS—the date you left for home). CONUS was the acronym for CONtinental United States. I forget what the first "O" stood for, but I wasn't going to volunteer to extend my tour in Vietnam to find out. But I get ahead of myself. Vietnam was after Fort Sill.

Fort Sill is pretty far south, but I've never been colder than out on the ranges as the January wind blew unchecked from the polar regions right into my face. No one at Fort Sill was shooting at me, however, while I was shivering in my inadequate field jacket out on the ranges. The biggest danger out on the ranges was dying of boredom while waiting for the next fire mission or choking to death on what was supposed to be hot coffee. At least, the cup warmed my fingers before the liquid in it cooled and became the consistency of motor oil with about the same taste. To this day, I can't drink coffee. Maybe if they had had Starbucks deliver (had it existed back then), I could have stood it, but the foodstuffs served by the aptly named "Roach Coaches" had to have been designed to make you tolerate C-rations once you got to Vietnam.

Upon reporting to the 4th of the 30th, I was assigned to Company B. The battalion adjutant told me that I was lucky because its commander, First Lieutenant Isaac Harris, was just back from Vietnam and was really "squared away." He had earned an excellent reputation as a platoon leader in the First Cavalry Division and, although very tough, was generally liked by his officers and troops because he was fair.

Feeling lucky to get a tough, but fair, commander, I walked down the sidewalk, past the well-manicured lawns with white-painted rocks around the trees, bushes, and military monuments and statutes, to Bravo Company. I bounded up the steps, feeling quite cocky in my pressed fatigues with my brand-spanking new Jump Wings over my left breast pocket and my highly shined jump boots. My cockiness lasted about five minutes.

The company clerk took a copy of my orders and led me down the hall to Lieutenant Harris's office. I knocked on the door and then walked in at the terse "Enter." I stepped around a soldier standing at attention in front of Lieutenant Harris, who was seated as his desk, and came to attention and saluted smartly. "Lieutenant Thomas reporting for duty, Sir!" An Army axiom was that there was no difference in rank between second and first lieutenants. But he was my commander, so I saluted.

Lieutenant Harris looked up from what he was reading and returned the salute, somewhat casually, I thought. I would later find myself returning salutes with the same casual flair, but only after I had seen some of the same combat that he had. My new commander was about my height, 6', but even skinnier than my 150 pounds. Proud as I was of my Jump Wings, they didn't hold a candle to the Combat Infantry Badge and First Cavalry Division combat patch on his perfectly pressed fatigues. He told me, many weeks later, that he had been impressed with my Jump Wings—he hadn't gone to Airborne School—believing that the wings showed that I had at least enough balls to jump out of a perfectly good airplane. He wasn't impressed, however, by my spit-shined boots. It would take me several months before I could even approach the perfect mirror shine that he had on his.

"Sit down, Lieutenant," he ordered. "I have some disciplinary matters to attend to."

"Yes, Sir," I replied in my best command voice, taking the only seat available, to the left of the commander's desk. Although my 150 pounds and thick, black-framed military glasses did not make me look much like a warrior, my voice could have been Patton's. I could project it as far and as authoritatively as I wanted—probably the only reason that I was an officer, what with my undergraduate degree in commercial art earned while I was an ROTC student.

A tough-looking sergeant first class stood to the right of the desk, blocking two other chairs. I quickly deduced that the SFC was the company First Sergeant, the senior non-commissioned officer in the unit and the real second-in-command. His name tag read "Burks." He also wore a Combat Infantry Badge, but his had a star in the center of the wreath around the rifle in the center of the badge, meaning a second award. He had fought in Korea and Vietnam or maybe the Dominican Republic and Vietnam. A CIB with Star was as good as it gets in the Infantry—there were damn few of them. I didn't know a whole lot about the Army, but I did know enough to not want the First Sergeant against me. And he would think that a second lieutenant, Airborne Jump Wings or not, was a dud until the lieutenant had proved otherwise and maybe then not even change his mind.

As soon as I sat down, Lieutenant Harris got up from his chair, strode swiftly around his desk with the taps on the heels of his blindingly shined boots clicking loudly, and walked in front of the soldier standing at attention before the desk. The commander quickly got the one percent of my attention that I wasn't already paying him when he grabbed the soldier by his fatigue shirt, backed him up, and started bouncing him against the wall, yelling, "Hit me, you motherfucker!" The First Sergeant looked on impassively, as if this activity were a daily occurrence.

I thought that I had been scared the second time that I jumped in Airborne School. I had been too stupid to realize what I was doing the first time. But it was nothing compared to watching Lieutenant Harris bounce one of his soldiers off the wall. I halfway expected him to do the same thing to me the first time I fucked up or maybe as part of a welcoming ceremony to ensure that I didn't fuck up.

Well, the soldier, a private first class, whether he was a motherfucker or not, was not so stupid as to hit a commissioned officer who was his commander. I was somewhat impressed at how he remained largely at the position of attention as he was being bounced off the wall. But I was not impressed enough to stop shaking like a leaf and wondering what the fuck I had I gotten myself into. Even though I had been struck by the best of them, Master An, the instructor of my Korean Karate class, who had done such fun things to me as stick a spear hand in my eye while saying, "They don't stop on the street when you are blind," this scenario seemed worse. At least, with Master An, I could strike back, futile as it was. When your commander hit you, what could you do? I was to find out.

Finally, Lieutenant Harris let go of the PFC and stomped back to his chair with a disgusted look on his face as if he were pissed off that the PFC hadn't hit him. I couldn't tell whether he was mad because he hadn't been given an excuse for a good old-fashioned fistfight or because, if the PFC had swung at him, he could have charged him with assault on a superior commissioned officer. SFC Burks would no doubt testify that the assault was entirely unprovoked by Lieutenant Harris.

Once behind his desk, Lieutenant Harris shoved the document that he had been reading at the totally cowed PFC and said, in a scary monotone that left no room for disobedience, "Sign this, you doofus fuck." I didn't know whether doofus fuck was a synonym for motherfucker or a new term, but was hardly going to ask. I later learned that doofus fuck was synonymous with fucking dud. Somehow my 99th percentile on the verbal Scholastic Aptitude Test had not accurately projected a working knowledge of an infantryman's vocabulary.

The PFC, who seemed about as scared as I was, signed immediately. I eventually learned that he had signed an Article 15, which allowed his commander to summarily punish him without the formalities of a court-martial. Much later, I learned that the commander was supposed to inform the troop who had screwed up of his rights, including his right to refuse the commander's punishment, to demand trial by court-martial, and to present evidence to show why he shouldn't be punished. Lieutenant Harris obviously was trying to save the PFC the strain of deciding which would be better, nonjudicial punishment, a court-martial, or how to put on evidence of innocence, by demanding that he sign, accepting the commander's punishment. The commander wasn't supposed to have the punishment, which was a one-grade reduction, forfeiture of seven days' pay, two weeks' restriction to the barracks, and two weeks' extra duties, filled in until after the troop had had the chance to show why he shouldn't be punished. Even though this punishment was the maximum that a commander below the grade of major could impose, the PFC looked relieved when Lieutenant Harris said, "Dismissed." I suppose that the Article 15 punishment beat getting bounced off the wall repeatedly.

By the time that the same drill had occurred twice more, I was beginning to become blasé, thinking that this military justice routine must be a regular part of being in a troop unit and feeling grateful that at least he hadn't started in on me as yet. But my terror quotient hit the maximum when Lieutenant Harris handled the final disciplinary problem that I was to witness that first day.

The final troop who was in trouble was a Sergeant E-5. I later learned his name and that he would be my platoon sergeant, my second-in-command. Sergeant Blasingame was in his Class A uniform, with all of his ribbons and badges. In addition to his Combat Infantry Badge, he wore ribbons showing that he had been awarded five Bronze Stars with "V" for valor and two Purple Hearts, among other awards. If he had five Bronze Stars with "V" device, he had seen some shit. An officer would have ended up with a Silver Star or two with that much valor in combat.

Well, Sergeant Blasingame may well have seen some heavy shit in 'Nam, but Lieutenant Harris chewed him out so bad that he fainted, falling forward and hitting his head on the commander's metal desk, putting a significant dent in the medal modesty panel—a concept that I didn't learn of for another twenty years when we started getting female officers who wore skirts with their Class A uniforms.

Perhaps, I should leave it up to the reader's imagination how bad a chewing out has to be to make a sergeant with five Bronze Stars with "V" device and two Purple Hearts faint. But this book is subtitled as being nonpolitically correct, so here it is.

"Sergeant Blasingame, you are the sorriest excuse for a non-commissioned officer I have ever seen. My fucking sister could lead a squad better than you. My fucking dog could lead a squad better than you. How in the fuck did you survive a year in the 'Nam? You are the biggest fucking dud I've ever had under my command. You are a pussy, bronze stars or not. I ought to rip those fucking stripes right off your fucking sleeve. If you weren't a sergeant, I'd bounce you off the fucking wall until you pissed all over yourself. What the fuck do I need to do to get your attention? What do I have to do to square your sorry ass away? I know. Reach up, you fuckhead, grab your ears, and pull your head out of your ass."

I never learned whether Sergeant Blasingame would have grabbed his ears preparatory to pulling his head out of his ass or not, because it was at this point that he fainted, denting the desk. Nor did I ever learn what he had done to earn this ass-chewing from his commander. I did know that I had never heard so many permutations of the word "fuck."

After the First Sergeant had dragged the fainter out of the commander's office, Lieutenant Harris started briefing me. He told me that I would be the mortar platoon leader, that I'd better get Sergeant Blasingame squared away, and that I'd better not fuck up. Cowed as I was from the military justice proceedings, I said, "Yes, Sir!"

Apparently, the ass-chewing from Lieutenant Harris had squared Sergeant Blasingame away for a while, because he really helped me as his clueless weapons platoon leader. How I got assigned as a mechanized infantry weapons platoon leader is beyond me because I have no mechanical ability whatsoever. Every girl in my high school class had scored higher on the mechanical ability portion of aptitude tests than I had. Nor did my command voice help me at all because I had no clue what to say when one of the troops reported some mechanical problem with the half-tracks other than, "Well, fix it." So here I was, responsible for keeping my platoon's armored personnel carriers functioning. But Sergeant Blasingame did it for me, so smoothly that it appeared that I knew what I was doing. So notwithstanding my initiation as to Lieutenant Harris's brand of military justice when I reported in, I was feeling pretty good—at least until Post Housing called to tell me that they had a room for me at the Bachelor Officers Quarters. I moved my few belongings from the Post Guest House into the BOQ and slid the name tag into the slot next to my door. The military always made you wear a name tag and place one where you were staying so that your commander or anyone else who needed to find you could do so. As I turned to go back into my room, I glanced at the name tag on the next door and about pissed myself. "First Lieutenant Harris," it read. Oh shit, I was right next door to my commander. Was there no justice? Well, there was no justice, but it turned out to be a good thing.

After unpacking, I put on my Karate gi and went down to the dayroom to practice my kata. I had earned the highest grade of red belt in Karate from Master An a year before entering the Army and had been just about ready to test for my black belt when I had to report to Fort Benning for Infantry Officer Basic and Airborne School. So my gi had a red collar and was tied around my waist with a red belt with three black stripes at each end. I wanted to keep my technique as polished as possible for the unlikely event that the Army would station me in a place with a Korean Karate school so that I could get my black belt.

As soon as I had worked up a good sweat going through the first black belt kata—the ritualized series of attacks and defenses that had as much in common with dancing as with fighting, Lieutenant Harris poked his head in, observed me for several minutes and said, "So, Thomas, you think you're a fucking warrior. Let's find out!"

I mentally quailed at what that might mean—I didn't know whether he was going to fight me or whip out a gun and shoot me. I had wished for a dollar for every time someone had asked me what good my Karate would be against a pistol and didn't know whether my commander had the same mindset. He whirled around, stalked down the hall to his room, and disappeared inside.

I didn't know whether to be relieved or not when he came out without a gun, but dressed in sweat clothes. He stood in front of me and said, "Let's go, motherfucker. Let's see what you've got."

He had always been scrupulously formal with me before this moment, calling me "lieutenant," but now I had apparently been demoted to the same category as the PFC that he had bounced off the wall. I must admit to some qualms about fighting my commander. I had learned that he had earned the Silver Star in Vietnam, so I was pretty sure that he could fight. But I didn't know how good he was at hand-to-hand combat. I also didn't know what it was going to do to my relationship with my commander and to my Officer Efficiency Report if I did show him what I had, particularly if it was better than what he had. Taking up a ready position, my mind raced furiously, wondering whether I should let him beat me or kick his butt. I felt that perhaps it was more important that he respect me as a warrior than anything else, so I decided I would not insult him by letting him win.

He attacked, using techniques that I recognized as Army hand-to-hand combat techniques, like the ones that we had been taught in Infantry Officer Basic. These moves were loosely based on Karate and other martial arts, but were to Karate what high school volleyball was to the Olympics. So fending off his attack was fairly easy. But I must say that he was relentless. The apparent ease with which I blocked his punches and kicks did not deter him at all. All it did was make him try harder. After five minutes or so, it dawned on me that he was not going to quit until he beat me or died of exhaustion. So the next time he came at me, I blocked his right hand punch at my face with my left hand, carrying his arm past my face with my left hand, exposing his armpit, in which I planted a stinging round-house kick with my left foot. This move staggered him for a moment, and while he was off-balance, I swept his legs out from under him, followed him down, and struck at his temple with a killing back-fist, pulling the blow just before contact.

I stood up, not even breathing hard, and waited for the explosion. But Lieutenant Harris simply bounced up, grimaced as he rubbed his armpit, smiled, and said, "Air-fucking-borne, you can fight! Let's go to my room and have a cold one."

So this incident turned out to be how bunking next door to my commander turned out to be a good thing, because while we drank beer, he told me how both to survive and to be a good Infantry platoon leader in Vietnam. "If you walk into an L-shaped ambush, assault through either line, and then you are free. If you walk into an X-shaped ambush, kiss your ass goodbye, because you are fucked because, no matter which way you go, you still face flanking fire from another line. Don't wear your rank. Your men will know who you are, and there's no sense in advertising to Viet Cong snipers that you are the officer. Your first night in the bush, dig your own foxhole so that your men will know that you're willing to do what they do, but don't do it every night. You've got to keep some distance from them, and you've got better things to do, like checking the placement of the claymores and trip flares. Forget the rank of your troops, a Spec 4 who's been in the bush for six months knows a hell of a lot more than a shake-and-bake Sergeant E-5, and you should make the Spec 4 squad leader even though the sergeant outranks him."

A shake-and-bake was a sergeant who had gone straight from Basic and Advanced Individual Training into the Non-Commissioned Officers Course and had skipped several ranks upon graduation and promotion to sergeant. Apparently, squad leaders had about the same life expectancy as lieutenants in 'Nam.

Well, if I had to fight Lieutenant Harris nightly for his real world guidance—nothing like what they had taught us in Infantry Officer Basic—it was a hell of a bargain. Infantry School doctrine would never permit you not to wear your rank or to put a Spec 4 over a sergeant as squad leader. And it certainly had not told us to kiss our young Infantry asses goodbye if we blundered into an X-shaped ambush. Even though my commander was a National Guard Officer Candidate School graduate from Stillwater, Oklahoma, with a high school diploma and no college, he had me, with my college degree in commercial art and advertising and my Regular Army commission, highly motivated to live up to his expectations of what his officers should be. I spent hours polishing my boots, trying to equal his mirror shine. Eventually, I almost did.

Fighting my commander every other night or so led me into my second experience with military justice. Although I can't say that Lieutenant Harris ever won, he certainly never quit. He almost seemed to relish fighting outmatched. He would brag to the other company commanders, "Lieutenant Thomas can kick my ass. That's how I like my officers—tough!"

At least, none of the other officers decided to see whether I was really so tough. But my Karate skills inspired Lieutenant Harris to suggest that I teach the men in the company Karate. He said that it would keep them fit and maybe out of trouble. While they were in my class, he said, they wouldn't be drinking and getting into trouble in the Lawton bars. So two nights a week, I held a class for about twenty members of the company at the post gym. They seemed to enjoy it, and I know that I did.

One day, Lieutenant Harris called me into his office and said, "Your platoon sergeant is doing marijuana. I want you to kick the shit out of him at your Karate class tonight and get him off the shit."

I was surprised to hear that Sergeant Blasingame was on drugs, because I couldn't fault his duty performance. Not only, however, did I trust my commander to see things that I didn't, I wouldn't have contradicted him even if I hadn't trusted him. After the bouncing off the wall incident, this order seemed like a perfectly logical course of action to me, so I quickly replied, "Yes, Sir!"

After we had warmed up with stretching exercises, we worked on defensive techniques. First, I taught them how to break the hold if someone wrapped their arms around them from behind, pinning their arms to their sides (clasp your fists together, throw your elbows up and out, pivot, and drive your elbow into your opponent's solar plexus). Next, we worked on how to break the hold if the attacker grabbed them from behind under the arms (grab their left wrist with your left hand, form your right hand into a ball peen hammer by forming a fist and sticking your bent index finger out braced by the other fingers, strike the middle of the back of their left hand, which I guarantee will break the grip—lot of unprotected nerves there—straighten and pull back your left arm, pulling their arm away from their body, exposing their armpit, and pivot and strike or kick that armpit). We finished up the self-defense moves with the defensive move to use if someone grabbed you from the front, pinning your arms to your sides. This move was fairly simple, form two fists with your thumbs extended and braced against your first finger and drive it into your opponent's gonads. And now it was time for kumite—free style sparring—and Sergeant Blasingame's comeuppance.

Master An, in contrast to many lesser-qualified black belts, had taught us control, so that we pulled the killing or disabling blow a quarter-inch from the temple, bridge of the nose, armpit, or the like. And I had been quite good with control. One time at an exhibition, I had used a jumping front snap kick to kick a playing card out of the mouth of another student, who was standing on a chair so that the card was about nine feet in the air, without missing the card and breaking the student's jaw or his nose. But although I didn't use lethal force on Sergeant Burlingame, I did make contact. Enough contact to hurt. After kicking the shit out of him like Master An used to kick it out of me, I swept his legs out from under him, dropped my knee into his solar plexus, and, while pressing my knee painfully into him, whispered in his ear, "We're going to do this every fucking day unless you stop doing drugs."

I think he believed me—I was dead serious—and I am 99 percent certain that he stopped doing drugs, at least for the remainder of his enlistment in the military. My belief was based on Lieutenant Harris's compliment on a good job in squaring away my platoon sergeant and Sergeant Blasingame's invitation to visit him at his parent's home in Toledo, Ohio, during my 30-day leave before going to 'Nam. I accepted that invitation and went to

Toledo, where Sergeant Blasingame introduced me to his parents as having saved him from drug addiction, thereby saving his honorable discharge and veterans' benefits—a powerful testimonial to that old-fashioned military justice. The reception that I received from my former platoon sergeant and his parents was certainly one of the highlights of my first year on active duty.

I also got to see the officer version of Lieutenant Harris's old-time-military justice. As he had told me to do with regard to putting a more competent, but lower ranking, soldier in as squad leader, he made me the company executive officer ("XO") when Shazam left, even though I was the lowest ranking lieutenant in the company by date of rank. The outgoing XO wore a 25th Infantry Division combat patch, which had what appeared to be a lightning bolt striking down through it—hence, the name Shazam from some comic book character. We didn't call him that to his face, however, because he came across as a baby-faced stone killer with his Combat Infantry Badge and next to total disrespect for anything approaching rear-echelon soldiering, which, of course, was all we did at Fort Sill.

As XO, I was supposed to handle all of the administrative details of running a company—ensuring that the mess hall food was at least barely edible, ensuring that the supply room more or less functioned, making sure that all of the paperwork got done—all so that the commander could concentrate on accomplishing the mission of supporting the Artillery School's training of new redleg officers and new redleg soldiers. Redleg had been the Infantry's derogatory term for artillerymen since the 1800s, when artillerymen wore uniform trousers with a two-inch red stripe. Of course, the First Sergeant was the real second-in-command, but I was unduly proud of being the nominal second-in-command and the real third-in-command. In fact, when Lieutenant Harris went on leave or pass, I was the acting commander.

As nominal second-in-command, I was brought into the loop when one of the officers fucked up, on the old military axiom that you didn't chew out an officer in front of an enlisted man. So SFC

Burks was not present when Lieutenant Perry reported to the commander after having been written up for DUI.

Back in the late 1960s, DUI was not the career-killer that it became in the 1980s when MADD and other groups pressured the military into believing that DUI was only slightly less reprehensible than murdering the commanding general and raping his daughters.

In the late 1960s and for many years before that for all I knew, the military hardly discouraged drinking. Although we were not nearly so bad as the British Army of the 1800s—we didn't issue brandy or rum before the battle to help the troops march into volley fire from the French or the Americans—the Army did not see much wrong with allowing soldiers to blow off a little steam by having a tot. Although the Uniform Code of Military Justice did make it a crime to be drunk on duty or drunk and disorderly, a little off-duty drunkenness was no big deal, unless you got drunk and tried to fondle the general's daughter.

The best evidence of this fairly permissive attitude was the ubiquitous happy hour—Friday night drinking bouts at the Officers' Club, where you blew off steam from a week of hard duty by drinking half-priced drinks. Also, a dining-in or a unit party, such as a hail-and-farewell to welcome new personnel and say good-bye to departing ones, was little more than an excuse to get roaringly drunk under the guise of building unit cohesion.

Unfortunately, however, at least for the roaringly drunk, the Military Police loved to bust officers for any reason and had little compunction against busting their fellow enlisted men. Thus, the MPs would be out in force on the road—typically the only road—exiting the O Club or the NCO Club to pull over any vehicle that crossed the center line, was a mile over the speed limit, had a defective taillight, or exhibited any other excuse to pull the car over. This stop would almost invariably lead to a field sobriety test—an easy way to humiliate an officer—just call him "Sir" when telling him to walk the line—and an arrest for DUI. When such an arrest happened to one of Lieutenant Harris's officers, he would have to go to the MP station to sign him out of the lockup—something not calculated to raise one's status in the commander's eyes.

Such had happened to Lieutenant Perry, and now the bill was due. The MP blotter report had come down through the chain of command, and Lieutenant Harris now had to take appropriate disciplinary action. As XO, I was the witness, not the First Sergeant. I watched with bated breath, wondering whether we would have a second dent in the front of the commander's desk. But apparently, Lieutenant Harris had chewed his first platoon leader out enough when he had signed for him at the MP station, releasing him to his commander's custody, because Lieutenant Harris did not chew the miscreant out. He simply said in a tone that brooked no argument, "Donate $100 to the Army Emergency Relief Fund, and this goes away." Not being a total moron, Lieutenant Perry quickly replied, "Yes, Sir. AER will have my check today."

Now, although I am a total heathen, I thought that this order was the greatest act of Christian charity that I had ever seen in the Army. Yes, Lieutenant Perry was out a hundred bucks—a lot of money in 1968 when a lieutenant's pay for the whole month was only three hundred and change. But the alternative, the—it doesn't go away—was nonjudicial punishment for the lieutenant or, at the minimum, a poor officer efficiency report, which would have killed any chance of promotion. So the $100 contribution to a worthy charity was a gift to the offending officer.

I didn't learn until much later, after I had become an Army lawyer, that Lieutenant Harris's action was also a crime—extortion. Article 127 of the Uniform Code of Military Justice ("UCMJ") makes the act of obtaining something of value—a $100 contribution to AER—by threatening something—ruining one's career—the crime of extortion, punishable by dishonorable discharge (dismissal for an officer), forfeiture of all pay and allowances, and confinement for three years.

Now, I doubt that Lieutenant Harris knew that his effective method of discipline—taking a lot of money out of the pocket of one of his officers and giving it to an Army charity so that he didn't ruin the offender's military career—constituted the crime of extortion. But even if he had known, I doubt that the knowledge would have deterred him. He knew that bouncing his men off the wall and ordering them to sign an Article 15 was illegal. But he also knew that his methods were effective. And whatever you might say about him, and I'll never say anything bad about him, he was a soldier and a leader, and he got the job done, one way or the other. And he will always be on my short list of about five soldiers that I would want to go into combat with.

But according to the Uniform Code of Military Justice and the Judge Advocate General's Corps officers who did not have any prior service in the combat arms but applied military law to situations where they had no personal experience, he was probably a war criminal, having committed assault consummated with a battery, maltreatment of a subordinate, and extortion. Because I had yet to meet a JAGC-Off, however, I took his "I will put a hurt on you, but I won't kill your career unless you force me to" as good leadership and took it with me to Vietnam, to, what I thought was fate—the same division that he had served in—the First Cav.

But before I leave Fort Sill to tell you about Vietnam, I must mention a darker side of military justice that had reared its ugly head. Another soldier was on drugs. This soldier had not wanted to attend my Karate class and was not in the weapons platoon when I was platoon leader, so I had no semicolorable way of assaulting him and arguing, if he complained, that it was training. After both Lieutenant Harris and the first sergeant had failed to improve Private Matasar's performance, Lieutenant Harris told him that he was going to process him for an administrative discharge with an other-than-honorable discharge—the administrative counterpart of a bad-conduct discharge. Effectively, such a discharge would take away all of his military and veterans' benefits. Well, Private Matasar did not take kindly to this proposal and went AWOL. When the First Sergeant tracked him down and suggested that he return to the unit or face court-martial, Private Matasar responded by saying, "I'll return to Fort Sill but only to kill Lieutenant Harris and his wife."

A week or so before Private Matasar went AWOL, Lieutenant Harris's wife had finished nursing school and had moved from Tulsa to join him. I felt a real sense of loss at losing my BOQ companion, even though I was getting somewhat tired of having to kick the crap out of him every other night. But I was glad that he could get some connubial bliss after his tour in the 'Nam.

Of course, Murphy's law played into this scenario, and Private Matasar made this threat a day and a half before the Inspector General inspection. This IG inspection, announced way in advance, was meant to demonstrate how good a unit could be when it had time to get everything perfect as opposed to an unannounced inspection to see the day-to-day reality. With a definite day by which we had to be perfect, I had not slept for three days, trying to ensure that the IG inspectors couldn't find an incorrect entry on the maintenance records, a missing piece of equipment that a Report of Survey was not pending on, and the like. So I didn't know whether to be complimented, relieved, or concerned when Lieutenant Harris called me into his office and said, "I'm ultimately responsible as commander for how we do on the IG inspection. You've done a great job getting us ready, but I need you to stay with my wife and guard her from Private Matasar because I must be here for the inspection. Here's the key to the gun cabinet. Don't let that motherfucker in the door, much less anywhere near my wife. If he shows up, do what you have to do."

Well, I had no clue whether that set of instructions was a lawful order or not, but I can't say that I gave a shit. If Lieutenant Harris trusted me enough to guard his wife from an expressed threat, I'd die before anyone harmed his wife.

The only problem with my bold resolve was that I couldn't stay awake. I went to his quarters, and his wife, who was pathetically grateful for my assistance (minimal though it was) let me in. I retrieved every weapon known to an Okie gun nut like Lieutenant Harris from his gun cabinet—several pistols, a shotgun, and a rifle. I made sure that they were loaded, sent her to bed, stationed myself on guard duty at the front door, and promptly fell asleep, clutching the shotgun to my chest. But at least I fell asleep propped up against the wall in the hallway across the hall in front of the front door, effectively blocking it from any disgruntled private who might try to break through. None did, whether from fear that I was lying there on the other side ready to wake up from a deep sleep and let loose with a shotgun blast or from fear that you didn't fuck with Lieutenant Harris. Regardless, the next morning I accepted with a straight face Mrs. Harris's gratitude for having saved her life and went back to the company to find out that we had miraculously passed the IG inspection. Private Matasar never did show up. I like to think that he is still in hiding, afraid to join American society for fear of being prosecuted for being AWOL.

So all of these experiences influenced how I enforced discipline in Vietnam. In other words, I was not predisposed to take any shit, especially because I was assigned to Lieutenant Harris's division—the First Cav. I took this assignment as a good omen, although my assignment probably actually meant that the First Cav had lost more Infantry platoon leaders than any other division.

I didn't have any military justice problems for some time. As a new platoon leader, I followed Lieutenant Harris's guidance religiously. I dug my own foxhole the first night in the field. I didn't wear my rank on my uniform. I didn't stand next to my radio telephone operator, where the platoon leader would normally stand, because if Viet Cong snipers could not see any rank insignia, they would shoot the soldier closest to the RTO because the leaders were the ones who used the radio. And I managed to avoid an X-shaped ambush although I did manage to blunder into some L-shaped ones and escape without significant friendly casualties. These and other tips from my former commander apparently worked, but they didn't stop Private First Class Bennie Sutton from talking at night.

The Viet Cong ruled the night. Large, noisy Americans who were not used to the jungle were largely worthless at night. So my rule was that we did not talk at night. Voices carry at night. I didn't want to give away our location any more than we already had by moving into our night defensive perimeter under their clandestine observation. So one night, from nearly 50 meters away, I heard PFC Sutton talking to the troop who shared his foxhole. So I crawled from my foxhole to his and whispered in his ear that we don't talk at night. Not being sure that he was really in agreement when he whispered, "Yes, Sir," I added, "If I have to come over here again to shut your fucking yap up, my boot is going six inches up your ass."

Sure enough, ten minutes later, I heard him talking again. So I went to his foxhole, drew my foot back, and, with no warning, executed a front-snap kick that would have pleased Master An. I placed my foot, well, maybe not six inches, but definitely up his ass as he lay on his belly with his legs spread. Although I later learned that this maneuver was also an illegal assault, it was effective. He didn't talk at night in the bush again that night or any other night that we spent together. And my platoon never lost a man because of the enemy's knowledge of exactly where our NDPs were. Nor did Private Sutton end up in disciplinary trouble that would have resulted in a black soldier facing a discharge that would have denied him military and veterans' benefits and that would have made it much more difficult for him to get a civilian job when his enlistment was up.

I had a few contacts with Army lawyers in 'Nam because I testified on behalf of one of my soldiers who had been convicted of going AWOL, testifying that he had done a good job before going AWOL and that I would take him back in my platoon. I wasn't particularly impressed by the JAGC defense counsel who called me as a witness. I ended up having to tell him what questions to ask me, which seemed backward to me, especially because he was the one who had been to law school. But my first contact with a JAGC officer after Vietnam left me very impressed.

While I was on leave after I had returned to the states, I got a letter in the mail saying that a Report of Survey had found that I was liable for twenty-three missing M-16 rifles. After my platoon leader stint had ended, the battalion commander moved me to the XO position in another company, Charlie Company. The executive officer has to sign for all of the company's equipment. A good XO would conduct a thorough inventory before signing for the equipment. But because the battalion was moving to another firebase and was spread out over hundreds of kilometers of jungle and because I stupidly believed that making sure that the company's troops had enough food, water, ammunition, and mail—don't even fuck with the mail in a combat zone—was more important than accounting for every mess kit, canteen, and helmet, I had conducted a half-assed inventory.

Of course, when I got my orders to rotate back to CONUS, the new executive officer who took over from me conducted the anal inventory from hell. Although we had the total number of the M-16 rifles that we were supposed to have, twenty-three of them had the wrong serial numbers. So the battalion commander appointed a Report of Survey officer to investigate whether I was liable for not having the correct twenty-three M-16s.

What had happened was that Charlie Company had combat assaulted into a landing zone along with my old company, Alpha Company, on a joint search and destroy mission. While setting up a night defensive perimeter, the North Vietnamese Army took umbrage to this excursion and attacked. Each troop snatched up whatever M-16 was closest without bothering to check the serial number to make sure that it was the one that he had signed for and that had been on the XO's inventory. After the two companies had beaten off the attack, the battalion commander, orbiting above the attack in his command and control helicopter, ordered Charlie Company to pursue the retreating enemy and Alpha Company to go in the opposite direction to check out a report of an enemy supply cache. So twenty-three rifles went with the wrong owners.

Well, the survey officer quite properly, I thought, found that I was not liable for twenty-three missing M-16s and wrote off the other missing stuff as combat losses. So I was off the hook, I thought. But after I had happily left the battalion on my way home, the battalion commander disapproved the findings of the Report of Survey and found me liable for twenty-three missing M-16s. So my welcome home included a bill for the cost of twenty-three M-

16s—a bill that would have taken more than six months of my lieutenant's pay to pay off.

Being less than thrilled by this bill, what with knowing that the M-16s weren't really missing, I went to the closest Army base, found the JAGC office, and barged in on the Legal Assistance Officer. I explained the situation to him and showed him the correspondence disapproving the Report of Survey and charging me for the loss. After he had stopped laughing, although I didn't see the humor, he said, "Leave your paperwork with me and forget about it. I'll take care of it."

I thought that this solution sounded pretty good. This lawyer obviously had his shit together. I never heard anything more about it, so he must have taken care of it. So I had a fairly positive view of Army lawyers.

But notwithstanding my limited experience with JAGC lawyers after Vietnam, following Fort Sill, I still believed in that old-time military justice. That belief would last until I became a military lawyer and had to integrate that old-time military justice into the post–1969 Manual version. The 1969 Manual tried to civilianize the military justice system—which was not always a good thing. But understanding how Lieutenant Harris and his ilk thought and acted became incredibly valuable in the successful practice of military law, a benefit that most Army lawyers had not had and a benefit that won me my first cases as a JAGC-Off, an Army Judge Advocate General's Corps officer.

2

No Evidence? Who Cares!

"The time to strike is when the opportunity presents itself."
—Master Anko Itos

"It don't mean nothing."

(Starting off this story of my first court-martial as an Army Judge Advocate General's Corps ("JAGC") officer with this sentence would have given my Army writing instructor a cross between a stroke and a hissy fit. I knew that it would. I had managed to break every rule of good writing in one sentence. First, I started with a weak pronoun rather than a strong noun. I can still hear her say, "It what?" I don't know what. Apparently, if the reader can't tell what "it" refers to, you've given your editor Excedrin headache number fifty-three. Instead of some wimpy pronoun, I'm supposed to have used some strong noun, such as "verdict." My next writing screw-up was that I had followed the weak pronoun with a verb that did not agree in number with the wimpy pronoun subject. I should have used "does not" because the wimpy pronoun subject is singular. Finally, I should have used "anything" rather than "nothing" so that I wouldn't end up with a double negative. So grammatically, the sentence should read, "The verdict does not mean anything." But the grammatically preferable sentence doesn't capture the flavor of the saying. And the saying is a quotation even though I'll have to commit yet another writing error of failing to attribute it to whoever said it. I first saw it scrawled on a helmet liner in Vietnam. Apparently, infantrymen in

Vietnam, where the saying was ubiquitous, didn't care about grammar or perhaps simply didn't have room on their helmets to write, "Whatever the brass did to screw me over today does not mean anything." Yeah, and I said it myself more than a few times as the Army screwed me over one way or another. So the first sentence stands as written.

This story starts with that thought. It was running through my mind as I awaited the verdict in my first court-martial as a trial counsel, a military prosecutor, trying to convince myself that I didn't care whether the jury found the accused, the military term for the defendant, guilty or not. Apparently, to me that day, "it" referred to losing the case, having the jury return a verdict of not guilty. I was trying to tell myself that I wouldn't be the first one to lose a court-martial presided over by Military Judge (Colonel) Savage. But telling myself that "it," the verdict, didn't matter did not seem to work. I was more nervous than I had been before making my second parachute jump (I was too stupid to realize what I was doing the first time), before and during a firefight in 'Nam, or before opening up what usually turned out to be rejection letters from law schools. But I get ahead of myself.

My Army career up to this point had hardly been distinguished, Vietnam combat medals notwithstanding, although I had done better at ROTC than I had done in my college major, commercial art. Somehow, I had failed to work up any interest in designing artwork for feminine hygiene product ads, and my grades were as low as the professors could make them without flunking out someone who would then get drafted. Professors in the 1960s did not like to provide cannon fodder for Vietnam. But I did ok in ROTC. ROTC paid $50 a month—big bucks in the late 1960s. So I did well enough in ROTC to get a scholarship, which not only paid twice as much, but also paid tuition and supplies—the only way that I could afford to get a degree in something that I no longer had any interest in. But I had no interest in dropping out and going to Vietnam as a draftee, either. I took the scholarship because I thought that the war in Vietnam might be over by the time that I graduated and that, if I earned a Distinguished Military Graduate award, I would have my choice of branches and would not end up in the Infantry. I did earn that award and, because I was fascinated by Ian Fleming's James Bond books, chose Military Intelligence—yeah, it's a contradiction in terms, but it gave me a certain cachet among the other cadets that I was going to be a "spook." But although my plan was brilliant in theory, it failed miserably. Apparently, the Army had lost so many second lieutenants in combat in Vietnam that it had instituted a new policy under which all Regular Army second lieutenants in noncombat arms branches, such as Military Intelligence, had to spend a two-year detail in the combat arms. And the Infantry is as combat arms as it gets.

So my brilliant plan to be James Bond ended with Infantry Officer Basic, Airborne, and Jungle Warfare schools, a platoon leader under Lieutenant Harris at Fort Sill, followed by the real thing: Infantry Platoon Leader, Alpha Company, First Battalion, 8th Cavalry, First Cavalry Division, Republic of Vietnam. But I survived, thanks to Lieutenant Harris's beating into my head what to do, without killing any of my men by my stupidity. Then, lo and behold, the Army sent me to spook school. After Vietnam, I reported to the Area Intelligence Officers Course at Fort Holabird, Maryland. The six-month course was in humint—human intelligence—using human sources to gather information. My most indelible memory of that course is tailing the "rabbit," a black officer, through the slums of Baltimore in August in the early 1970s, dressed in coat and tie. I was in the coat and tie. The rabbit wore jeans and a T-shirt. The student spooks were the only ones in coat and tie in the whole city at that time. The high point occurred when the rabbit went into a fish market and sat down at a two-chair little snack bar and ate a leisurely lunch. Have you ever tried to feign interest in fresh fish for forty-five minutes in an unairconditioned market in humid Baltimore in August while dressed in a coat and tie? One of the sales staff finally asked me whether she could help me find someone. So much for being clandestine.

At graduation, I found myself screwed again as the faceless beings that assigned Military Intelligence officers decided that, what with my combat experience, I should command the Military Intelligence detachment of an Infantry division in Germany rather than work in what I had just been trained to do. So while most of the rest of the class—those who were not Regular Army and, consequently, had not been detailed to the combat arms—went off to humint assignments, I got to command a unit consisting largely of enlisted men who had returned from Vietnam and were just waiting for their enlistments to be up, hardly a motivated crew. Because Vietnam was getting all of the resources, a tour in Germany sucked as far as the military part, although taking leave in France, Austria, Holland, and so forth almost made it worthwhile. After almost being relieved of my command because fifteen of my eighteen vehicles met the criteria for salvage, even though I had requisitioned new ones and even though any vehicles that the Army had were going to Vietnam, not to Bad Kreuznach, I somehow finished my command tour and got a real humint job.

Once again, my timing was off. I got the real humint job just as the Army decided that it didn't need humint and started cutting it way back. Even back then—long before 9/11 and Al Qaida hiding in caves in Afghanistan—I knew that doing away with human sources was a mistake. Spy satellites and signal intercepts aren't much good when the enemy is talking around a campfire in a cave in the Hindu Kush mountains of Afghanistan. But no one was going to listen to a dumb Army captain. So being totally uninterested in combat intelligence or aerial imagery interpretation, I knew that I had to find a new home and decided to get out of the Army and go to law school. Law school couldn't be any harder than coming up with a plan to place a human source inside the Soviet Group of Forces Germany's headquarters in Potsdam-Geltow overnight. The brand new Deputy Chief of Staff for Intelligence for U.S. Army Europe, an Infantry general, had actually tasked my unit to come up with this plan as his initial salvo to prove that he was the equal of "M," James Bond's boss, and, consequently, deserved another star. Although I came up with some half-assed plan by working all night, it would have been the intelligence feat of the century to place a human source inside that headquarters. And if we had any possibility of doing so, the CIA spooks would have taken the operation away from us and run it themselves. As I recall, our biggest military intelligence coup was the revelation that certain Russian railroad engines had changed lubricants.

In hindsight, I should have acquired some of that lubricant because I managed to skewer myself again. I allowed someone to talk me into applying for the Judge Advocate General's Excess Leave Program, under which the Army sent twenty-five officers to law school every year. Because some colonel had arranged for the Army to pay for his law school degree just before he retired, some law forbade the Army to pay for law school. But the time in law school counted for promotion and retirement, and I could earn my full pay and allowances when performing on-the-job-training when school was not in session. So I wimped out and applied for the program.

To this day, I have no clue how I was selected. My military career, as shown by my Officer Efficiency Reports, was mediocre. Not only was I not highly rated for having had so many unserviceable jeeps, but also my having told my company commander to fuck himself when he gave me an idiotic order that would have gotten my men killed for nothing in Vietnam and for having hit my Military Intelligence battalion commander in the back of the head with my racquetball racket during a hotly contested match seemed to cause them to rate me as less than stellar. Yeah, I had some neat combat medals, but the Military Intelligence officer assignment pukes—any pencil pushing assignment officer was automatically a puke—had told me that my OERs were in the bottom third of those of Regular Army Military Intelligence officers. So I didn't think that I had any chance to get into a program that chose approximately twenty-five officers from about 2,000 applicants. I think that someone must have mistakenly put my application and Official Military Personnel File ("OMPF") in the "accept" file rather than the "reject" file for the Excess Leave Program. I was so certain that applying had been a waste of time that I almost threw the envelope from the Student Detachment at Fort Sam Houston into the trash before opening and reading it. The letter that notified me that I had been selected was beneath a pamphlet titled "Student Officer Guide" that I did throw away as being irrelevant to my life before finding out that the Army was sending me to law school.

The only problem was getting into law school. Incredibly, no one was impressed with my C+ average in commercial art even though I had an excellent Law School Aptitude Test (LSAT) score—above the median for Harvard Law School. With Vietnam still going on, it may not have helped that my mailing address was 430th Military Intelligence Battalion, 66th Military Intelligence Group, Munich, Germany, because law schools were not known for having conservative, pro-Vietnam war faculties. But I finally got into a bottom-tier law school that educated me very well, and I became a full-fledged Judge Advocate General's Corps officer, a JAGC-Off, as other branches of the Army not so fondly called us. Commanders don't like to be told that what they want to do is illegal. "What do you mean I can't fire my tank guns without getting an environmental impact assessment?" So JAGC officers are not universally loved by the rest of the Army.

So I reported to my first JAGC assignment—the Office of the Staff Judge Advocate (the chief attorney of a post or unit), Fort Knox, Kentucky. The Staff Judge Advocate, Colonel Olgin, welcomed me and assigned me as a trial counsel—a military prosecutor. Thank God. I had been afraid that I would get some boring assignment like administrative law or, worse yet, legal assistance. Helping soldiers write wills and advising them on legal matters that I could not represent them on in court (I wasn't licensed in Kentucky, and JAGC regulations prohibited representing soldiers in civilian courts) struck me as worse than waiting on the flight line for eight hours in the German winter to board the perfectly good plane that I had to parachute out of. I wanted courtroom experience. After all, if I couldn't be James Bond, I could at least be in court like Perry Mason. Another benefit of being a trial counsel was that those JAGCs were about the only JAGCs that the rest of the Army liked. Commanders liked lawyers who put their problem troops in jail or got them kicked out of the Army. And I got my chance—I would be a trial counsel. But I wasn't sure that I was going to be like Perry Mason right off because I received my first case with the comment that, because it was unwinnable, it would be a good case to start out with because I couldn't mess it up. I wasn't particularly thrilled by this theory because I had used my Military Intelligence training to figure out what was really going on in the Fort Knox courtroom. Judge Savage, a full bird colonel, was the Chief Military Judge. He even looked the part: 6' 4" with a lion-like mane of silver-gray hair and an imperious face with dark, bushy eyebrows. And Judge Savage did not suffer fools in his courtroom. Mounted on the wall in his chambers, a plaque titled "You've been Savaged!" listed the names of anyone who had, in his sole opinion, screwed up in his courtroom. My primary interest as a JAGC-Off was avoiding having him list me on that board. But my G-2 (military slang for intelligence) was that, if you blew your first case before Judge Savage, you were forever deemed a dud. So the last thing that I wanted was to start off with a loser case.

In the Army, commanders, not lawyers, decide what cases go to trial. Good commanders listen to their lawyer's advice when deciding, but it is ultimately the commander's call. So I decided that the only way to avoid looking like a dud before Judge Savage was to get the commander, called the Convening Authority in this capacity, to dismiss the charges. So I got an appointment with Colonel Rock, the Commander of the 194th Armored Brigade. I entered his office, stood between two large and, I hoped, inert tank gunnery shells in front of his desk, and saluted.

Colonel Rock was about as aptly named as Judge Savage. He was a hulking bear of a man chewing on an unlit cigar, with a butch haircut that was so close that it looked as if he had shaved his head. Although I was in my class A uniform with all of my combat badges and ribbons in the hope that they would give me some credibility, he was dressed in fatigues. His web gear with ammunition pouches and canteens hung off the back of his chair as if he might have to leap to his feet and fight off a Russian invasion of Fort Knox at any moment. Colonel Rock finally returned my salute and growled, "Well?"

But I had faced the North Vietnamese Army, Master An, and Professor Creed, who would question one student in law school until the student had broken (he had broken me, but it took the whole hour instead of the usual ten minutes), so I jumped right in. "Sir, Captain Thomas, Sir. I need to talk to you about the Turner court-martial. I'm the trial counsel on the case. Although I certainly agree that possession of marijuana may properly be referred to a court-martial, the search that found the marijuana was illegal, and Judge Savage will throw out the evidence. And without any evidence, I can't win. I don't think that it would be good for discipline for Specialist Turner to be running around your brigade saying that you had tried to court-martial him and couldn't do it."

Colonel Rock fixed me with a baleful glare, slapped his oversized fist down on his desk, and said, "Captain Thomas, I'm surprised at you. You've got a Combat Infantry Badge on your chest and Jump Wings. I've read your OMPF. You've got the Silver fucking Star for Christ's sake! What the hell is this defeatist attitude? Go win the motherfucker!"

Using my best Military Intelligence gathering capability, I quickly decided that I was out of options. "Yes, Sir!" I saluted and beat a hasty retreat.

Well, I worked on the case until it was as polished as a jewel, but even with my brilliant argument that Colonel Savage should not apply the Exclusionary Rule to exclude the evidence of the bad search because none of the policy reasons behind the rule applied, Judge Savage threw the marijuana out as being the result of an illegal search. Normally, I would have asked for a recess to get the Convening Authority's permission to dismiss the case at that point, but I knew that any effort in that regard would be as futile as trying to block one of Master An's spinning back kicks, and I had just enough circumstantial evidence to continue, although not enough to win.

Judge Savage, perplexed, asked me whether I had any motions, expecting me to move to dismiss the case. I said, "No, Your Honor."

He shook his head, looked at me as if I were a total idiot, and said, "Call the court members."

Because I was the trial counsel, I had to instruct the bailiff to get the court members, the military's term for jurors, and bring them to the courtroom. A general court-martial had to have at least five members, and a special court-martial, at least three. Most of the time, Army lawyers persuaded convening authorities to detail more than the jurisdictional minimum to avoid aberrant—that is, not guilty—findings. The greater the number of officer court members on the panel, the less likelihood that the defense could prevail.

As the jury filed in, I realized that I had won the case. In the Army, you wear the patch of the unit that you are assigned to on your left sleeve. If you serve in combat, you can wear that unit patch—your combat patch—on your right sleeve for the rest of your career. So I had some nondescript patch for Fort Knox on my left sleeve and the big, bold, yellow shield of the First Cavalry Division on my right sleeve with its horse's head and saddle roll. The rest of the Army said about the patch, "The horse that was never ridden, the stream (the diagonal representing the saddle roll) that was never crossed, and the color speaks for itself."

Well, that saying wasn't going to impress the court members because, lo and behold, all six of them also wore the First Cav combat patch on their right shoulder. Not being a total dud, I immediately rotated my right shoulder so that they could see that I was a Cav buddy, someone who had served in combat in the same division that they had. I was thankful that I had worn all of my ribbons and badges. I almost felt sorry for the poor defense counsel with no combat patch and his lone National Defense Service Medal, called the "I was alive in '65" or, if not '65, "whatever year it was when you entered active duty" medal.

If I had been the defense counsel, seeing that all of the court members had the same combat patch as the trial counsel would have made me move to challenge the whole panel for cause because they were going to take care of their Cav buddy. But not having served in combat, the poor defense counsel didn't even notice the combat patches, much less the court members' military histories displayed on their uniforms. But I could read their decorations like a book. The President of the Court, an Armor lieutenant colonel, had three Bronze Stars with "V" (for valor) and two Purple Hearts. The next senior member was an Infantry major with a Combat Infantry Badge, Master Blaster Parachutist Wings, and a Ranger Tab. One captain had Artillery brass on, which, combined with his combat patch and his ribbons, told me that he had been an Artillery forward observer, humping the bush in 'Nam with the Infantry. Another captain was an Armor officer who must have been assigned to an Infantry position in 'Nam because he had a Combat Infantry Badge. Yet another was a helicopter pilot with a Distinguished Flying Cross, among other decorations. Because he was wearing Medical Service Corps brass, I knew that he had been a hero when extracting wounded soldiers from the field as a Medevac pilot. The final captain, the meanest looking of the bunch, was Airborne, Ranger, and Special Forces, with a Combat Infantry Badge and Silver Star ribbon atop the dozen or so other ribbons on his chest.

Confidently, I put on my shaky case, managing to approach the court members to hand them exhibits several times so that they could focus on my Silver Star, Bronze Star, Air Medal for twenty-five combat assaults, Combat Infantry Badge, and Jump Wings, among other awards. I could almost hear them thinking, "A JAGC who's been there and done that and whose shit doesn't stink. Plus, we know this dirt-bag is guilty whether there's any evidence or not. And we don't want this wimp-ass JAGC defense counsel to beat our Cav Buddy."

The defense counsel had done a pretty good job of pointing out that there was not enough evidence to convict beyond a reasonable doubt, but he had already lost when the court members entered the courtroom and saw my big yellow combat patch. Gamely, he argued on, but they weren't listening. Even so, after I had presented my rebuttal argument and after Judge Savage had given the jury instructions, I nervously awaited the verdict, telling myself, "It don't mean nothing," although I knew that it did. Not wanting to face the other trial counsel's inevitable questions about how it had gone in court, I couldn't bring myself to leave the courtroom to go back to my cubbyhole of an office. Fortunately, I didn't have to wait long. Within about ten minutes, the bailiff notified me that the court members had reached a verdict. After having notified Judge Savage and the defense, I nervously watched the court members as they filed into the courtroom, still afraid that I had lost. But my Cav buddies took care of me. Not only did they convict the accused, but also they gave him the maximum sentence at a special court-martial of six months' confinement, forfeiture of two-thirds pay per month for six months, and reduction to the lowest enlisted grade. To this day, the defense counsel doesn't know how he lost. Even Judge Savage nodded to me as I left the courtroom.

When I returned to the trial counsel offices, the four other, more experienced trial counsel rushed up and asked, "Well, how bad was it? How bad did you lose?"

"Me lose? The word is not in my vocabulary. I maxed the motherfucker!"

From that point on, I had it made. I could go to court and screw something up, and everyone would comment about the brilliant new trial tactic that I had come up with. The defense counsel almost always pled their clients guilty rather than face my unbeatable tactics. But the thing I wonder to this day is whether Colonel Rock had stacked the jury with First Cav veterans or whether I had just gotten lucky. I did know that now-Private Turner wasn't lucky. He had been steamrolled by the First Cavalry Division.

3

The Mummy Case

"The wimp who made it through the eliminations on luck alone will suddenly turn into Bruce Lee when you're up against him."
—*Murphy's Law of Karate*

The not-yet-a-mummy had finished Basic and Advanced Individual Training (AIT) at Fort Knox, Kentucky. Fort Knox was a training base with Basic Training and AIT for new enlisted men and Armor Officer Basic and Advanced for officers. The only combat unit on post, the 194th Armored Brigade, was in school support, just as the Infantry battalion that I had served in at Fort Sill was in school support of the Artillery School.

Just before graduation with a Military Occupational Specialty (MOS) as a tanker, the mummy had received orders to his first duty station, the Replacement Battalion, U.S. Army Vietnam, for further assignment upon arrival in country. The mummy had hardly been an honor graduate who got to choose his first assignment. So he was going to be a tanker in the 'Nam. One might wonder why the U.S. Army needed tankers in Vietnam with its jungle terrain from swamps to triple canopy to mountains, but it did. Tanks could operate in some parts of the country, and they could provide security to convoys moving supplies around the country. But they made big targets, especially when the topography of Vietnam took away their mobility. I wasn't wild about tanks because the closest that I had come to getting killed in 'Nam occurred when a "friendly" tank crashed the firefight that I was in so that it could get a body count. The tank knocked a tree over while driving through my position. The tree missed me by less than a foot. It would really suck to get killed by a tree hit by one of your own tanks. But be that as it may, back to the Mummy Case.

With the war winding down, the soon-to-be-mummy, Private E-1 Hazels, decided that he didn't want to be the last tanker to get blown off his tank by a Soviet RPG (rocket propelled grenade) before the war ended. So he decided to go AWOL. But privates don't make much money, and he couldn't wait until payday to get his pittance, so he decided to engage in a little armed robbery to finance his flight to Canada.

Private Hazels, a draftee from the South Side of Chicago, was about as effective a robber as he was a soldier. After he had robbed two trainees at knifepoint, he tried to rob a third, but picked the wrong victim. This third target surrendered his money all right, but then chased Private Hazels down the middle of Gold Vault Road, screaming, "He robbed me! Catch him!" The victim might not have had Master An's self-defense skills, but he certainly had his heart! At least, Private Hazels didn't try to rob the Gold Vault at Knox—he wouldn't have lived long enough to be chased down the road, James Bond's "Goldfinger" movie notwithstanding.

Two military policemen who were driving by in a patrol car were more than happy to oblige, and Private Hazels soon found himself in pretrial confinement pending general court-martial for three specifications of violation of Article 122, UCMJ, robbery, each carrying a maximum punishment of a dishonorable discharge, forfeiture of all pay and allowances, reduction to the lowest enlisted grade, and confinement for ten years.

Presented with the seriousness of the offense, the thirty years of confinement that Private Hazels faced, and his handwritten plan for robbery to finance going AWOL, the Military Magistrate had little difficulty in finding pretrial confinement warranted because the accused was both a flight risk and a danger to the community.

Having previously decided to have nothing more to do with the Army, which he manifested by beginning to execute his plan to go

AWOL, Private Hazels decided to have nothing whatsoever to do with the military justice system either, which he manifested by becoming the Mummy. He would not dress himself in the stockade, would not shave himself, would not follow orders, would not talk to his defense counsel, and the like. About all that he would do was use the latrine, chew food that was spooned into his mouth, and masturbate. He was not to be my last stockade masturbator—must be something about the confinement in a military stockade.

Captain Ostend was appointed the Mummy's detailed defense counsel, and I was assigned to prosecute. Captain Ostend was a good guy. He had entered the JAGC to avoid being drafted and going to Vietnam as an enlisted man, but he did his job competently enough. I particularly liked him because, like me, he sported a mustache. Every platoon leader in my battalion of the First Cavalry had a mustache, and I refused to shave it even though the military frowned on officers having such facial hair. I suppose that keeping it was my one rebellion against the military that I now owed four more years of my adult life after having let them send me to law school.

Even though the Mummy was totally uncooperative with the stockade personnel and with his defense counsel, the wheels of justice ground on. During the Article 32, UCMJ, investigation (the military version of a grand jury proceeding), the stockade guards would dress and shave the Mummy, carry him to the courtroom where the Investigating Officer was conducting the hearing, and tie him in a seated position in a chair at the defense table. Absent this bondage, he would just slide off the chair and collapse on the floor. For some reason, the Investigating Officer, an Armor major, had felt that the Mummy lying prostrate on the floor would not show appropriate respect for the dignity of the proceeding and ordered him tied to his chair. Predictably, the Investigating Officer determined that sufficient evidence existed to recommend trial by general court-martial, and the Commanding General, Fort Knox, agreed. The CG was the General Court-Martial Convening Authority for all units on the fort.

So the day that the court-martial started for the Mummy, the guards again dressed and shaved him and carried him to the courtroom. Because Captain Ostend and I had briefed Judge Savage on the Mummy's shenanigans, Judge Savage was able to control his irritation at someone who was totally failing to act respectfully in his court. And it is not difficult for a military judge to preside over a mummy case—not nearly so hard as over a disruptive defendant. The military judge simply exercises the mummy's rights and choices in a manner that does not require an affirmative response from the accused mummy.

Normally, the "script" that the military judge follows, after an explanation of the accused's rights to counsel, requires the judge to ask the accused, "Do you understand?" Judge Savage first asked the Mummy whether he understood in the faint hope that the Mummy would decide to un-mummy himself and cooperate. When the Mummy continued to mummy, Judge Savage continued, "Unless you tell me differently, I am going to assume that you understand your rights to counsel. Let the record reflect that the accused did not respond." I've got to give Judge Savage credit. Not only did he not show any irritation at the accused's lack of cooperation and respect for the military judicial system, but also he never slipped and said, "Let the record reflect that the Mummy did not respond."

Judge Savage continued in this vein, entering a plea of not guilty, because a plea of guilty required the accused not only to so state, but also to answer questions to demonstrate that he was knowingly, intelligently (well, that word might have been a stretch in the Mummy's case), and voluntarily pleading guilty because he really was guilty. This inability to plead guilty was arguably the worst part of being a mummy, because the mummy could not plea bargain for a lighter sentence.

Because a court composed of officer court members was the default and a court consisting of not less than one-third enlisted required an affirmative request as did a request for trial by military judge alone, Judge Savage again said, "Unless you tell me differently, I am going to assume that you understand your rights to request trial by military judge alone or a court composed of not less than one-third enlisted members and that you want to be tried by a court composed of officer members. Let the record reflect that the accused did not respond."

Eventually, all of the preliminaries were out of the way, with a lot of "let the record reflect that the accused did not respond" observations by Judge Savage to protect the record. If the court-martial resulted in sentencing the accused to a punitive discharge—dishonorable or bad conduct—or confinement in excess of a year, a definite possibility with this mummy routine, a verbatim transcript was required. But the court reporter could not record answers that were not oral. Thus, the judge and counsel had to describe motions, nods of the head, and lack of response for the record.

Eventually, it was time for the trial itself to start. Judge Savage called for the court members. As they filed in, the court members looked somewhat taken aback at seeing the accused tied to a chair at the defense table with his head lolling back and his eyes closed. Judge Savage had reluctantly ordered this restraint as being preferable to having the Mummy slide out of his chair onto the floor anytime the bailiff didn't hold him in place. During his opening instructions to the court members, the judge emphasized that they could not hold his being restrained against him in any way on the issue of whether he was guilty of the charges that he was facing. The court members all responded that they could follow that instruction. Yeah, right.

My case wasn't hard to prove. All three of the victims all positively identified the Mummy as the person who had robbed them. The knife, which the military police had recovered from the Mummy, established the necessary force and violence to turn a mere larceny into a robbery. The two MPs were good witnesses, giving a stirring recounting of the chase that captured the Mummy. Captain Ostend did a good job of cross-examining the witnesses—yes, it was dark; yes, it was hard to see; yes, the accused looked much like any other soldier dressed in fatigues—but without the

Mummy presenting some lame defense, there wasn't much else that his lawyer could do.

I wasn't particularly worried while the court members deliberated. Yes, Judge Savage had instructed them that they could not draw any adverse inference as to his guilt from his behavior, but even if they followed that instruction, I had more than enough evidence to convict beyond a reasonable doubt. And I did.

Because the Mummy had just finished Basic and AIT, I didn't have much evidence to put on during the sentencing portion of the case. The Mummy hadn't had time to accumulate nonjudicial punishment or other disciplinary measures before committing his robberies. But on the other hand, the defense didn't have much to put on, either, because the Mummy continued to mummy, and Captain Ostend had been unable to find anyone to say anything good about the Mummy. I had actually been hoping that the defense would call a military witness to testify on the Mummy's behalf so that I could have a friendly discussion with the witness about an armed robber who was so disrespectful of the military that he had to be tied to his chair in the courtroom. But Captain Ostend was no mummy—I mean no dummy. He wasn't about to open the door for me to bring out evidence about how the Mummy was a dud before he became a mummy. His only witness was the Mummy's mother, who testified that, even though her son didn't want to be drafted, he had told her that he was going to try to do a good job in the Army. It was not until he got orders to Vietnam that he freaked out. She asked the court members to let him come home to her because she was in poor health and needed his help. As Captain Ostend knew I wouldn't, I didn't cross-examine the Mummy's mother. She hadn't hurt my case, and attacking her could get sympathy for the Mummy.

In my sentencing argument, I urged that three robberies at knifepoint involved such a high risk of death or serious bodily injury that a severe sentence was warranted and that, in arriving at an appropriate sentence, the court members could consider the accused's demeanor at his trial: "Gentlemen of the jury, Judge Savage properly instructed you that you could not consider the accused's demeanor as evidence of his guilt. But you can consider it as evidence of his lack of remorse, his disrespect for military service, and his total lack of rehabilitation potential when you deliberate on an appropriate sentence. And that appropriate sentence is the maximum."

I really wondered what Captain Ostend could even argue as to why the Mummy should get a light sentence. I've got to admit, however, that he did a good job with what he had—nothing. He mentioned that the Mummy had successfully completed Basic and Advanced Individual Training and had committed these crimes only out of fear of dying in Vietnam. He asked the court members to arrive at a sentence with only a short period of confinement so that the Mummy could help his poor, sick mother.

The court members did not deliberate long. They came back and sentenced the Mummy to a dishonorable discharge, forfeiture of all pay and allowances, and confinement for 30 years—the maximum sentence because they couldn't reduce him in grade because he was already at the lowest enlisted grade. Shortly after the trial, one of the members told me that, if he had acted halfway normal and had expressed some remorse or offered some half-assed mitigating factors, such as that he had just gotten religion or that his mother used to kick him with combat boots, they would have given him somewhere between five and eight years' confinement. But he wanted to play hardball, and the court members were happy to accommodate him.

As the stockade guards were carrying the Mummy out of the courtroom to begin his journey to the United States Disciplinary Barracks at Fort Leavenworth, Kansas, the Mummy finally broke his silence, "Duh, I think I fucked up."

Indeed. But at least he hadn't turned into the Bruce Lee of defense lawyers.

4

The Said Willie K. Lower

"According to all the laws of aerodynamics, the bumble-bee should not fly, but the bumble-bee does not know this and so flies anyway."

—*Kung-fu principle*

If *United States v. Turner*—my first prosecution—was the case that I won with the least admissible evidence, *United States v. Lower* was the case that I won with the most inadmissible evidence. Private First Class Willie K. Lower was facing three pages of charges, each with multiple specifications, such as this one:

> Charge: Violation of the UCMJ, Article 91.
>
> Specification: In that Private First Class Willie K. Lower, U.S. Army, Headquarters and Headquarters Company, 194th Armored Brigade, Fort Knox, Kentucky, did, at Fort Knox, Kentucky, treat with disrespectful language Staff Sergeant Mark M. McBride, his superior noncommissioned officer, then known by the said Willie K. Lower to be a superior noncommissioned officer, who was then in the execution of his office, by saying to him, "Why don't you pull a rubber over your head so I don't have to see your ugly face," or words to that effect.

Willie's charges included disrespect, disobedience, breaking restriction, going from his appointed place of duty without authority, and malingering—feigning illness to avoid duty. Having already suffered punishment from his company commander for going AWOL, Willie was obviously not a candidate for Sergeant Major of the Army.

The next manifestation of Willie's antimilitary view occurred when he fired his defense lawyer, Jim Preston. Captain Preston was probably the best of the four defense counsel at Fort Knox. He certainly put up a great battle every time he faced me—the one defense counsel that did not try to plea bargain on every case that I tried. But Willie did not want anything to do with an officer, even an officer who was going to defend him before a special court-martial.

At the trial, Willie showed up promptly for a change, dressed properly in his Class A uniform. Willie was a scrawny black man with an afro coif that pushed the boundaries of a proper military haircut. Captain Preston sat beside him, but not for long. Military law does contemplate representing oneself at a court-martial, so Willie set out to prove the old adage that one who seeks to represent himself has a fool for a client. When Judge Savage asked the accused whether he understood his right to counsel and whom he wanted to represent him, Willie said that he did understand his rights and wanted to defend himself. Judge Savage, either out of concern that the accused was an idiot and would severely damage his case or, more likely, out of concern that he would be reversed on appeal for somehow denying Willie his right to the effective assistance of counsel, grilled the accused to make certain that Willie's waiver was both knowing and voluntary. When the accused stubbornly refused to be badgered into keeping Captain Preston on the case, Judge Savage threw up his hands, said, "Very well. You are excused, Captain Preston. Continue, Trial Counsel."

After I had gone through the remaining preliminaries, including reading all of the charges against Willie, he pled, "Nolo contendere," which is Latin for "I will not contest." Apparently, he had watched too much television. Judge Savage promptly informed him that the military did not have a "no contest" plea, whereupon Willie changed his plea to "not guilty."

Then, we sat the jury. Just as Willie's brilliant plea had done, his challenge to the court members as being biased because they were officers and were assigned to Fort Knox left Judge Savage unmoved. Judge Savage told Willie that he should have exercised his right to one-third enlisted upon request at the proper time if he did not want an all-officer military jury.

The jury had shown some surprise at a private first class representing himself, but upon hearing Judge Savage's instruction that they could not hold it against the accused that he was representing himself, they acted pretty much the way that any other typical military court-martial panel would, half-relieved to be away from the field or whatever other less-than-thrilling duties they had or nervous about taking time away from their duties—the stellar performance of which they believed would get them promoted if they didn't have to waste time as a court member.

I called my first witness, Captain Bill Hunt, the commander of Headquarters Company, to prove that Willie had broken the restriction that Captain Hunt had imposed. Captain Hunt's medals and badges showing that he had spent two tours with the Infantry in Vietnam trumped his short stature. I had only a few questions to prove that Captain Hunt was Willie's superior commissioned officer, had lawfully restricted him, and had informed him of the restriction and that Willie had been found outside the limits of the restriction without permission. "No further, questions. Your witness, PFC Lower."

Willie slowly rose to his feet, grabbing both lapels of his Class A blouse, which was like a suit coat except for having extra pockets, PFC stripes on the arms, a 194th Armored Brigade patch on the left sleeve and a few ribbons and badges above the left breast pocket. He stuck out his chest, still clutching his lapels like some old-time movie shyster, and strutted up to the witness.

"Now, Sir," he began his cross-examination, "when the said Willie K. Lower, meaning me (pointing at himself), disrespected you, why did you need to restrict him?"

This question was the one that Captain Hunt had been waiting for all of his military officer life. "PFC Lower, you are the worst excuse for a soldier that I have ever known. The first day that you reported to Headquarters Company, you were late, out of uniform, unshaven, without a proper haircut, sullen, and disrespectful. And that probably was the high point of your career."

Well, this answer was the equivalent of one of Master An's roundhouse kicks to the temple for ending one's defense. For the next fifteen minutes, we got to hear Captain Hunt's scathing denunciation of the witness. None of his tirade would have been admissible as being uncharged misconduct if I had asked the question, but the defense can bring out as much bad shit about the accused as it wants.

Willie initially reeled back from this verbal onslaught. Soon, however, he realized that he was Perry Mason Lower and would recoup his fading chances of an acquittal with his next insightful cross-examination question. He drew himself up, fixed the witness with a stern look, and said, "Well, besides that."

The jurors had their fists to their faces, trying to stifle laughs. Judge Savage was notorious for losing it if anyone dared to laugh in his courtroom, and every trial counsel briefed new court members not to laugh under any circumstances. So the court members were pinching themselves, biting their fingers, and covering their mouths with their hands as Captain Hunt launched his second salvo. This one lasted only eight more minutes, but it was obvious that Willie had committed every crime charged and dozens that had not been charged. Willie nodded sagaciously at each new revelation as if it somehow proved his innocence. Finally, he said, "That's all, Cap," and sat down.

Because Willie had brought out 90 percent of my case, I called only two more witnesses instead of the six that I had standing by. Master An had taught me Sun Tzu's precept of economy of force—don't waste your strength on unnecessary offensive or defensive actions. After I had elicited their testimony, Willie reprised his unusual cross-examination technique. As he finished with my last witness, I finally figured out Willie's brilliant strategy. He was going to bring out so much evidence of his misconduct that the court members would be so confused as to which evidence went with which charge that they would throw up their hands and find him not guilty of any of the charges. Yeah, right.

After I had I rested my case, Willie, believing that he had accomplished enough with his probing cross-examination of my witnesses, rested his defense without putting on any evidence.

Countering Willie's strategy of confusing the jury with all of his misconduct, my argument methodically focused on which evidence proved which element of which specification, telling the jury to ignore the other misconduct that had not been charged.

As a lawyer, I should be able to describe Willie's argument. After all, because the prosecution has the burden of proving guilt beyond a reasonable doubt, I argued first and last—a rebuttal argument to knock out any points that he might have made in his argument. His argument started with the illegality of the Vietnam War, ran through the racial prejudice that allegedly resulted in more blacks dying in 'Nam per capita than whites, to the lack of leadership in the 194th Armored Brigade. Because he hadn't served in Vietnam, the first two points seemed too irrelevant to bother rebutting, and because all of the court members were officers in the 194th Armored Brigade, I hardly thought that Willie's attack on them would gain him anything, so I said, "No rebuttal, your honor," when Judge Savage looked at me with a look that said, "If you waste my time with a rebuttal argument, you will make the 'I've Been Savaged,' board." Maybe the judge followed Sun Tzu's principles of war, too.

Sure enough, the jury convicted Willie of all of the charges and specifications, deliberating for about five minutes. Now, here's where I continue my string of maximum sentences, I thought, because all of the uncharged misconduct that Willie had brought out was relevant on the issue of sentencing. I put on my sentencing case, getting Willie's prior nonjudicial punishments admitted against him and bringing Captain Hunt back to testify that he would not want Willie back in his unit under any circumstances.

Willie's sentencing phase defense case consisted of making an unsworn statement that mostly reprised his argument on whether he was guilty or not. A military accused can testify under oath during the sentencing proceeding or make an unsworn statement. The trial counsel cannot cross-examine an accused who makes an unsworn statement, but may introduce evidence to rebut any untrue statements made. Again, I saw no need to bother rebutting anything that he said.

In my sentencing phase argument, I strongly contended that the maximum penalty, a bad-conduct discharge, confinement for six months, forfeiture of two-thirds pay per month for six months, and reduction to the lowest enlisted grade, would be the only appropriate sentence. Then, Willie countered by again repeating his findings argument and unsworn statement—hey, maybe repetition would make some part of it sink in to the factfinders. After Judge Savage's instructions, the court members retired to deliberate.

This time, their deliberations took longer than their deliberations on whether Willie was guilty. What was taking them so long? I worried. It has to be the most open and shut give-the-SOB-the-maximum-sentence case in the history of military law, I thought. Finally, after an hour and a half, the members came back and sentenced Willie to a bad-conduct discharge, forfeiture of two-thirds pay per month for six months, reduction to the lowest enlisted grade, and confinement for *five* months. Oh, no. Not six months—the maximum sentence—only five months! My streak was gone!

Crushed, I went up to the court members to find out what had happened. Military law prohibits asking them how they had voted, but I could ask more general questions. The first member, a captain whom I did not know, told me that they had cut one month off Willie's sentence because of the entertainment value of his defense. The President of the Court, a major whom I had spent some time with at the Officers' Club, said, "Come on, Captain Thomas. Don't be pissed. We took care of you. We knew that you were worried about having to compete with PFC Lower if and when he gets his law degree, so we gave him a Big Chicken Dinner (military slang for Bad Conduct Discharge) so that he couldn't get into law school!"

Thanks a lot. I'd have preferred taking my chances facing Willie again in court instead of having to listen to the ribbing of the other trial counsel for losing my string of maximum sentences. I will say one thing for the said Willie K. Lower, however. He fared better than the Mummy—even if he was a bumble-head who could not fly.

5

The Sensitivity Test

"Do not let your opponent see your spirit."

—Miyamoto Musashi.

My days of easy wins prosecuting as a trial counsel came to an end when the Chief Defense Counsel at Fort Knox, Kentucky, left military service. I was apparently the only captain senior enough by date of rank to take over because the second most senior defense counsel to the outgoing Chief was a rabid defender and the Staff Judge Advocate ("SJA") thought that he might, if appointed Chief, instill too much fighting spirit into the other defense counsel. Even though I had a great reputation for fighting hard in the courtroom as a trial counsel, the SJA could not envision that a former infantryman like me could fight for, charitably speaking most of the time, the problem children that his trial counsel were court-martialing. The only problem with the SJA's theory was that I hated to lose, no matter which side I was on. I had always believed in Red Auerbach's adage when he coached the Boston Celtics to NBA title after NBA title, "Show me a good loser, and I'll show you a loser." And neither combat nor Master An had done anything to dispel my belief that losing was for losers, whatever side of the matter one found himself on. So I approached the defense with the same intensity with which I had prosecuted soldiers.

Of course, defending accused soldiers turned out to be a whole lot harder than prosecuting them. First, I had to move from my spacious office on the second floor of the building that housed most of the JAG office (legal assistance, being beyond the pale, was in a World War II barracks a mile or so away) to a cubbyhole on the third floor. Second, the commanders who loved me when I was prosecuting their troublemakers now viewed me as a traitor. Worst of all, commanders quit offering me free drinks at the Officers' Club.

But the best thing about being Chief Defense Counsel was that I got to assign the cases. Thus, I had assigned some of the doofus cases that I didn't want to try to whoever happened to be on my shit list at the time. For example, Captain Dale had gotten me chewed out by the Staff Judge Advocate for having an unkempt uniform and a nonregulation mustache. So I promptly assigned him the "wrongfully dumping pickle relish on the mess-hall floor" case, apparently a violation of Article 134, Offenses Prejudicial to Good Order and Discipline in the Armed Forces or of a Nature to Bring Discredit upon the Armed Forces. I also assigned him the case of Specialist St. John, who had been accused of stealing a dozen whole chicken carcasses from the mess hall, so that Captain Dale could have a chicken thief to defend.

When the case against Second Lieutenant Wyndham came across my desk, my first instinct was to assign it to someone else without even reading the charges. No one wanted to defend officer clients. They were too difficult. They were so used to leading their platoons, commanding their companies or higher units, or supervising a large staff that they wanted to run their defense, as well. I may have occasionally followed some of the strategies outlined in Sun Tzu's *The Art of War,* such as concentrating my forces at the most vulnerable part of my opponent's case, a tactic similar to Master An's theory of kicking them in the balls. But in general, one couldn't successfully try a case the way that one could wage a military campaign. And I knew Wyndham. He had been the legal officer for the 194th Armored Brigade, which meant that he was responsible for the administrative processing of the courts-martial that we had tried from that unit. Knowing him as being particularly anal, I definitely did not want to be the defense counsel. But trying to be thorough, I flipped to the second page of the charge sheet to see what the Butterbar had allegedly done.

The first charge was a violation of Article 134, with two specifications: (1) indecent assault, by touching one JoAnne Williams on the breast, with intent to gratify his lust, and (2) willfully and wrongfully exposing in an indecent manner his penis. The second charge was a violation of Article 133, Conduct Unbecoming an Officer and a Gentleman, by doing the two acts alleged in Charge I.

Well, even though I was irritated at Captain Dale, I couldn't dump this case on him. It would be too high profile—an officer sex case. So if I didn't take it, it would have to go to Captain Bob Reilly, the most experienced defense counsel. We were pretty good friends, but not good enough for me to take the case myself, so I gave the case to him.

But Captain Reilly had the last laugh. A couple of days later, he came into my office, smiled evilly, and said, "Lieutenant Wyndham was so impressed by your performance when you prosecuted cases that he had forwarded to you in his capacity as legal officer for the 194th that he's requested you as his Individual Defense Counsel."

"Oh, shit."

"They say that misery loves company, so now you and I can share."

"Can't we just plead him guilty?" I begged, already conceding that I had no choice but to find myself reasonably available so as to be eligible to be Wyndham's Individual Defense Counsel.

"No, then he would have to admit to his bride of less than a year that he had been fondling another woman's breasts."

"Fuck me," I said, having learned an infantryman's vocabulary during my year in Vietnam.

"I just did," Captain Reilly laughed as he left my office.

So being stuck with the case, I began reading the file that Captain Reilly had so graciously left on my desk. My spirits sank farther with every page that I read.

The first page was the DA Form 3997, Military Police Desk Blotter, which read as follows:

> CONDUCT UNBECOMING OF AN OFFICER:
>
> SUBJ: PI
>
> WHEN: 1830 hrs, 24 Jun 77
>
> WHERE: Qtrs #3655B, Eighth Armor Div Road, Prichard Place Housing Area, Fort Knox, KY
>
> DETAILS: COMP stated that, while at the above location, she was approached by SUBJ who stated he was conducting a survey. COMP further stated that SUBJ made harassing remarks towards her, at which time he fondled her breasts and exposed his genitals by unzipping his pants. SUBJ was apprehended, advised of his rights, and charged. SUBJ rel to unit (COL Rock) at 2100 hrs. CID (Millar) ntfd at 2145 hrs, 24 Jun 77. Investigation continues.

By this time, I could read military acronyms as easily as real words. Surely, military acronyms must have been the precursor to texting. The SUBJ PI meant that the subject's identity was protected identity ("PI") because he was an officer. The offense had taken place in the Complainant's ("COMP") quarters ("qtrs") at 6:30 P.M. ("1830 hrs"). The Military Police had notified ("ntfd") the Criminal Investigation Division's ("CID") Agent Millar at 9:00 P.M. ("2145 hours"). My client had not been placed in pretrial confinement, but had been released ("rel") to his commander, Colonel Rock. From my experience with Colonel Rock in my first case, I wouldn't have wanted to be an officer suspected of a sex crime and released into Colonel Rock's custody.

A supplemental CID report of investigation revealed another Military Police blotter report indicating that Mrs. Williams, the wife of Staff Sergeant Williams of the 194th Armored Brigade, had been arrested in the Non-Commissioned Officers' Club parking lot for oral sodomy. As 194th Armored Brigade Legal Officer, my illustrious client would have received all blotter entries relating to members of the 194th and their families to help ensure that proper disciplinary action was taken, if appropriate.

Well, there was nothing to do but get going on the defense. First, I had to talk to the client, make certain that he really wanted me (as if I had any hope that he didn't), and get his side of the story. So I told my paralegal to get the lieutenant to my office ASAP.

About an hour later, Lieutenant Forrest Wyndham knocked on my open door, looking somewhat sheepish. Reporting to your defense counsel for a sex crime isn't calculated to make you appear confident. He didn't look much like a warrior to begin with, being somewhat short and scrawny, with sharp features. But his uniform was immaculate, for whatever that was worth. And he wasn't even unzipped.

After we had finished the preliminaries and, yes, he definitely wanted me to represent him, I asked him what had happened.

"Well, Sir," he began, "as you know, I was the 194th Brigade Legal Officer before this happened, and I had a whole bunch of extra duties. One of them was morale officer. I was supposed to find ways to improve the morale of the soldiers in the 194th. Because I am also the safety officer, I noticed that we had been having a number of heat-related injuries. I knew that we were doing pretty well at fixing the problem with the troops, but was concerned about their families. So I thought that I would do a survey to see whether families in government quarters were susceptible to heat injuries. So I went to the Prichard Place Housing Area and started asking questions about whether the air conditioning worked, whether the children had enough light-weight summer clothing, whether they were getting enough liquids, and so on."

"What about the allegation by the complainant, Mrs. Williams, that you touched her and exposed yourself on June 24th?"

"I had interviewed Mrs. Williams on the 23d, but I never saw her on the 24th."

The words to the old song "Straighten Up and Fly Right!" came to mind: "The monkey looked the buzzard right dead in the eye and said, 'Your story's touching, but it sounds just like a lie!'"

Because I believed in Santa Claus more than I believed in my client's ridiculous story about a heat injuries survey, I didn't immediately follow up on what might prove to be a defense—an alibi. Instead, I focused on what I saw as the weak points in his story, that is, any and all of the story.

"Who authorized this survey?"

"No one."

"Whom did you tell that you were going to do this survey?"

"No one."

"How many different quarters did you visit to conduct this survey?"

"I had only completed Mrs. Williams's quarters."

"So let me get this straight, Lieutenant. After you, in your capacity as legal officer, get an MP blotter telling you that Mrs. Williams had been arrested for oral sodomy, you just happened to pick her quarters out of the blue to perform the only heat injury survey—a survey that was not only unauthorized by, but also unknown to, your superiors?"

"I know that it looks bad when you put it that way, Sir, but I didn't touch her or expose myself."

"It may be bad when I put it that way, but it's going to be devastating when the trial counsel puts it that way."

The L-T, slang for lieutenant, looked so woebegone at this point that I decided that I'd better leave the issue of guilt or innocence for a while and get all the required preliminaries out of the way, such as making sure that he understood his rights, getting contact information for potential character witnesses, and the like.

Finally, I tried to end the meeting. "Ok, Forrest, let me do some digging, and I'll get back to you when I know more or when they schedule the Article 32 investigation."

"An Article 32! Doesn't that mean a general court-martial? Maybe it won't go to a general court."

"Forrest, the chance of Colonel Rock not recommending that the Post Commander refer an officer sexual misconduct case to a general court-martial is only somewhat less than my chance of being promoted to four-star general in the next five minutes. Sorry, but that's the way it is. You just have to hang in there and keep your mouth shut. No talking about the case with anyone but me. Although the government couldn't compel your wife or your priest to disclose conversations with you about the case, I don't even want to risk having the prosecution try to do so. Now, get back to your duties and do the best job that you can so that we can get some good character evidence."

Although good character evidence might be admissible on the issue of guilt or innocence on the theory that good soldiers do not commit crimes, I was really focusing on sentencing—so-called E & M for extenuation and mitigation. Extenuation in military law refers to extenuating circumstances—things that make the crime less serious, such as the fact that Mrs. Williams did not appear to be a nun. Mitigation refers to mitigating factors aside from the facts and circumstances of the offense that indicate that the punishment should not be so severe. A good military record, no prior punishments, mental problems not amounting to an insanity defense, not mummying before the judge and court members, and so forth could be mitigating in a particular case.

So I got to work. More accurately, I put my paralegal to work. I assigned him to dig up any more dirt that he could find on Mrs. Williams that might impeach her testimony and to interview all of the character witnesses that Lieutenant Wyndham had listed. My paralegal, Staff Sergeant Carrette, was, for no reason that I could fathom, intensely loyal, so loyal that I had to constantly turn down his offers to fabricate favorable evidence for the accused, intimidate prosecution witnesses, and the like. He really topped himself in the Wyndham case, however, by volunteering to get Mrs. Williams arrested again after performing oral sodomy on him at the NCO Club parking lot so that we would have more evidence of her bad character. I had to ruin his day by turning down his magnanimous offer because I did not want to lose my law license, face a court-martial myself, and/or be kicked out of the Army. Nor did I think that one more such arrest would really damage her credibility all that much more. In law school, they call stacking evidence "bolstering," and in real life cases, it doesn't usually work.

Well, nobody that Sergeant Carrette interviewed thought that the lieutenant could possibly be guilty of this type of conduct unbecoming an officer. But neither did they have such great things to say about him that we could put on the so-called "good soldier defense." The theory was that good soldiers didn't expose themselves or grab breasts—at least not without some type of invitation. After all, the lieutenant was a lieutenant—and a second lieutenant at that. The nickname Butterbar was not a term of respect. Second lieutenants were expected to screw up most everything. Although Lieutenant Wyndham was not that bad, he was a typical second lieutenant who had performed moderately well in a fairly unimportant job. So no one had enough good things to say about him for me to rely on the good soldier defense. And I didn't think that creating the Butterbar defense—that second lieutenants were so dumb that we should forgive them their stupidities—was likely to work, either. Fortunately, the Uniform Code of Military Justice did not have a charge for criminal stupidity, or my client surely would have faced that charge, too.

So I was reduced to checking out his story to see whether a defense was lurking around somewhere. And lo and behold, he had an alibi. He wasn't at Mrs. Williams's quarters the day that she said that the incident had happened—just as he had said.

At the Article 32 Investigation—the military's version of a grand jury investigation except that the accused and his lawyers get to be there—I found out quite a bit more about her story.

She testified, under oath, as follows. Lieutenant Wyndham had come to her quarters, in uniform, wearing his gold bars and nametag, and carrying a clipboard. He had said that he was conducting a safety survey to prevent heat injuries. Thinking it a bit strange, but not suspecting anything sinister, she had let him in.

He started asking her questions: "Does the air conditioning work? Do your children have enough lightweight clothing?" He wrote something down on the clipboard after each response. After only a few questions that might be related to preventing heat injuries, he asked her how sensitive she was.

She initially thought that he meant how sensitive was she to heat injuries, but upon asking him what he meant, he said that he was referring to a sensitivity touch test. He said that he had studied physiology in college and was always trying to learn more about human reactions to sensory stimuli. He continued, "Some women, for example, have much more sensitive breasts than others." Then, he tried to slide his hand inside her blouse and under her bra.

She pulled away, saying, "Don't do that."

Then he backed away, unzipped himself, displayed his erect penis to Mrs. Williams, and asked her whether she knew where he was sensitive. She pointed to his penis. He asked her whether it embarrassed her.

She replied, "Does this look like I'm embarrassed?" as she grabbed his penis.

Thereupon, the lieutenant apparently beat a quick retreat—no pun intended—putting his penis back into his pants and saying that he'd have to return another day.

Now, I don't know about you, but this story sounded too credible for Mrs. Williams, with her high school education, to have fabricated.

Mrs. Williams had been so unconcerned by this incident that she had not called the Military Police.

But when her neighbor came over several hours later, she had asked Mrs. Williams, "Who was that officer? What was he doing here?"

Mrs. Williams told her the whole story, and the neighbor called the Military Police.

I did not want to cross-examine Mrs. Williams too much at the Article 32 investigation, preferring to save it for the actual trial. So I merely brought out that, yes, she was guilty of oral sodomy at the NCO Club parking lot, had otherwise had a checkered sexual history, and had had an AWOL soldier living with her in her quarters at the time of the incident. I also locked her in, in sworn testimony, as to the exact date and time: 1605 hours, not 1600, and not 1610, on June 24th—at 4:05 P.M., not a moment before and not a moment later.

The neighbor testified as to having seen the lieutenant in the housing area, but did not remember the date, and to having received Mrs. Williams's report of the incident.

And that was it for the 32 investigation. But it was enough for the investigating officer to recommend trial by general court-martial. His conclusion was fairly damning:

> In the investigator's view and with some circumstantial evidence involved, it is most probable that Lieutenant Wyndham did know of Mrs. Williams's reputation and decided to see for himself. The heat survey was a very poor excuse for an officer to be in an enlisted area. Interviews without the presence of a husband are questionable even with a valid survey. Even though Mrs. Williams may have "come on" to Lieutenant Wyndham, all of the elements of the offenses are met, and he deserves a general court-martial for these actions, which are not becoming of an officer in the United States Army."

The entire chain of command, quite naturally, agreed, and the Commanding General referred the matter to a general court-martial. So my first general court-martial defense would be an officer sexual misconduct case—in front of Judge Savage.

The only motion that Captain Reilly and I could come up with of any consequence was one that the charge of conduct unbecoming an officer was multiplicious with the other two charges and amounted to stacking charges—charging the same thing several ways, not because of uncertainty as to what the evidence might show but, rather, to increase the punishment or to cause the court members to think that, what with so many charges, the accused must be guilty of something. Either Captain Reilly had a very good day or Judge Savage had a very bad one, because the judge actually granted the motion. Judge Savage was not known for granting defense motions unless they were meaningless ones so that he could look as if he were fair to the defense or unless he had absolutely no choice. We called most of his favorable rulings, rare as they were, "tossing the defense a bone." I never thought that Judge Savage would grant this motion, but maybe he liked Lieutenant Wyndham for having sent so many cases to court when the lieutenant was the legal officer for the 194th Armored Brigade.

The ruling was huge for the defense, because the court members could have decided that our client had not indecently assaulted the alleged victim or exposed himself, but that, nonetheless, even performing such a stupid survey was conduct unbecoming an officer.

The trial started in earnest at 0900 the next day. Promptly at 9:00 A.M., Judge Savage ordered the trial counsel, Captain Yoder, to get the court members. Even though the order convening the court had listed all of the court members, so I knew whom to expect, watching them parade in with all of their ribbons and badges was quite daunting for my first big defense case. The President of the Court was a full colonel. Because the accused was an officer, the Convening Authority had packed the court with more high-ranking officers than usual—three lieutenant colonels, three majors, and five captains, in addition to the full colonel. All but two of the captains had served in Vietnam. One of the court members was a rear echelon type, an Adjutant General officer—a paper pusher—but even he wore Airborne Wings. The rest of the court members were combat arms officers, Infantry, Armor, and Artillery.

Because military juries convict when two-thirds of the court members vote guilty, a common defense tactic was to play the so-called "numbers game." This tactic involved using your challenges to get a total number of court members that made it hard to get to a two-thirds majority. For example, if you got the court down to five members, four of the five or 80 percent had to vote "guilty" to convict because three of the five was only 60 percent, not two-thirds. Twelve members, as we had here, favored the prosecution, who had to convince only eight members to get a conviction. So I wanted to use my challenges both to get a more favorable number of members and to get any members off the panel that might be too hard-core to vote for an acquittal.

First, the trial counsel got to question the members, a process called voir dire. As I would have done if I had been prosecuting, he didn't ask the court members any questions that they could view as impugning their fairness or integrity. But I didn't have that luxury. The only fact I that brought out that would disqualify a juror was that the Adjutant General captain had read reports of the matter. The other members were too savvy to say that, no, they didn't think the fact that the military police, the Article 32 investigating officer, the accused's company, battalion, and brigade commanders, and the Commanding General of Fort Knox had recommended a general court-martial was any indication that Lieutenant Wyndham was guilty. Yeah, right. All of them knew that the military justice system didn't send cases to general courts-martial unless the accused was facing some fairly damning evidence. But they also knew that, if they answered that way, they would be bounced off the court, and the Commanding General, by God, had chosen them to be on the court, and they intended to stay on the court.

Captain Yoder had no challenges for cause, announcing it as if he were personally blessing all of the court members. Even though the trial counsel had done a good job of rehabilitating the Adjutant General officer, getting him to say that he could ignore what he had read about Lieutenant Wyndham's crimes, Judge Savage granted my challenge for cause. He likely decided that granting that challenge didn't really hurt the government and why create an issue on appeal that could get him reversed.

Under military law, each side had only one peremptory challenge—one that didn't need a reason. Again, Captain Yoder unctuously intoned that he had no peremptory challenge.

So I got up to use my peremptory challenge to get rid of Colonel Boychuck. Every Army lawyer on post knew that Colonel

Boychuck was the most hard-core senior officer on the post. If there was a badge that he wasn't wearing, I didn't know what it was. In addition to a Silver Star, a Bronze Star with "V" device and many Oak Leaf Clusters denoting multiple awards, and two Purple Hearts, his filled-to-overflowing Class A blouse displayed Airborne Master Blaster Wings, a Ranger Tab, a Special Forces Tab, a Combat Infantry Badge with Star denoting combat in both Korea and Vietnam, and a Pathfinder Badge. Colonel Boychuck was of Ukrainian extraction (he was rumored to have been a partisan who had fought against the Nazis) and looked like a perfect warrior—compact build, thick neck, heavy shoulders, muscular arms, and a shaved head. The G-2 (intelligence) on him was that he always voted to convict and always voted for the maximum sentence—hardly your most desirable President of the Court if you were an accused, particularly an officer accused of sex crimes.

So even though eleven members made a more favorable number for the defense than ten, I rose to my feet to challenge Colonel Boychuck peremptorily. Just as I opened my mouth, however, I got a flash, "Don't do it!" So I awkwardly converted my "the defense challenges Colonel Boychuck" to "The defense challenges no one," hardly the proper, "the defense has no challenges for cause." Judge Savage looked at me as if I had suddenly sprouted horns, but put the court in recess so that the trial counsel could reseat the court members.

Under the ritualized court-martial procedure, the President had to be seated in the middle of the jury box with the next senior man to his left, the next senior to his right, and so on. So when someone was excused as a result of a challenge, the trial counsel had to assist the court in playing musical chairs to correct the seating order. Because I'd managed to get the AG officer booted off the panel, we had to go though this drill.

During this exercise, what we called a cluster-fuck in Vietnam, a complicated military movement with no real purpose, Captain Reilly took me aside and told that me I was nuts for not getting rid of Colonel Boychuck. I could only respond with a weak, "I know, but I had a flash not to."

Captain Yoder gave his opening statement, and then Judge Savage nodded graciously in my direction and said, "Defense?" The good judge always appeared gracious to defense counsel in front of the court members even if he had denied every defense motion up to that point. His question was whether I wanted to make an opening statement right after the trial counsel or wait until the start of the defense case. The decision was seldom an easy one. If you made your statement right after the prosecution, you might promise something that you might not be able to deliver or might not want to. For example, if you promised that the court members would hear the accused testify, and the prosecution's case ended up much weaker than anticipated, you might want to change your tactics and not put the accused on so that the trial counsel would not have the chance to shore up his case by cross-examining your client. If, however, you had promised the members that they would hear from the accused, they might hold it against the defense if they didn't, notwithstanding the judge's instruction that they could not hold it against the accused if he didn't testify. And officer court members expected a not guilty officer to look them in the eye and tell them that he hadn't done it no matter whether the judge instructed them until he was blue in the face that they couldn't hold a failure to testify against the accused.

I had once attended some defense counsel workshop at the JAGC School in Charlottesville, Virginia, that featured an expert on jury selection. But because in the military, the defense had no say in selecting the court members and had only one peremptory challenge to get rid of ones who might be too pro-prosecution, the workshop at the time seemed largely irrelevant. But the one thing that I did take away from the course was that military juries always fit the model that the expert called "the authoritarian jury." Who is going to be more authoritarian that military officers and sometimes high-ranking noncommissioned officers? According to the expert, authoritarian juries believed the first thing that they heard—the prosecution's opening statement, followed by the prosecution's witnesses and other evidence. So their minds would be made up before they ever heard from the defense. The only way to get around this tendency was to get the jury to identify with the defendant—not an easy task when he was a black private facing a jury of twelve high-ranking officers, or as in this case, a dumb second lieutenant. So I had always tried to get some kind of transferred identification—getting the members to identify with me as a fellow combat veteran. And I tried to get my side of the case out and into the court members' minds as early as possible by never postponing my opening statement until the start of the defense case.

"Mr. President, members of the court, I am Captain Thomas, the individual defense counsel who, along with Captain Reilly, the detailed defense counsel, has the honor of defending Lieutenant Wyndham. The purpose of an opening statement is to let you know what we intend to prove. As you know, however, there is no obligation on Lieutenant Wyndham's part to prove anything. The entire burden of proving guilt beyond a reasonable doubt rests upon the prosecution. As the defense intends to show you as this trial progresses, however, what the trial counsel has told you is not necessarily the way things happened. Not only will we show you that the government has failed to meet its burden, but also we will prove to your satisfaction, through the testimony of Lieutenant Wyndham and other witnesses, that he is not guilty of any of these charges.

"Of course, the defense would ask you to keep an open mind during the presentation of the government's case and not merely wait for the defense to put on its evidence. Ask yourselves whether the government's witnesses are credible and whether their story is believable. The defense feels that, long before the defense ever puts on its case, you will see that the government's evidence is nothing more than a clever fabrication from a witness, Mrs. Williams, who was mad at an officer being in her housing area.

"The defense will show you that the survey that the trial counsel talked about in his opening statement, although perhaps ill-advised, was not a pretext to have sex with Mrs. Williams. It was for a legitimate purpose—protecting military family members from heat injuries. The defense will show that Lieutenant Wyndham could not possibly have committed the offenses listed on the charge sheet.

"You will note the pencils and writing tablets in front of you. I would ask you to take careful notes of the times and dates testified to by all of the witnesses. Their significance may not immediately be apparent, but those dates and times will become very important as the case progresses.

"Thank you for your attention and for remaining open minded until all of the evidence is in."

"Call your first witness, Captain Yoder," Judge Savage said.

"Your Honor, the government calls Mrs. Williams."

The bailiff went out to the witness waiting room and returned with Mrs. Williams. If this case had involved rape, I would have been happy at how she was dressed—not like someone who would resist a sex act. But the more like a slut she looked, the more likely the court members would think that my client thought that he could get away with groping her and exposing himself. Mrs. Williams came into the courtroom wearing some sort of form-fitting sundress with spaghetti straps. The bodice barely held her ample breasts in, and the material in the skirt part of the dress was so sheer that you could see her panty line. No bra straps were visible. After the trial counsel swore in the witness, Mrs. Williams, smiling at the court members, settled into the chair in the witness box with a loud sigh that threatened to spill her breasts out of their fragile confinement. Judge Savage looked pissed at this breach of decorum, but could hardly reprimand the government's star witness before she answered the first question.

So Mrs. Williams told her story. And she told it pretty well. At this point, I had no doubt that if neither side put on any more evidence, Lieutenant Wyndham was going to end up under the jail for a long time. Mrs. Williams's sultry appearance only made her story more believable. Even I believed her except for the small problem that my client had an alibi for that day.

The trial counsel, trying to take the wind out of my sails, elicited Mrs. Williams's conviction for oral sodomy at the NCO Club parking lot on the theory, I surmised, that it would less damning if he brought it out than if I made a big deal about it in cross-examination. I had thought that her sexual history was much more damning to my client than it was to her because it demonstrated why he thought he could get away with groping her and exposing himself. So I didn't say my usual, "Objection, Your Honor, trial counsel is impeaching his own witness." Such an objection would only highlight the matter and cause the court members to believe that I was trying to hide things from them—not the way to ingratiate one with an authoritarian jury.

The key part of her testimony focused on the alleged crimes. Captain Yoder methodically took her through her version of the events. "What, if anything, did the accused say after he had finished talking about the air conditioning?"

"He sat down next to me on the couch and told me that he was also working on a sensitivity test. He said he had majored in psychology and asked whether I would like to help him keep current in the field."

"What did you say?"

"Well, I first thought he had meant allergies and said that I didn't have any, but if I could be helpful . . . ."

"Then what happened?"

"He said, 'No, I meant a touch sensitivity test.' He asked if the human body's receptiveness to touch embarrassed me. I said that it didn't. Then, he asked me if fellatio would embarrass me. I told him that I didn't know what that word meant. He said that it meant oral sex, and I said that it didn't embarrass me. So he asked if I had a few minutes for him to show me some of his sensitivity test. I said, 'Yeah.' He said that it would seem a lot like sex, but that it was all very scientific. My baby started fussing, so I went over to the crib and picked him up. The lieutenant stood up too and stroked my neck and told me that I had a soft neck and that he could tell that it was sensitive."

"Please continue."

Mrs. Williams took another deep breath, riveting the eyes of the court members on her chest, and continued, "Then, he ran his hand down alongside my breast and said something about women having a very sensitive spot alongside their breasts."

"Let me back up a minute, Mrs. Williams. Would you please tell the court members what you were wearing during this incident?"

"I was wearing what I call a kerchief top which is just a square piece of material off the shoulders with a square neckline, a pair of slacks, no bra because the kerchief top is real full and it's gathered. I don't remember whether I was wearing panties or not."

"Then what, if anything, did the accused do?"

"He went over and closed the front door. Then he came back to me. He tried to pull my top down and look down it and made some comment about not being able to see or something like that. It was kind of awkward holding my baby, so I stepped back. He said he was going to show me something. He walked up to me, reached up underneath my blouse and started to fondle my breast. I backed up and told him that his sensitivity test would have to wait because the baby was fussy.

"He told me that he was having marital problems with his wife because they didn't have sex very often because he was too large and it was uncomfortable for her. My baby seemed to calm down at this point, so I set him down. When I straightened up, I looked at Lieutenant Wyndham, and he had his pants unzipped and had his penis out. His wife must have really been tight, because if that was too large, I'm a virgin. He asked me whether I could tell where he was sensitive, and I pointed at his prick and said, 'right there.'"

I looked over at the court members who were listening raptly. They certainly hadn't expected this much fun at a court-martial. Mrs. Williams continued.

"He looked at me and said that he thought that I was getting embarrassed. It sort of irritated me, so I grabbed his penis, looked him right in the face, and said, 'Now, do you think I'm embarrassed?' It seemed to panic him when I grabbed him because he pulled up his zipper and started to leave."

"Did he leave?"

"Yes, after I told him he would have to wait until Monday to finish the sensitivity test."

"Why did you want him to come back on Monday?"

"I didn't really, but I thought that it would give me time to report the matter and find out whether the survey was real or not."

After Captain Yoder had finished and looked at me, saying graciously, "Your witness" (he could cut the heart out of any defense counsel, but would always appear courteous in front of the court members), I rose to cross-examine Mrs. Williams.

According to Mrs. Williams's direct testimony, my client had come back a second time, the next day, which was when the alleged indecent assault and indecent exposure had occurred. So I had two things I that wanted to establish by my cross-examination of her: (1) lock in the time of the alleged indecent assault and indecent exposure to set up the alibi defense and (2) minimize, insofar as possible, the alleged offenses in case the alibi did not work. If the court members did not believe the alibi, Lieutenant Wyndham was toast, and all I could do for him was try to minimize his jail time by showing that Mrs. Williams had not really been harmed. I decided to minimize the crimes first, so that the time sequence would be fresher in the minds of the court members when it came time for them to deliberate.

"Mrs. Williams, I'm Captain Thomas, and I will be representing Lieutenant Wyndham. You may remember me from the Article 32 investigation."

"Yes."

"I'd like to draw your attention to the first time you say that Lieutenant Wyndham showed up at your quarters—on July 23. He was in uniform, was he not?"

"Yes."

"Wearing his name tag?"

"Yes."

"He introduced himself as Lieutenant Wyndham from the 194th Armored Brigade?"

"Yes."

"So would it be correct to say that he made no effort to conceal his identity?"

"Yes, that's correct."

"Now, when you would go out into the NCO Club parking lot for sex with someone who was not your husband, you didn't give your true name, did you?"

"No."

"And other than that it may have seemed strange to conduct a survey in dependent housing, Lieutenant Wyndham did nothing improper on 23 July, did he?"

"No—except officers shouldn't be in NCO housing areas."

"Are you aware of any regulation that puts NCO housing areas off-limits to officers?"

"No."

"And haven't some of your neighbors had officers they serve with over for dinner or a picnic on occasion?"

"Yes."

"But even though there's no rule against it, you just don't like officers around your quarters?"

"I guess you could say that."

"Now, turning to the next day, the 24th, you testified that Lieutenant Wyndham came back and that he was still in uniform with his name tag?"

"That's correct."

"Now, when he allegedly touched your breast, how long did he touch it?"

"A second or less."

"Was there any force or violence involved?"

"No. He didn't grip it, and there was nothing physically strong about it. He was telling me about the sensitivity test, and he was very cautious like he didn't want to upset me."

"Other than this one alleged touching of your breast, did he make any other attempts to touch you?"

"No."

"Did you ever feel physically threatened by him?"

"No."

"Now, when Lieutenant Wyndham allegedly exposed himself, was there anyone else who could have seen him?"

"No—just the baby, but his eyes were scrunched up crying."

"Was there any one else in the quarters?"

"Yes. Private Chris was hiding in the bedroom."

"Why was he hiding?"

"He was AWOL, and he was afraid that the lieutenant might find out and arrest him."

"And isn't it true that he was at your quarters because your husband was away on temporary duty and you two were having an affair?"

"We were having sex, yes."

"When you grabbed Lieutenant Wyndham's penis, how long did you hold it?"

"Only a matter of seconds."

"Would it be correct to say that you were not shocked or embarrassed at this display?"

"I actually thought it was kind of amusing, but I was kind of pissed at the whole sensitivity test nonsense."

"Did you notice whether Lieutenant Wyndham was circumcised or not?"

"No, I didn't."

"Do you know what circumcision is?"

"Yes, but I didn't pay any attention to his penis."

"You had to look at it to know where to grab, didn't you?"

"Yes, in order to grab it, I had to know its location, and I did look at it at least that much, but I don't remember from touch whether it was circumcised or not. I just remember that it wasn't very big."

If it were possible for Lieutenant Wyndham to look even more mortified than he was from the humiliation inherent in being an officer on trial for indecent assault and indecent exposure, he managed it. He sat there accused of indecent assault, indecent exposure, and a non-macho dick. I almost felt sorry for him.

Having spent enough time on Mrs. Williams's lack of knowledge of the characteristics of my client's male organ and after having gotten her admission that she had not been disturbed enough to call the Military Police, the rest of my cross-examination locked her in as to the exact time that Lieutenant Wyndham had allegedly been in her quarters on the 24th. Captain Yoder must have worked with her a lot, because she had expanded her 1605 on the dot to from 1600 to 1625. She testified that the accused had left no later than 1630—four-thirty P.M. She testified that, if she was wrong about the time, it was off by only five minutes or so. I got her to admit that in her prior testimony at the Article 32 investigation she had said 1605 on the dot.

The government called a neighbor, Mrs. Couch, who had seen my client at Mrs. Williams's quarters, but she could not remember whether it was on the 23rd or the 24th. She had called the Military Police when, over coffee, Mrs. Williams had told her the story. The AWOL soldier also testified that he had overheard talk about a sensitivity test, but didn't know the exact date. The only other thing that he could remember was that Mrs. Williams seemed especially horny that night.

On cross, I brought out the fact that Lieutenant Wyndham had talked briefly with Mrs. Couch and another neighbor just before leaving the area.

After the government had rested, I made my usual futile motion for a finding of not guilty. The military judge will deny such a motion unless all of the evidence, viewed in the light most favorable to the government, fails to establish an essential element of the offense. Mrs. Williams's testimony alone established every element necessary to convict my client.

Now, it was time for my case. I had decided to put Lieutenant Wyndham on first and then support his story by my other witnesses. That way, if he came across as a jerk—a real possibility—some other witnesses supporting his story would help, and his smart mouth would not be the last thing that the members of the court would hear before deliberating.

After I had brought out his youth, education, and military career up to this point, I honed in on the heat injury survey.

"Lieutenant, how did this safety survey come about?"

"I first got interested in it when my wife suffered a heat stroke. It really scared me. Then, one of my extra duties besides being the legal officer for the 194th was being safety officer. I had the duty of compiling data on training heat injuries for our soldiers for a report that the XO, Major Marsh, had to submit, so because of what happened to my wife, I started wondering about whether there were other problems with family members in the heat. I thought that, if I compiled data that showed heat injuries in family housing, I could submit it to the post safety officer and maybe prevent what happened to my wife from happening to someone else."

"Did you get any approval for this survey?"

"No, I didn't think that I needed any. I thought that it was within the scope of my duties as safety officer, and I was doing it on my own time."

"How did you happen to pick Mrs. Williams's quarters?"

"It was just chance. Her quarters were the first one on the right in the cul-de-sac."

I had to deal with the issue that my client had picked out Mrs. Williams because of her sexual history. "Had you seen the blotter entry that she had been arrested at the NCO Club for oral sodomy?"

"I may have seen it, but because it wasn't an entry about one of the Brigade's soldiers, I didn't pay any particular attention to it. I certainly didn't know that the quarters I stopped at were those of Mrs. Williams's sponsor. There must be dozens of Williamses on post."

None of the jurors appeared as if they were buying this theory, so I decided to move on before doing any more damage.

"Tell the court members what happened on 23 July."

"It was pretty much like Mrs. Williams testified. I went there, but she was kind of distracted, so I said that I would come back at a better time."

Anticipating Captain Yoder's cross-examination and wanting to defuse it, I continued, "Why didn't you go to any other quarters in the housing area?"

"It was dinner time, and my wife is pretty fussy about my being home when dinner is ready."

"Now, Lieutenant Wyndham, did you return to Mrs. Williams's quarters?

"No, I didn't."

"Did you return on the 24th?"

"No, Sir."

"What did you do on the 24th?"

"I went to work at 0700 at the headquarters building. I pretty much worked at my desk until 1200, when I went to lunch with Lieutenant Conrad, the Assistant S-3. Then, I went back to my desk and worked until 1800. At 1800, I left and went straight home."

"How long did it take you to get home?"

"No more than 10 minutes."

"What time did you arrive home?"

"About 1810."

"How certain are you as to the time?"

"Very certain. My in-laws were in town from New York, and we had an 1830 reservation at the Officers' Club for dinner. I knew that I would be in big trouble with my wife if I was late."

"What did you do once you got home?"

"I changed from my uniform to a sports coat and we left for the club."

"What time did you arrive at the club?"

"Right about on time at 1830."

"I now hand you what has been marked as Defense Exhibit A for identification and ask you whether you recognize it."

"Yes, Sir." Now that he realized that his neck was on the line, Lieutenant Wyndham was not going to fail to call a superior officer "Sir" in front of the court members who would decide his fate.

"What is it?"

"It is my credit card receipt for dinner at the Officers' Club on July 24th."

“The defense offers Defense Exhibit A for identification into evidence as Defense Exhibit A.”

Captain Yoder had no valid objection, so he continued to try to appear magnanimous to the members by not only not objecting, but also by stipulating to admission of the document.

“Now, Lieutenant Wyndham,” I continued, “does this receipt reflect the number in the party?”

“Yes, four, Sir.”

“Who was at the Club with you?”

“My wife, Deborah, and my in-laws, Roger and Esther Deutsch.”

“How long did you stay at the O Club?”

“Until almost 2200 hours. They had a piano player who was pretty good, so we stayed around after we had finished dinner.”

“What time does the receipt show that you paid for the evening’s food and drinks?”

“2145, Sir.”

“Where did you go when you left the Club?

“Straight home.”

“Did you go out again?”

“No, Sir.”

At this point, one of the court members raised his hand and said that he had a question. In military law, the court members, not just the judge and counsel, could ask questions. Because, however, the answer to the question could be inadmissible, the drill was for the court member to write out the question, the bailiff to take it first to the trial counsel, then to the defense counsel, and finally to the military judge. As I read the question, my heart sank. It read, “Why is Captain Thomas trying so hard to show that Lieutenant Wyndham was not there on the 24th?”

To me, this was intuitively obvious. If he wasn’t there, he could have hardly touched Mrs. Williams’s breast or exposed himself. It’s called an alibi. But apparently, I had not gotten that point across. So I’d better be more definite.

“Did you see Mrs. Williams on July 24th?”

“No, Sir.”

"At any time on the 24th of July or any subsequent time, did you visit Mrs. Williams's quarters for a second time?

"No, Sir."

"At any time whatsoever, did you touch Mrs. Williams's breast?"

"No, Sir."

"At any time whatsoever, did you expose your penis to Mrs. Williams?"

"I never exposed my penis to anyone, Sir."

This was not a good answer. I had beaten my Butterbar client around the head and shoulders with just answering the question and not making broad statements that he could be cross-examined over. He had finally lost it, so it was time to end my client's direct examination while we were still slightly ahead on points.

"Your witness, Captain Yoder."

Sure enough, Captain Yoder immediately started in on Lieutenant Wyndham's penis. "So, Lieutenant, you have never exposed your penis to anyone?"

"Well, not improperly, Sir."

"Didn't you testify, and I quote, 'I never exposed my penis to anyone?'"

"Yes, Sir."

"How long have you been married, lieutenant?"

"Six months, Sir."

"How many times have you had intercourse with your wife?"

Time to get involved, so I said, "Objection, your honor. The question violates Article 31(c) in that it degrades the witness."

Not wanting to quit having this much fun, Captain Yoder responded that the witness had opened the door by his answer—much like he had unzipped his pants.

Judge Savage, not wanting the trial to turn into any more of a farce than it was already, issued a split decision that the trial counsel could inquire whether the accused had had intercourse with his wife, but could not get into the number of times or the details of the sexual encounters."

"Have you had intercourse with your wife?"

"Yes, Sir."

"More than once?"

"Yes, Sir."

"And did you have sex fully clothed?"

"No, Sir."

"Is it possible that your wife may have seen your penis?"

"Yes, Sir."

"So when you testified that you had never exposed your penis to anyone, that wasn't true, was it?"

"I guess not. I meant that I never improperly exposed it."

"So if you have already lied to the court members, why should they believe anything that you say?"

"Objection, argumentative," I interjected.

"Withdraw the question," Captain Yoder responded. The question had been asked and effectively answered whether he had received an actual verbal response from the witness or not.

Fortunately, that was the best salvo that Captain Yoder could come up with. He hammered away at the unauthorized nature of the survey, the next-to-impossible coincidence that Lieutenant Wyndham had magically ended up only at Mrs. Williams's quarters after he had read the blotter entry about her oral sodomy at the NCO Club, and the lieutenant's whereabouts all day during the 24th of July but didn't score any major points.

Then, I called my first three witnesses, one after another. First, I called Sergeant First Class Surendorf, who had shared an office with my client on the day in question. He corroborated my client's testimony that he had arrived at the office at 0700, worked until noon, left for lunch with Lieutenant Conrad, returned with Lieutenant Conrad, and worked until 1800. Other than leaving his desk for a couple minutes here and there to use the latrine or get a drink, Lieutenant Wyndham was constantly in his sight. Lieutenant Conrad testified that, yes, they had gone to lunch and that, no, they did not go to Mrs. Williams's quarters over lunch. Major Varney, the S-1, my client's boss, testified that, every time he walked past on the 24th of July, he saw my client working at his desk. Captain Yoder's cross-examinations did not shoot any holes in their stories, so it appeared that I had ruled out my client having gone to Mrs. Williams's quarters before 1800.

The time period between 1800 and 1830 was crucial—the exact time period that Mrs. Williams had said that the indecent assault and indecent exposure had occurred. First, I called my paralegal to testify that, at my direction, he had driven from Lieutenant Wyndham's place of work to Mrs. Williams's quarters two dozen times on different days during the time period of 1745 to 1800. With the rush hour traffic, the fastest he had been able to make the trip was 15 minutes, and the average was 20 minutes. So I hoped that the court members realized that if my client had left work at 1800 as he and Sergeant Surendorf testified, he could not have gotten to Mrs. Williams's quarters until 1815 and, more likely, 1820. He also testified that, again at my direction, he had measured the distance from Mrs. Williams's quarters to Lieutenant Wydnham's quarters and that they were more than two miles apart—a good 10-minute drive. Finally, he testified that it took a minimum of 15 minutes and an average of 20 minutes to get from the Officers' Club to Mrs. Williams's quarters. Other than bringing out that I wrote Sergeant Carrette's efficiency report, so he would want to please me, Captain Yoder's cross didn't make many points.

Next, I called my client's wife, Deborah. She testified that her husband had arrived home shortly after 1800. She was certain of the time and date because she was nervous about taking her parents to dinner at the Officers' Club and did not want to be late. She testified that they had left for the O Club shortly after he had arrived, getting to the O Club right on time for their 1830 reservation. She said that they had stayed at the O Club until almost 10:00 P.M. and that her husband had never left the table for more than five minutes, she said. Once they had arrived home, she said, Forrest—she could call her husband by his first name while testifying—went straight to bed with her and remained in bed the rest of the night.

Captain Yoder didn't have much to ask on cross. He could not appear less than chivalrous when questioning an officer's wife. He stuck to the stock questions as to whether she loved her husband—"yes"—would lie for him—"no—and whether I had rehearsed her testimony with her—"yes." I didn't even bother asking her on redirect if I had suggested that she tell anything other than the truth.

My client's in-laws were next. The good thing about calling his wife and his in-laws as family members was that it kept them out of the courtroom because of the usual rule, although it could be waived for close family, that witnesses could not watch other witnesses testify because it might taint their testimony. I did not want his family to hear Mrs. Williams and the other prosecution witnesses because they could reasonably conclude that he was a guilty S.O.B., which would hardly be good for family harmony. I wanted them to be strong witnesses as to how much they loved him if he was convicted in a probably futile attempt to get a light sentence. Both of Deborah's parents corroborated the time sequence from the time my client got home at a little after 6 P.M. until they returned home from the Officers' Club around 10:00 P.M.

Captain Yoder did a pretty good job on cross-examination. "Lieutenant Wyndham is your son-in law, isn't he?"

"Yes."

"And you love him very much, don't you?"

"Yes."

"And it would be pretty devastating to Lieutenant Wyndham and you and the rest of the family if he was convicted, wouldn't it?"

"Yes."

"And you are aware he facing years in Leavenworth and a dismissal, aren't you?"

"Yes."

"And if the court dismisses him, he will lose substantially all military and veterans' benefits?"

"Objection, Your Honor," I interposed. "The administrative consequences of a punitive discharge are irrelevant."

"Sustained," Judge Savage intoned, having no real choice because the law was clear.

Captain Yoder could care less whether the witness got to answer or not. The jury had heard the question.

"You rehearsed your testimony with Captain Thomas, did you not?" Captain Yoder, realizing that the alibi was pretty solid on the facts, was trying to imply that I had put the words in my witnesses' mouths.

"Yes, we did." I had warned them of this eventuality and that they should be truthful because we had rehearsed.

I had only two questions on redirect. "Given that you love your son-in-law, would you lie under oath for him?"

"No."

"When we rehearsed your testimony, did I ever tell you to lie or even to shade the truth?"

"No, you said to tell the absolute truth."

Now, it was time for my star witness, Mrs. Keeler. She testified that, on the 24th of July, she had looked out her window at exactly 1810 and had seen Lieutenant Wyndham drive up, get out of his car, and go into his quarters. About 10 minutes later, she said, she saw the lieutenant and his wife and an older couple get into the lieutenant's car and drive off. She said that she was certain of the time and date because it was her anniversary and she had cooked her husband's favorite meal and, if he didn't get home by 1830, it would be spoiled. So she was looking at the kitchen clock and looking out the window watching for him almost constantly between 1800 and 1830. Mrs. Keeler was my star witness because she could not be impeached by being a family member or even a friend of the Wyndhams. Captain Yoder barely even bothered to cross-examine, just asking a few questions so that it did not appear that the witness was so credible that the court members should just accept her story at face value.

After Mrs. Keeler, I rested my case. Captain Yoder's only rebuttal witness was his paralegal, who testified that he could drive from Lieutenant Wyndham's office to Mrs. Williams's quarters in under 10 minutes at that time of day. I only had a few questions.

"What speed were you traveling at to arrive in under 10 minutes?"

"40 M.P.H., Sir."

"What's the posted speed limit?"

"25 M.P.H., Sir."

"Do the Military Police aggressively enforce that speed limit?"

"Yes, Sir."

"Isn't it true that they always have radar guns on the main thoroughfares leading to the family housing areas at rush hours?"

"Most, if not all, of the time, Sir."

"Did you find any traffic tickets issued to Lieutenant Wyndham for speeding on the 24th of July of this year during your investigation?"

"No, Sir."

"So isn't it unlikely that he could have somehow managed to drive from his office to Mrs. Williams's at that high speed on the 24th?"

"Objection, argumentative," Captain Yoder interjected.

"Withdraw the question." Two could play that game.

Neither side had any more witnesses, so Judge Savage asked the court members if they had any witnesses that they wanted called or re-called. They did not. Now, all that remained were final arguments, the judge's instructions, and the court members' deliberations.

After having excused the court members so that they wouldn't hear any arguments about the proposed instructions, Judge Savage told us what instructions he proposed to give and asked us whether we had any objections to the instructions as stated or requests for additional instructions. Remembering the court member's question as to why I was trying so hard to show that Lieutenant Wyndham was not at Mrs. Williams's quarters, I asked for an alibi instruction. I submitted Appellate Exhibit 9, which spelled out the proposed instruction:

> The evidence has been raised concerning the defense of alibi. "Alibi" means that the accused could not have committed the offenses charged

> because the accused was at another place when the offense occurred. Alibi is a complete defense to the offense of indecent assault and indecent exposure. There has been testimony by the accused, his co-workers and superiors, and his family that he was not at Mrs. Williams's quarters on the date and time alleged. The burden is on the prosecution to establish the guilt of the accused. Unless you are convinced beyond a reasonable doubt that the accused was present at Mrs. Williams's quarters on July 24th, 1977, you must acquit.

The trial counsel had no objection, so long as the instruction added that, if the court members found that my client was present at Mrs. Williams's quarters, the defense of alibi did not exist.

After a short recess, the court reconvened for closing arguments. Because the prosecution had the burden of proof, it went first and last. The defense was sandwiched in the middle. Captain Yoder gave his usual, methodical argument:

"Mr. President, members of the court, thank you for your attention throughout today's proceedings. It is almost time for you to begin the toughest part of being a court member—deciding whether the accused is guilty. You should find the accused guilty, notwithstanding his attempt to escape responsibility by relying on Mrs. Williams's confusion over the date of his indecent assault and indecent exposure.

"First, let's talk about motive. You saw his prim and proper wife sitting there dressed conservatively, wearing white gloves. Lieutenant Wyndham wanted something hotter. And one day he found it on the MP blotter—a blotter that he admitted comes across his desk every day. A loose woman who gives blow jobs at the NCO Club parking lot.

"So he comes up with this ridiculous, totally unauthorized survey to get inside Mrs. Williams's quarters. And inside her blouse. He'd have you believe that he visited this one set of quarters out of pure chance. You know better than that. If he had visited a dozen or more other quarters, it might be coincidental that had he also visited Mrs. Williams. But he didn't. He went straight to her quarters and went nowhere else. Went straight to the hottie's house and felt her boob and exposed his penis.

"Her story rings true, doesn't it? She couldn't have made up this nonsense about a heat survey, oops, a sensitivity test. Yes, she couldn't remember whether the accused was circumcised or not. But she's seen and felt enough penises that she would be unlikely to remember one as unremarkable as the accused's."

Lieutenant Wyndham was trying to slide under the defense table—shades of the mummy—at yet another humiliating comment about his male organ, but I grabbed him by the arm and held him upright. Now that all the witness testimony was over, his family was sitting right behind him with only the waist-high railing between them and the defense table.

Captain Yoder continued hammering point after point. He concluded by noting that it was just as likely that my witnesses were confused on the time as Mrs. Williams was and asking what motive Mrs. Williams had to lie? He said that my witnesses did—to keep the accused out of Leavenworth. Thus, he said, the evidence established each and every element of indecent assault and indecent exposure beyond a reasonable doubt, and they must do their duty and convict Lieutenant Wyndham.

I had two objectives for my closing argument. First, I had to convince the court members that reasonable doubt existed. Second, I had to give Judge Savage an apoplectic fit to punish him for having embarrassed me. Judge Savage had two pet peeves—chewing gum and laughing in his courtroom. A week before this trial, I had been sitting in the spectator section of the courtroom watching one of my subordinate defense counsel try a case so that I could rate his performance. I had just returned from the dentist, who had filled a cavity. I was, as dental patients are wont to do, feeling the tooth with my tongue. Judge Savage erupted from his seat behind the bench and bellowed, "Captain Thomas, you are chewing gum in my courtroom."

"No, Your Honor. I would never chew gum in your courtroom. I was seeing whether my dental anesthesia had worn off by feeling around with my tongue."

Well, Judge Savage didn't believe me and ordered me to open my mouth so he could see whether I had any gum in it. I found this whole scenario to be very humiliating, letting my mouth hang open so all could see—no gum. The court members looked amused at this exchange. I didn't want court members to remember me with my mouth hanging open instead of as a brilliant trial lawyer. So I wanted to get revenge on Judge Savage. I couldn't get everyone to chew gum, so I decided I would make everyone in the courtroom laugh, including Judge Savage. He would suffer a fit at being unable to punish the injudicious laughter because he would be equally guilty. And the Wyndham case was the perfect case to make a closing argument that would make everyone laugh except me.

After I had thanked the court members and pointed out that the government had failed to mention that it had the burden of proving guilt beyond a reasonable doubt, that it had not done so, and that it had, instead, attacked the defense case, I said that the defense did not have to prove its case beyond a reasonable doubt, that all the defense had to do was raise a reasonable doubt.

Then, I asked the court members to pick up the charge sheets lying on the bench before them and continued:

"I'd like to draw your attention to the charges. Lieutenant Wyndham is not charged with carrying out an unauthorized survey, with carrying out an ill-considered survey, with carrying out a stupid survey. He is charged with serious sexual offenses. This survey is only in evidence because the prosecution has no evidence worthy of belief that any of these acts happened and has to hope that you will bootstrap these serious crimes on top of this stupid survey.

"We do not contend that anyone authorized this survey. Yes, maybe it is a very unlikely coincidence that my client ended up only at Mrs. Williams's quarters. But if he had had some nefarious purpose, he hardly needed to concoct a fictitious survey to get Mrs.

Williams to engage in sexual activity. No, the survey was a valid, although unauthorized one, to respond to his wife's heat injury and to perform his duties as safety officer. The survey is simply a Butterbar screw-up, nothing more. Your job is not to decide whether Lieutenant Wyndham's commander should have chewed him out for this survey, but to determine whether he is guilty of these sex crimes beyond a reasonable doubt.

"Remember when I questioned you about whether you could be fair and impartial court members, you indicated that, if you thought my client had made an error in judgment but had not committed the sex crimes, you would acquit him?

"Before we even get to the defense evidence, there is enough reasonable doubt inherent in the government's own evidence to mandate findings of not guilty on all charges.

"The trial counsel would have you believe that the young second lieutenant sitting here read this MP report and that the report fostered in him the urge to go out and attempt to engage Mrs. Williams in this sexual misconduct, *two months later*. The prosecution would further have you believe that Second Lieutenant Wyndham cold-bloodedly dreamed up this survey as a pretext to do so. From the content of the report on what Mrs. Williams did at the NCO Club, why would it be necessary for anyone to think that he needed a pretext to engage in sexual activity with her?

"Finally, the government spins this wild yarn about how Lieutenant Wyndham fondled Mrs. Williams's breast and exposed himself while wearing his uniform with his name tag on it and after enough contact with others in the neighborhood to ensure that everyone knew who he was.

"Why would Mrs. Williams make this story up? She may have made it up to keep Lieutenant Wyndham from finding the AWOL soldier hiding in her bedroom during his only visit. She may have feared losing her government quarters for harboring a fugitive in those quarters. She admitted that she didn't like officers in the enlisted housing area. Perhaps, she enjoys recounting fictional sexual exploits or those she has engaged in with others at the NCO Club parking lot. We don't know her motive for sure, but it is not the defense burden to prove beyond a reasonable doubt that she is lying. You have to believe her beyond a reasonable doubt, and I've outlined a number of reasons to discredit her testimony.

"So what really happened? Lieutenant Wyndham's wife suffers a heat injury. Then Major Marsh tells my client that he has to submit a report on soldiers' heat injuries in the battalion. Lieutenant Wyndham, as safety officer, gets the idea to expand the data to include family members. He chose Pritchard Place because he knew the conditions in his own housing area. On the 23rd, he followed the main road, turned into the housing area, and stopped at the first house in the cul-de-sac, which happened, unfortunately for him, to be Mrs. Williams's quarters.

"As he admitted, he talked briefly about the survey, but left when Mrs. Williams seemed distracted. And he wasn't being very clandestine, wearing his uniform and stopping to talk with Mrs. Couch and another neighbor. So nothing improper or even suspicious occurred on the 23rd.

"What about the 24th? He goes to work. He's there all day. He left work at 1800. He arrived home at 1810. He changed clothes and got to the Officers' Club at 1830 and stayed there until almost 2200.

"Now, Mrs. Williams testified that my client was at her quarters from 1800 to 1830. That's just impossible. He was at work until 1800. He, according to Mrs. Keeler, drove up in front of his home at 1810. He went inside and came out with his wife and two older people at 1820 and drove off, according to Mrs. Keeler. By 1830, he was at the Officers' Club with his wife and in-laws. Remember the driving times to Mrs. Williams's quarters? Superman could not have gotten from my client's duty station to Mrs. Williams's quarters, to his home, and to the O Club in a half hour. Not only is his alibi totally corroborated by his coworkers and military superiors and by his family, but also by Mrs. Keeler, who has no motive to lie. And don't forget Defense Exhibit A, the O Club credit card receipt.

"How logical is it that Lieutenant Wyndham is going to come back on the 24th to fondle Mrs. Williams's breast and expose himself when his in-laws had just arrived and were going out to dinner with the lieutenant and his bride?

"The defense believes that His Honor will instruct you that unless you are satisfied beyond a reasonable doubt that Lieutenant Wyndham was present at Mrs. Williams's quarters between 1800 and 1830 on July 24th, you must acquit him.

"Thus, the government has the burden of proving that he was there. To the contrary, the defense has proven that he was not there. Certainly, the family member witnesses could be affected by a guilty finding. But it is far less likely that these respectable people would concoct an alibi than that the complainant concocted her version. Would a young wife testify falsely for her husband if she believed that he had touched another woman's breast or exposed himself to her? And other than the family members, the other defense alibi witnesses are unimpeached and unimpeachable.

"The one inescapable fact in this case is that, at the same exact time that Mrs. Williams claims that Lieutenant Wyndham was exposing himself to her, he was climbing out of his car at home to change clothes and then back into his car in his sport coat to go to the Officers' Club with his wife and in-laws.

As I wrapped up my argument, I decided that it was time to drop my bombshell to get everyone to laugh. Totally dead-pan, I said, "Mr. President, court-members, the only thing that rings true about this tale that Mrs. Williams concocted, in light of her character, is that she would certainly grab a penis if one was exposed to her," accompanied with a grabbing motion by my right hand. "But one was not available at the time because my client wasn't there."

All the court members burst out laughing, as did the spectators and there were quite a few of them for an officer sex crime case. Even Judge Savage burst into a loud guffaw, which he hurriedly bit off. His face reddened as he contemplated holding the entire courtroom in contempt except for me because I remained stone-faced. I even managed to look perplexed, as if I couldn't understand what was so funny. Judge Savage just gave up. He didn't even bang his gavel to stop the laughter.

When the laughter died down, I quickly finished my argument, ending with pointing out the injustice of convicting an officer on the word of someone like Mrs. Williams.

Perhaps the levity had thrown Captain Yoder off, because his rebuttal argument was weak for him. As the military judge instructed the court members, I tuned out. Captain Reilly would follow the instructions to determine whether any of them differed from the agreed-on instructions, and I was brain dead. My brain felt as if I had gone ten rounds with Master An.

Finally, Judge Savage finished his instructions, asked counsel whether we had any requests for additional instructions or any objections to the instructions as given. Because we had already gone through the instructional conference, we did not. Judge Savage instructed the bailiff, a second lieutenant bailiff for an officer accused, to take the court members to the deliberation room. They could not leave the room for any reason without having the bailiff bring them back into open court. The judge terminated the proceedings by announcing, "The court is closed."

After the court members had left, I tried to sneak out. Unfortunately, the door to the defense counsel offices was beside the judge's bench. As I sidled out, hoping to avoid Judge Savage after my closing argument, he looked down imperiously at me and said, "I suppose you think that was a good argument, Captain Thomas, and I guess it was. But it would have been more effective if your client had not been unzipped."

Faced with this revelation, I just smiled weakly and said, "Yes, Your Honor," and got out of the courtroom as quickly as possible. I had always checked my clients to make certain that they were wearing the correct badges and ribbons, that they didn't have a flying epaulet, and that they had a military haircut, before letting the judge and jury see them. But I had never checked whether they were zipped up. Something else now to add to my mental pretrial checklist—at least with officer clients charged with indecent exposure.

Waiting for a jury verdict always strikes me as the hardest part of the case. I can only imagine what it must have been like for

Lieutenant Wyndham, knowing that, if the court members found him guilty, the best he could hope for was dismissal—the officer version of a dishonorable discharge. And a sentence to the U.S. Disciplinary Barracks at Fort Leavenworth was hardly out of the question. Perhaps worst of all would be facing his wife and family. All I really had to worry about was my won-lost record.

Well, as it turned out, neither of us had to worry. The court members came back to open court in an hour and half and found the now-zipped-up lieutenant "not guilty."

After the obligatory handshakes from my client and his father and the hugs from his wife and mother, they went off to the Officers' Club to celebrate. I promised to join them later. After I had cleaned up the mess of papers on the defense table and my desk from the case, I decided that I might as well go to the party. I wasn't going to get anything constructive done because I was still brain dead. On my way out, I saw Colonel Boychuck come out of Judge Savage's office. This sight was a little troubling because I had never before seen the President of the Court talk to the Military Judge after the case. I was afraid that they were deciding whether to report me to the Staff Judge Advocate for my over-the-top closing argument.

But Colonel Boychuck smiled at me and said, "Good job, counsel." I thanked him and walked out of the JAG office with him. I really wanted to know how the court members had voted, but military law prohibits asking that question. So I compromised by asking the Colonel what he thought of the case.

He smiled wryly and answered. "We all thought he was guilty, but I convinced the members that we could not convict him because, even if he did it, it wasn't his fault."

This theory came as a complete shock to me as I could not think of any possible defense that I had not explored. But I didn't want Colonel Boychuck to think that I was not astute, so I just nodded wisely.

Fortunately, he continued to enlighten me, "Yes, it wasn't really his fault. If the Post Commander had done his job and terminated Mrs. Williams from government quarters for her misconduct at the NCO Club, your client could never have gone to her house. All the other court members wanted to vote to convict, but I wouldn't let them."

This theory was the nuttiest theory I had ever heard, but it validated my decision not to challenge Colonel Boychuck for cause. If I had, Lieutenant Wyndham would have learned about indecent assault on the receiving end at Fort Leavenworth.

So I bid goodbye to the good colonel, thanking him for his insights, and walked across the quadrangle to the O Club. Some brilliant planner had put the club a short, five-minute walk from the JAG office. With a single-malt scotch reviving me, I graciously accepted the no-longer-an-accused and his family's congratulations on my brilliant alibi defense that conclusively proved what they had known all along, that he was innocent. I did not have the heart to tell them that my brilliant defense was not the reason for the not guilty finding but that, rather, it was because I had not challenged Colonel Boychuck, as any sane defense counsel would have, and because he had come up with some flaky theory that, although Lieutenant Wyndham was a pervert, it wasn't really his fault.

Lieutenant Wyndham's father was very subdued, however. He had figured out that his son was guilty, regardless of the court's findings. But the rest of the family was on a high, and I gratefully accepted several more single-malts, the only free drinks that I had received since I had become a defense counsel.

The next strange turn in the case came about a month later. I ran into my star witness, Mrs. Keeler, at the Post Exchange. We exchanged a few pleasantries, and I thanked her again for her testimony. She told me that I was welcome and added, "Did you know that he had tried the same thing on me?"

No I hadn't. And if I had, I would never have called her to testify. Why hadn't she told this to me, to my paralegal, or to the trial counsel when he had interviewed her? I can only surmise that she must have enjoyed the sensitivity test.

Anyway, I had got Lieutenant Wyndham off—even if Mrs. Williams hadn't.

6

D^{3}FM

"TRADITION – The explanation for a technique that has no other reasonable explanation."

—Unattributed karate saying

In some ways, defending soldiers was easier than prosecuting them—even if winning the case was harder. The trial counsel had to prove each and every element of a court-martial charge beyond a reasonable doubt. But the defense counsel only had to raise enough reasonable doubt to knock out one element of the charge or come up with an affirmative defense, such as the alibi that I had used to get Lieutenant Wyndham off. One such affirmative defense was psychological—that the accused either did not have the mental capacity to cooperate in his defense or, as a result of a serious mental disease or defect, lacked the capacity to know right from wrong and to adhere to the right.

If a defense counsel thought that his client was nuts, the proper tactic was to request a sanity board—what would later be known as a 706 board. The board members, military psychologists, or other mental health professionals would render an opinion as to the accused's mental state—an opinion that was almost always that, although his behavior was aberrant, he could cooperate in his defense, he did not have a severe mental disease or defect, and he knew right from wrong—in other words, he could not avoid a conviction by reason of insanity. The sanity board members usually reached this diagnosis after an hour interview and a few diagnostic tests, such as an MMPI (Minnesota Multiphasic Personality Inventory).

The first time that I requested a sanity board was for Private Kimbell. Private Kimbell was facing general court-martial for lewd and lascivious conduct. Apparently, he had, while in uniform and wearing his name tag (shades of Lieutenant Wyndham), gone into the women's restroom at the Post Exchange and lain on the floor so that he could look up under the bottom of the walls of the toilet stalls at the women who were using those stalls. Not surprisingly, the military wives who had stopped shopping at the PX long enough to use the facilities were somewhat upset at looking down to pull up their pantyhose and seeing Private Kimbell looking up at them, grinning broadly. Their screams quickly brought the Military Police, who dragged Private Kimbell to his feet—he was trying to stay on the floor and get one last peek for as long as possible—and apprehended him. His commander found that he was a threat to the female population of the fort and ordered him into pretrial confinement.

Because I had been stupid enough to take a week's leave after the Wyndham case, the acting Chief Defense Counsel decided to assign me this Peeping Tom case either because I appeared able to get perverts off as a result of having successfully defended Lieutenant Wyndham or to get revenge for my having assigned him the "wrongfully dumping pickle relish case." That accused servicemember had not liked the food in the mess hall and had dumped a big jar of pickle relish on the floor of the mess hall to the prejudice of good order and discipline in the Armed Forces or of a nature to bring discredit on the Armed Forces in violation of Article 134, Uniform Code of Military Justice. Yes, if civilians found that out we were running around dumping pickle relish on the mess hall floor on purpose, the military's reputation would be ruined.

When I went to meet my client in the stockade, I quickly deduced that this case might be the one case in which a sanity board might actually find that my client was incompetent to stand trial. Talking to Private Kimbell was almost like talking to a goldfish. He kept opening and closing his mouth, but nothing intelligible came out, not even bubbles. So I requested a sanity board. The board's report quickly came back with a finding that he was perfectly normal, just exhibiting attention-getting behavior to avoid a court-martial. So I decided that I had to defend on some other ground or enter into a plea bargain. I fought off the offers of help from my trusty paralegal, the same one who had wanted to see whether Mrs. Williams would actually engage in oral sodomy. He now thought that he should investigate what color panties each of the victims had on to see whether they somehow had enticed Private Kimbell. I was about to approach the trial counsel to see what kind of plea bargain I could get when my phone rang. It was the senior correctional NCO, a very level headed sergeant first class who, I thought, had seen everything in his more than twenty years in the Military Police. So I was surprised to hear the panic in his voice when he said, "Captain Thomas, you've got to do something about your client. He's been masturbating 24 hours a day, and we've put him in a strait jacket, but he still keeps masturbating!" I was experiencing déja vu again, this time shades of the Mummy, who would only eat, sleep, defecate, and masturbate while in confinement.

Trying hard not to think about how one could manage to masturbate in a strait jacket in a prison cell, I replied, with great legal acumen, "Well, exactly what do you expect me to do about it?"

When SFC Gore had no ready answer, I added, "Let him beat off—who's he hurting? If he starts hurting himself, call the medics to sedate him."

Armed with this new information about my client's "attention-getting behavior," I thought I'd better not rely on the sanity board's finding. So I contacted Private Kimbell's mother and learned that he had been committed to a psychiatric ward for almost a year for severe depression with paranoid ideations. He had been released for only a few months before he had joined the Army. So much for the Army's screening of potential recruits. I got his psychiatric records from the psych ward and, armed with them, was able to get the sanity board to change its mind and find him unfit to stand trial. So the Army gave Private Kimbell a medical discharge, freeing him to peer under civilian toilet stalls and to masturbate without the hindrance of a strait jacket.

My next foray into the world of mental health defenses was even weirder, involving just my second female client. I had not been lucky with my first female client, a big, raw-boned, blonde haired, Pennsylvania Dutch farm girl named Private Doris Hildegard. She was court-martialed for selling PCP (phencyclidine) to other soldiers, something that the Army thought was worse than a garden variety mass murder. Because I had a reputation of turning any trial into World War III and because Judge Savage liked my many and complicated motions because it kept him on the bench longer—he was trying, for no good reason that I could see, to report more hours in court than any other judge—trial counsel would usually give me a great plea bargain. Why such a record mattered to Judge Savage, who was a full colonel who was not going to make general, escaped me, but it caused trial counsel who didn't want to spend hours doing legal research to shoot down my motions to give me sweet deals. So I got Doris a deal that the convening authority would suspend all confinement in excess of two months. Considering that her co-conspirators in the PCP drug ring, who had better military records than she did, could only get suspension of confinement in excess of one year, it was a hell of a deal. I even got the convening authority to defer starting her confinement so that she could do some family reunion nonsense before going to jail. The court-martial sentenced her to a bad-conduct discharge and one year's confinement, so the plea bargain was a good one for her, saving her an additional 10 months in the stockade.

Well, Doris decided that she didn't want to serve even two months. So she got herself pregnant while home with her family, thinking that the Army wouldn't incarcerate a pregnant woman. Yeah, right. Although the convening authority might defer the confinement of a woman in her third trimester until after she had delivered, Doris, who was in her first trimester and a drug dealer, wouldn't get such a break.

As a zealous defense counsel, I dutifully filed a petition for clemency, asking the convening authority to disapprove or suspend Doris's confinement. The only thing that I could think of in my short military career that was more futile was asking to be assigned to Germany for my first assignment as opposed to going to Vietnam. The convening authority probably took a whole nanosecond to decide to deny the petition for clemency and order Doris and her alleged fetus to the stockade.

On the day that Doris was to begin her two-month sentence, she persuaded the two Military Police who were to take her to the stockade that she had to see her defense counsel. So the MPs brought my client up the two flights of stairs to my third-floor office. Apparently out of concern for her delicate condition, they had not handcuffed her as per regulations when transporting a prisoner. Once she was in my office, I told her that the convening authority had denied her petition for clemency and that I knew of no way to keep her from serving her sentence to confinement, pointing out that it was only two months—not the year or more that her co-accused drug buddies had received—and that, with time off for good behavior, she could be out in only 50 days. Doris was unimpressed with my legal prowess and told me to submit another petition for clemency. To humor her, I agreed, but told her that she would have to go with the MPs now and that if (ha ha) the convening authority approved the petition, the stockade would immediately release her.

"I'm not going to the stockade," Doris insisted.

"You can't avoid it. I'll walk the petition through as soon as we are done here," I replied.

"You don't understand. I'm not going."

"You have to."

"No, I don't," Doris insisted, grabbing a long pair of scissors from my desk and thrusting the sharp end up to the side of my throat.

Well, Doris picked the wrong wimpy lawyer to take hostage to avoid the stockade. Thank you again, Master An. He had taught me how to disarm someone holding you at knifepoint without stabbing yourself in the process. The move is hard to explain, but involves striking the inner wrist of the hand holding the knife with the heel of your hand a nanosecond before striking the top of the hand bending it across the fulcrum of the hand, immobilizing the inner wrist. Striking the inner wrist first moves the knife away from your body so that when you strike the top of the hand, the knife or scissors in this case can fly away without cutting you, as Doris found out. I picked up the scissors from the floor, walked quickly out of my office, and told the MPs that she was all theirs. I probably should have charged her with an assault on a superior commissioned officer—a crime carrying a ten-year sentence—but that move would only have inflicted her on another defense counsel. She already had a Big Chicken Dinner, JAGC slang for a BCD, Bad Conduct Discharge—so she would be put on excess leave until her appeals were exhausted and her discharge executed. Thus, charging her with another offense would have meant keeping her in the military longer, something that I, for one, didn't want. The next time, she might have a gun.

I went down to the trial counsel section to get away from Doris and her escorts, borrowed a typewriter, and cranked out another worthless petition for clemency. By some strange circumstance—perhaps a cosmic harmonic convergence—Doris, her guards, the convening authority, and I all ended up on the stairwell leading up to the Staff Judge Advocate's office at the same time. The MPs were carrying Doris down the steps, handcuffed and with a belt around her ankles so that she couldn't kick. Apparently, they still weren't going to handcuff her, out of concern for her delicate condition, but when she started beating on them and kicking them, they changed their minds. The two-star general convening authority was walking up the same stairs because the Staff Judge Advocate, a full colonel, had cancer and was facing a disability retirement. The general, who apparently had a heart if it didn't involve a pregnant drug dealer, would find excuses to walk over to the SJA office to keep the SJA from having to make the painful walk over to the general's office. So as the MPs carried Doris down the steps cursing and struggling against her restraints, I shoved the petition for clemency at the general, saying, "Sir, that's my client, Private Hildegard. You denied her petition for clemency yesterday. Here's another."

The general looked at me as if I were a lunatic, but took the petition and continued up the stairs. He ultimately denied the petition, and Doris was off to jail.

Lest I sound too macho for having disarmed her, I must confess that, two months later, after her release from the stockade, I saw her walking up those same stairs, possibly to ask me to help her appeal her Big Chicken Dinner. So I snuck out the fire escape.

My luck with female clients didn't improve with my second one, Captain Rockhill. Captain Rockhill was a short, stern-looking woman in an immaculate uniform, wearing Adjutant General's Corps branch insignia. She was the assistant S-1 (personnel officer) of the School Brigade, to which the instructors and students of the Armor School were assigned. She looked old for a captain—in her forties. I later learned that she had been enlisted for 12 years before completing college in her off-duty time and going to Officer Candidate School (OCS).

The captain was facing an administrative discharge board for frequent acts of a discreditable nature with military and civilian authorities. Apparently, she had three shoplifting convictions in Radcliff, Kentucky, the town just outside Fort Knox. Because she had managed to avoid jail time, the Army might never have found out about her convictions, except that the last time she faced the judge to plead guilty, when the judge asked her whether she understood her rights, she couldn't just say, "Yes." She had to say, "Of course. I'm an Army officer." The judge, who had been a platoon leader with Patton's Third Army in World War II, had an old-fashioned idea that officers did not stoop to shoplifting, so he called the Fort Knox Staff Judge Advocate, and the wheels of military justice started grinding for Captain Rockhill. Because the shoplifting had taken place off post and because the civilian courts had already prosecuted her, the command dispensed with a court-martial because it could discharge her with an other-than-honorable discharge, the functional equivalent of a dismissal (the officer version of a dishonorable discharge), based on civilian convictions, at an administrative board.

Defending Captain Rockhill made me long for the good old days of the Mummy case. She wanted to talk on ad nauseum about how perfect her military career was—all perfect Officer Efficiency Reports, letters of commendation up the wahzoo, a Meritorious Service Medal as a captain (very rare below the rank of major), and the like. Although I needed that information to try to convince a board of officers not to discharge her or, at least, not to give her an other-than-honorable discharge so that she would keep her military and veterans' benefits, I had a copy of her entire 201 file with all of those documents in it, and I didn't need to hear her recount each of them in excruciating detail laced with bravado, especially because I wasn't being paid by the hour. I found that I had a lot more patience when listening to clients drone on when I had gotten the point in the first few minutes after I had retired from the Army and discovered the joy of billable hours.

Captain Rockhill was adamant that she couldn't be kicked out of the Army. But a great military record wasn't going to outweigh three shoplifting convictions by a commissioned officer. The board of three senior officers who would hear the case undoubtedly would have some strange idea that officers should have a modicum of integrity and not steal.

"Come on, Captain Thomas," Rockhill demanded, "you're supposed to be such a hot shot. Figure out how to save my career."

So I did. Captain Rockhill had had a pretty tough year. First, her mother had died of a particularly nasty cancer, and then, her brother had died in an automobile accident. Finally, her fiancée had decided that he didn't want to get married and had jilted her. He probably got tired of hearing her brag about her career. I wondered whether all of these stressors could lead to a mental health condition that might cause a board of officers to forgive the shoplifting. So I pulled my handy-dandy DSM-IV down from my bookshelf. *The Diagnostic and Statistical Manual of the American Psychiatric Association, 4th Edition,* listed the recognized mental disorders and their diagnostic criteria. Although I thought that Captain Rockhill—she never told me to call her by her first name as any other officer of the same rank would have—had some of the diagnostic criteria of some of the disorders, she didn't have enough of any one that I thought that I could find a mental health clinician to agree and testify that she had that disorder. So I took an afternoon away from the office and went to the medical library at the University of Louisville College of Medicine and started going through the indexes to psychological periodical literature. Lo and behold, I found shoplifting in the title of an article in a Swedish psychological journal, "Shoplifting While in a Transient Dissociative State by Post-Menopausal Women Who Experience Significant Loss." Bingo! Of course, the library did not have such an obscure European publication, but I convinced the librarian that national security and the defense of our country depended on her getting me a copy. So she got me a copy through Interlibrary Loan in about a week.

The article postulated that some post-menopausal women who had experienced severe losses in their personal or professional lives turned to shoplifting while in a transient dissociative state to get things to compensate for their losses. Other than not knowing whether she was menopausal—and I wasn't looking forward to asking her whether she was—the article fit Captain Rockhill to a "T." And it had a great list of other articles on the same disorder—not PTSD (Post Traumatic Stress Disorder)—but rather PMWWSLD (Post Menopausal Women Who ShopLift Disorder—my acronym). One of them was even from an American journal.

As I had expected, Captain Rockhill did not appreciate being asked about whether she had undergone menopause. "Are you nuts! Asking me such a thing! It's none of your damn business! I should report you for sexual harassment!"

"Look, Captain Rockhill, you told me that, if I was such a hot shot, I could come up with something to keep your commission. I think I have, but unfortunately, whether you have undergone menopause is very relevant. I apologized for asking the question when I asked it, and I'll grovel some more if it makes you feel better, but I need to know to defend you effectively."

After chewing me out for another ten minutes (why clients want to alienate the one person between them and jail or a bad discharge from the military always escapes me), Captain Rockhill confirmed that she had had a somewhat early menopause and was done with all of that stuff. But despite her demands, I didn't tell her what the defense was yet. First, I had to get a mental health clinician to support my defense.

So I called Dr. George. Doctor (Major) George was an Army psychologist. I had worked with him on some other cases, and we had become friends. "Hey, Doc," my phone call began. "I've got a Post-Menopausal Woman Who Shoplifts While in a Transient Dissociative State defense that I need you to support."

"You're nuts," he laughed.

"Yeah, we know, but the question is whether my client is. If I send over some psychological literature, will you read it?"

"It will cost you several Chivas Regals at the O Club."

"You got it."

A few days later, Dr. George called and said, "Ok, I'll evaluate your client for this disorder. I'd never heard of it, but you've amassed enough literature that it may be legitimate. I'll give it a try."

So it was time for the real hard part of the case, convincing Captain Rockhill to let me put on the record that she had this mental disorder. I armed myself with language from the literature and Dr. George's opinion that the disorder was imminently treatable to be able to answer her inevitable question, why would the board vote to retain me if I'm nuts? The second part of my answer was that, if she were nuts, we might be able to get her a disability retirement with tax-free retired pay, which would certainly beat being kicked out without a pension or any other benefits.

Well, I had had easier fights with both Master An and the North Vietnamese Army in 'Nam, but I ultimately convinced her that her good record wasn't enough to avoid a discharge and that she needed some excuse for shoplifting three times. So she reluctantly agreed to make an appointment to see Dr. George.

He called me up just after her appointment and said, "I don't know how you come up with this shit, but I can honestly testify that she shoplifted in a transient dissociative state because of this syndrome that you found in the literature."

So I had my defense.

The good thing about administrative discharge boards back then was that most of the time the prosecutor, called the recorder, was not a lawyer. After the military became all volunteer, however, there was less work for military prosecutors, so they started acting as recorders. But back right after Vietnam, the recorder was usually some fairly inexperienced lieutenant who got the job as an extra duty. Nor was there a judge at an administrative board, just a legal advisor to the board president. The board president ruled on everything and often did not consult his legal advisor. And the defense counsel was a lawyer. So the defense could get away with some shit that they could never get away with in a court-martial. In a court-martial, I would have had to give the trial counsel all sorts of advance notice of a mental health defense, including allowing the trial counsel's experts to examine my client, as in Private Kimbell's sanity board.

But the recorder for Captain Rockhill's board was a reserve captain who had been given this duty for his two weeks' annual active duty for training. He simply asked me for a list of my witnesses so that he could make certain that they were present for the board proceedings. As at a court-martial, the prosecutor, whether trial counsel or recorder, was responsible for getting all of the witnesses to the hearing. The recorder, Captain Fugate, didn't even ask me what Dr. George was going to testify to. He probably operated on the usually correct assumption that, when an officer had a conviction for stealing, much less three of them, no evidence that the defense could put on would change anything. He did, however, seem pleased when I said that we would stipulate to the convictions so that he didn't have to get them admitted as official records. Anything that made him think that I was just going through the motions might prevent him from preparing his case better. I couldn't have sandbagged any of the trial counsel at Fort Knox—they knew me too well—but I knew that Captain Fugate, as an Armor officer Reservist attached to the School Brigade for two weeks of training, wasn't aware of my reputation in the courtroom.

After the board had convened and we had gotten the preliminaries out of the way, the President, Colonel Bailey, ordered the recorder to call his first witness. The recorder had no witnesses but handed copies of all three convictions to each of the board members, saying that the defense had stipulated that they were true copies of the record of conviction. Each of the members, an Armor lieutenant colonel and an Infantry major, and Colonel Bailey, also an Armor officer, frowned as they read the evidence that a commissioned officer had shoplifted three times. Actually, for an administrative discharge board, it was not even necessary to have a conviction, simply proving the discreditable acts by a preponderance of the evidence was enough. That requirement was why I had stipulated to the convictions. Otherwise, the reporter might have called the merchants and arresting officers and brought out all of the sordid details, details that were missing from the sterile records of conviction. I didn't think that evidence as to what my client had shoplifted, Gucci silk scarves and skimpy panties, would help her case much. On second thought, maybe admitting the panties into evidence would titillate the panel members enough to get my client some sympathy. Or not.

Because the Army had not even considered the issue of women in combat in the mid-seventies, a board composed of two Armor officers and one Infantry officer was obviously all male. The day before the board hearing, the recorder had asked me whether I was going to object to not having a female member of the board. I replied, "Oh, no. Although I normally would want a female board member, it is too late to put you through all that hassle. I will not object to the composition of the board." Actually, the last thing that I wanted was a female board member saying bull shit to my post-menopausal transient dissociate state defense, but I thought that I'd keep the recorder happy, thinking that I was easy to work with and only going through the motions.

My strong belief that we didn't want a female board member was the corollary of the defense axiom that, although it might seem counterintuitive, the defense did want female court members if there was a real contest about whether the victim was raped or not. By today's standards, I'm sure that none of this thinking is politically correct, but being politically correct is hardly the way to defend an accused soldier. The last thing that you wanted was a female court member if the accused had jumped the victim in a dark alley, knocked her out, and viciously raped her. But if the alleged victim had dressed provocatively, had flirted with the accused, and had not defended her virtue to the max, a female court member would often hold the alleged victim to the court member's standard—how she would have acted in that circumstance. She might have thought along the lines of how the alleged victim had not really put up any resistance because the female court member would have kicked him in the balls and clawed his eyes out in the same circumstances. Politically correct or not, as a general proposition, minority members, women or blacks, were much tougher on members of their own minority than anyone else. I guarantee, politically correct or not, that the last thing that a black private accused at a court-martial needed was a black colonel as President of the court-martial. The black colonel would, consciously or unconsciously, remember all of the shit that he had gone through to make it as far as he had in the Army and would not appreciate another black man making it harder for him and other law-abiding black soldiers by giving ammunition to those who said that blacks couldn't hack it in the military. The senior black officer or non-commissioned officer would hammer a black soldier that they found guilty at a court-martial. Similarly, women, regardless of race, did not appreciate other female soldiers giving ammunition to the critics of women in the military by committing misconduct, especially if they tried to excuse it by some flaky reaction from a few personal tragedies and menopause.

If there had been a female board member in Captain Rockhill's case, I would have found some way to challenge her for cause and get her off of the board.

So Captain Fugate rested his case, believing, quite logically, that uncontested records of three civilian convictions were enough to require the board members to immediately boot my client out of the Army. But he had not reckoned with the PMWWSLD defense.

My first three witnesses were superior officers in Captain Rockhill's chain of command, all of whom said, under oath, that she was an outstanding officer that they would be happy to have work for them at any time, notwithstanding the shoplifting convictions. All of them testified that shoplifting was entirely out of character for her and that there must be something that caused her to act out of character in that way. Getting the accused's supervisors to say that despite the misconduct they would take her back was what I would later come to call the "you-asked-for-it-you-got-it-Toyota rule." Later on in my JAGC career when I was a military judge, television stations often aired a Toyota commercial with that tag line. The rule said that, if the accused's commander or first sergeant testified that, notwithstanding whatever it was that the accused was convicted of, they wanted the accused back, they asked for it and got it, Toyota. I must admit, however, that, when I became a military judge, I formulated the Thomas corollary to the Toyota rule. It was, quite simply, that, when the supervisors were insane enough to want the accused mass murderer and rapist back, the Toyota rule did not work.

After my good character witnesses had testified for Captain Rockhill, the recorder did his best to get the board members to invoke the Thomas corollary by cross-examining them, "Let's get this straight, you are willing to have a three-time thief as the second-ranking officer in your S-1 shop?" But I had prepared them for this line of questioning, and they stuck to their guns.

Then, I put my client on the stand. As in a court-martial, she had the right not to take the stand, part of the Fifth Amendment right against self-incrimination and Article 31, UCMJ. But as a practical matter, an officer did not have that right if the officer wanted to avoid being slam-dunked. Any board of officers expected an officer to take the stand, look them in the eye, and tell, in this case, her story.

By asking a lot of leading questions, I got Captain Rockhill's story out. I wanted to use leading questions because my client didn't want to show any weakness, much less any form of mental disorder, and I wanted to control her testimony as much as possible. I also wanted to control her tendency to blather on and on about how great she was. I already had the evidence of how great she was covered, and the board members could easily get turned off if she bragged too much about herself. I couldn't have gotten away with leading questions in a court-martial, but the recorder didn't object much, and the board president overruled all of his objections. Even if they were going to slam-dunk a female captain, they would not allow any discourtesy to her, such as not letting her tell her story the way her counsel wanted her to. After I had brought out the usual preliminary drivel, where she was born, who her parents were, where she went to school, when she joined the Army, and so forth, I took her through her entire military career, getting her to identify her many great Officer Efficiency Reports, commendations, and citations for her medals, cutting her off when she tried to over-dramatize her accomplishments. Finally, I brought out the losses that she had suffered just before beginning her shoplifting career—a career that I did not think was likely to have more financial rewards than saving her military career would. She concluded by testifying that she had no idea why she shoplifted and hoped that the board could find it in their hearts to let her continue to serve. The board members looked somewhat sympathetic as she recounted her family members' deaths, but not sympathetic enough to keep her in the Army. The recorder's cross-examination did not hurt us much because I objected successfully to most of his questions because I knew the rules of evidence and he didn't—even the rules of evidence that I was making up on the spot. So it was time for Dr. George.

I always told any other defense counsel who asked how good Dr. George was at giving expert testimony, "Just wind him up and let him go." Because this hearing was in front of an administrative board and the recorder wasn't a lawyer who knew the rules of evidence, I could do just that without worrying about having him say, "Objection, the witness is testifying in narrative form." The problem with narrative form was that the witness just rambled on, without questions that the other side could object to.

So after I had established Dr. George's credentials, including a Ph.D. from the University of Chicago, I asked him whether he had conducted a psychological evaluation of Captain Rockhill. Instead of saying, "Yes," and waiting for the next question, he was off and running. Yes, he had conducted an evaluation consisting of taking a complete psycho-social history, an in-depth interview, a review of all Captain Rockhill's military, medical, and school records, and the administration of three psychological tests, including the MMPI. As a result of this evaluation, which had taken more than 75 hours to complete, he diagnosed her with PMWWSLD, making this obscure disorder sound like both the most well accepted mental disorder in the literature and the easiest to treat. He opined that Captain Rockhill shoplifted to compensate for the loss of her mother, brother, and boyfriend while in a transient dissociative state. In other words, she didn't know what she was doing. If she hadn't been caught, she would have wondered where the Gucci scarf in her bag had came from. Oops! Well, one little slip up in the brilliant narrative was no big thing. At least, he hadn't used the skimpy silk panties as his example. He even got the nexus with being post-menopausal out. I hadn't been about to ask Captain Rockhill about that on direct examination. The doc concluded by stating that, in his expert opinion, enough time had passed and Captain Rockhill was so embarrassed by the shoplifting and the administrative discharge board that she no longer suffered from PMWWSLD and would shoplift no more. He did recommend counseling, but said no reason existed that would prevent her from serving honorably as a commissioned officer.

The recorder's cross-examination did nothing but reinforce Dr. George's favorable testimony, and he had no witnesses to rebut Dr. George's opinion. So the only thing left was to argue the case.

The recorder argued that the offenses were clear and that the board had no choice other than to find that the misconduct had occurred and that no officer who had stolen, not once, not twice, but three times should remain an officer, psychological claptrap notwithstanding.

Well, I didn't bother arguing about whether she had shoplifted three times but focused on the fact that she didn't know what she was doing when she had shoplifted because of PMWWSLD, that she wanted to stay in the Army and make up for it, and that the unrebutted testimony of her entire chain of command was that they wanted her to remain and work for them in the S-1 shop. Further, the recorder's argument that, because she had shoplifted three times, she had to be discharged ignored the board regulation that allowed the board members to find that, yes, frequent acts of a discreditable nature had occurred, but that the respondent could be retained. I didn't think that it hurt any that Captain Rockhill sat there sobbing softly throughout my argument, the only time I had ever seen her show any vulnerability.

Apparently, two of the board members were somewhat chivalrous and did not want to see her cry again, because they voted two to one to recommend retention. Because the convening authority could not do anything worse than what the board had recommended, her career was safe for now or at least until she saw another Gucci scarf that she just had to have.

Feeling pleased with myself, I led her back to my office to bask in my richly deserved praise for having saved her career. As soon as we got into my office, however, the no-longer-an-accused slammed my door shut behind her and snarled, "You asshole."

I was somewhat more shocked at this attack than at Private Hildeguard trying to take me hostage at scissor point, expecting, as I was, if not a big hug at least a more complimentary greeting than "you asshole."

"What's the problem?" I asked. "I saved your career."

"You made me look bad in there, like I was some kind of nut case."

"Yeah, and we agreed to put that defense on, and it worked."

"I'll never forgive you for making me look bad. I'm going to put in a legal ethics complaint against you!" With that threat, she turned on her heels and stormed out. So much for the big hug.

Sure enough, a week later I got a call from someone who identified himself as Colonel Niedham from the Office of Professional Responsibility at the Office of the Judge Advocate General in Washington and who started the conversation by telling me that I was in big trouble unless I could explain my actions.

"Big trouble for what actions?"

"The Rockhill case."

"Tell you what, Colonel, I've got nothing to say. Why don't you talk to the President of the Board or the recorder about my performance in that case?"

I hung up, walked down to the SJA's office, and told him about the complaint. He said not to worry, because Colonel Neidham was an anal retired lieutenant colonel who was now a civilian employee in charge of ethics complaint investigations and that he would call the former colonel and square him away. I never heard another word about the complaint, so the big trouble that Mr. Neidham had said that I was in never materialized. But I was now 0 for 2 with female clients for whom had I achieved military justice miracles.

The final straw with Captain Rockhill was when she appeared at my office door a couple of weeks later, asking me to appeal the finding that she had committed the misconduct. I asked her whether she was really nuts and not just a victim of PMWWSLD because, if the convening authority disapproved the board findings, he could convene a new board that might not be as forgiving as the one she had already faced. I also asked why would she want me to appeal when she had lodged an ethics complaint against me? Ignoring the second question, she said that because I was her lawyer, I should do her appeal and that, if I wouldn't, she would do it without me.

"Be my guest, Captain, because I'm not making a frivolous appeal arguing that your three convictions are insufficient to demonstrate that you engaged in frequent acts of a discreditable nature with civilian authorities."

Just then my paralegal stuck his head in the office and said the military judge wanted to see me ASAP. So I told Captain Rockhill to knock herself out filing her own appeal, but to find another lawyer if she won the appeal and had to face another board. I left her alone in my office while I went to see the judge. Dumb move on my part.

Apparently, Dr. George's opinion that the good captain was done with shoplifting was only partially accurate. She didn't shoplift from my office because it could not be called a shop by any reasonable stretch, especially with no billable hours. But when I returned from the judge's office, the half-sized presentation saber that a more grateful client had given me upon saving his commission was missing. Consistent with my history of being a wimp when it came to accusing my female clients of assaulting me or stealing from me, I just let it go. I don't know what happened with the remainder of Captain Rockhill's stellar military career, but I expect that unexplained gaps continued to occur in the inventories of Gucci scarves in the local stores outside the military bases where the Army stationed her for the remainder of her stellar career. But at least, she had a half-sized presentation saber to tell all that would listen how her prior command had presented it to her for her outstanding performance as the assistant S-1 of the Armor School Brigade. And my trusty paralegal and I had to console ourselves by mounting my drawing of Edvard Munch's "The Scream," in the middle of a dart board with the caption, D^3FM under it, for Doofus Cubed Fucking Maureen (her first name that I had never been allowed to call her). We would throw darts at the board to relieve the stress whenever a client for whom we had performed a miracle was ungrateful—that is, 90 percent of the time—thinking about Captain Rockhill and her Gucci scarves and her complaint as to how I had made her look bad. That dart board sits in my office to this day, twenty plus years later. Get over it, you say. Well, I've long since gotten over any irritation over her complaining about my legal work on her behalf or the theft of my presentation saber. After all, I've always tried to follow my favorite alleged ancient Chinese saying, "The best revenge is to live a happy life." But the dart board is a good reminder not to expect gratitude from the clients for whom you have performed a miracle. After all, you are the clients' living reminder of the shit that they had gotten themselves into. And because they frame the situation as one in which you merely got an innocent person off, which should have been a no-brainer, you get little credit for it. Maybe I'd feel the same way if I ever had a defense counsel get me off from a court-martial charge, but the dart board was a great reminder not to expect a tapioca milkshake, a kiss on both cheeks, and a recommendation for an Army Commendation Medal for doing your job and getting a doofus off. You're more likely to get an ethics complaint and lose your personal property as I did in the PMWWSLD case. Ok, so maybe I shouldn't have asked her whether she was post-menopausal.

7

Yes, We Have No Burma, We Have No Burma Today!

"You win in battle by knowing the enemy's timing . . . and by using a timing which the enemy does not expect."

—Miyamoto Musashi

Because I didn't actually get involved with the wrongfully dumping pickle relish case because I had dumped it onto Captain Dale, the Lieutenant/Captain Menzies case has to be the stupidest that I ever managed to get involved with. Now, the Mummy was stupid, but the case wasn't—he deserved to be prosecuted for his crimes. Lieutenant Wyndham may have been a pervert and none-too-bright to grab Mrs. Williams's boob while in uniform and wearing his name tag, but the command had little choice but to court-martial him. And the other military accused servicemembers that I've written about here all probably deserved to be court-martialed or taken before an administrative discharge board. But Lieutenant/Captain Menzies didn't. His case should never have happened.

Not that Lieutenant/Captain Menzies would ever win a "my favorite client" award, if I gave one. In fact, he would be in the running with Captain Rockhill for the "least favorite client award." Lieutenant/Captain Menzies was an Army National Guard officer who had done everything warriorlike but actually serve in combat. He was Airborne Master Blaster, Ranger, Special Forces, Pathfinder, and Air Assault qualified. You get your basic Jump Wings, as I did, upon graduating from Airborne School after jumping out of a perfectly good airplane five times. I had gotten through Jump School largely because of Master An's karate training. Karate is way more mental than physical, and I used the technique of blanking my mind and just reacting to the jump command the way that I used to blank my mind during karate sparring. Doing that drill kept me from anticipating something other than the attack that was coming or the result if my parachute didn't open.

I viewed it as quite an accomplishment that, although I was assigned to an Airborne unit for almost two years, I had to jump only eight more times. I had to jump once every so often to get the $110 a month hazardous duty pay for jumping, and I hit the absolute minimum not to lose any jump pay. But Lieutenant/Captain Menzies had a different view of parachuting. Although I couldn't be certain that he had jumped eight times a day—as opposed to my eight times in two years—I knew that he had jumped five times in one day because he wore German Jump Wings. When I was stationed in Germany with the 8th Infantry Division (Airborne), I had toyed with the idea of getting German Jump Wings because they really looked good—three times the size of American wings—and jumping with the Germans would have counted for one of the jumps needed to continue to qualify for jump pay. Besides, earning them was not difficult because one didn't actually have to go to German Jump School. The Germans invited American officers to come to the school the last day and make five jumps in one day to earn the wings. But even this gentleman's version of a real Airborne course seemed too intense to me. I had spent enough time waiting on a flight line for hours for the weather to clear to make just one jump. I couldn't imagine five in a day.

It took me only about a day of Jump School at Fort Benning, Georgia, to realize that I had fucked up by volunteering. Don't ask me why I volunteered for Airborne training. I was 22 years old and stupid and had been browbeaten daily by parachute officers about being a sorry "leg." "Leg" was short for "Straight Leg." Parachutists had to land with bent knees, so non-parachutists were straight legs. If you doubt the need to land with your knees bent, lock your knees, raise up on your toes, and drop back on your heels—after, of course, you have signed a complete waiver of any claims against me for any injuries suffered during this demonstration. Now, imagine landing on your heels with your knees locked after jumping off the roof of a one-story building. It would put your femurs somewhere around your clavicles. That's how hard you land in military parachuting. The idea is to get you down as quickly as possible without killing you so that the enemy does not have a lot of time to shoot you while you are helpless in the air.

My first clue that volunteering for Jump School wasn't my brightest military decision occurred when I put the risers—the straps going up to the chute—over the wrong shoulder the first time that I put the parachute harness on. The instructor wrapped the straps around my neck, pulled me up on my toes like a hangman, and yelled in my ear, "Do you really want to jump like this, Sir?"

"No, Sergeant," I croaked.

After a few more tugs to make certain that I had gotten the message, he let me down. Airborne instructors—all sergeants—followed proper military courtesy and called you "Sir" when they shit all over you.

Finally, it was time to make the first jump. I was minding my own business, waiting to board the plane, when I heard, "First Lieutenant Thomas, front and center. You are the ranking officer, so you're the Aircraft Commander."

I hobbled to the front and center, weighted down by the parachute harness, and politely pointed out that I was a second lieutenant and thus, not the ranking officer. The instructor, not so politely pointed out that, if he said that I was a fucking first lieutenant, then I was a fucking first lieutenant and to shut the fuck up and assume my fucking duties. "Get your troops on fucking board!"

I learned that the only real duty of the high-sounding title of Aircraft Commander was that I got to lead the troops out of the door when it was time to jump. So after the "Stand up," "Hook up," "Check equipment," and "Shuffle to the door," commands, I found myself standing in the door in the proper jump position, waiting to be slapped on the butt when the light turned green as the signal to jump. Although I kept repeating *I'm not doing this, I'm not jumping,* when the slap on the ass came, I reacted with a good exit still telling myself that I wasn't going to jump. If I had tried not to jump, it would have been difficult with several dozen other new jumpers behind me ready to push me out of the door in response to the instructor's "Go, go, go."

I quickly figured out that it was a little late not to jump since "my knees were in the breeze" and went through the drill that the instructors had beat into us of checking the chute, making certain that I wasn't going to collide with another jumper, and so forth. For a few moments, I even thought that I was doing fine. My chute was open, and my risers were not tangled, so I must have exited the plane properly. But the only problem was that everyone else was descending while I was ascending. I had caught a thermal. This circumstance wouldn't have seemed so bad if it hadn't been for the legend about the student who had jumped and had never come down. He supposedly still floats over the drop zone to this day.

Eventually, I started descending and was the last jumper on the ground. The instructor ran up as I was gathering up my chute and, although he knew full well what had happened, berated me for being a poor excuse for a leader. "God damn it, Lieutenant! You're the fucking Aircraft Commander. You're supposed to lead your men. They are all squared away and assembled to march off the drop zone, and you're still fucking around with your chute. Get a move on."

Although I was probably the least gung-ho Airborne candidate ever to go to Jump School, I ultimately made my five qualifying jumps and (fairly proudly) pinned on my Jump Wings. Then, after a tour in Vietnam, I found myself assigned to a jump unit in Germany—the last thing that I wanted. I had this strange belief that I had been lucky in Vietnam and deserved a low risk assignment.

And parachuting in an actual unit was no more fun that at Jump School—hours of waiting for a 60-second jump.

You've heard of the military's "hurry up and wait" protocol. Parachuting was hurry up and wait at its worst. If you were supposed to jump at, say, noon, the division G-3 (staff member in charge of operations) would require the paratroopers to be on the flight line about two hours before noon so that there would be plenty of time to chute up, check the chutes, and so forth. So the brigades or other separate units providing the jumpers would back that up an hour so that they wouldn't piss off the G-3 (who had the commanding general's ear) by being late. So now, everyone has to arrive by 0900 hours for a 1200 hours (noon) jump. So the battalion commanders would back that up an hour to make certain that they didn't piss off the brigade commander by being late. The brigade commander wrote their efficiency reports, and keeping the Air Force idling, burning JP4 jet fuel, was not the way to foster interservice cooperation. So now, everyone had to be on the flight line by 0800. Now, we are down to the company level (my level as a company commander—my next to the last job before going to law school), and knowing that, if my jumpers were late, I wouldn't be a company commander very long, I backed it up to 0700, as did every other company commander.

Now, 0700 became the time to be on the flight line. The flight line was at Ramstein Air Force Base—more than an hour's drive away. So the operations order for the jump had everyone reporting to the assembly area at 0700 to allow time for travel delays so that the jumpers would be certain to get to the flight line by 1000 hours, 0900 hours, or 0800 hours, depending on what level was specifying the time. So cutting to the chase, company commanders had their troops reporting to the assembly area at 0600, which meant that reveille was 0300 to leave time for pissing, shitting, showering, shaving, dressing, eating breakfast, and getting to the assembly area.

As you can see, this sort of scheduling nightmare cannot help but result in a lot of hurry up and wait. And waiting is not a lot of fun when you are dressed in fatigues and helmet and strapped into a military parachute, which seems to be most similar to being confined in an iron maiden—the old medieval torture device. For example, you had to lift up your nuts and place them carefully over the straps between your legs if you ever wanted to have any sexual function again. The jumpmasters seemed to take a sadistic pleasure in tugging on those straps to make certain that they were tight enough as part of the inspection to determine whether you had put your parachute on properly, shades of today's Transportation Security Administration officers. And being there on time is no guarantee that the Air Force will be on time or that the weather will allow you to take off or to actually jump if you do take off. I'll probably never forget sitting on the flight line for seven hours waiting for the weather to clear so that we could take off. And don't even ask how you take a piss when you are all chuted up. Thank God, I never had to try a number two. Probably because it was scared out of me.

In fact, the closest I ever came to wishing for death was a parachute jump in Germany. It should have been an easy one. My company executive officer was friends with the assistant S-3, who coordinated jumps. Once in a while, he would set up a helicopter jump right at the Division Headquarters where my 8th Military Intelligence Company was located. Yeah, I know it's a contradiction in terms, and I haven't demonstrated any intelligence by getting involved in this Airborne nonsense, but bear with me. The assistant S-3 would set up these jumps so that the Commanding General wouldn't have to wait on the flight line. So if there was an empty slot or so, he would call my XO and tell him that, if anyone needed a jump to qualify for jump pay, he should report to the helipad in 30 minutes. Because I wrote my XO's efficiency report and decided whether he would get a three-day pass to visit Paris or not, he would pass this opportunity on to me. To me, this set-up was perfect. I didn't have to spend days being nervous about jumping. There was no time for nerves when hurrying to the helipad and jumping less than an hour after the call.

With all the skydivers and the like, why was I so uninterested in jumping? Well, you must understand that back then—before the

T-10 Maneuverable Parachute, the military parachute was designed to get you down as quickly as possible without killing you. If a few parachutists broke a leg, so what? It was better than having a whole company hanging in the sky like sitting ducks, being shot at by the enemy. If you didn't do a proper PLF (Parachute Landing Fall), you were going to suffer broken bones, at best.

Further, you jumped from very low altitude to minimize the time that you were in the air being shot at, as I mentioned previously. The first time that I jumped, I wasn't scared about how high it was. I was scared about how low it was. Twelve hundred fifty feet—lower in actual combat jumps. The Sears Tower in Chicago is higher. So once you exited the plane, your chute was supposed to open in ten seconds. If it didn't, you had a couple of seconds to pull your reserve or splat. Once your chute opened, you had a whole list of things to check. For example, was your riser looped over the chute so that it looked like a big bra rather than a round cone? If the riser was looped over the chute, you would not land as if you had jumped off a one-story building but rather off a three-, four-, or five-story building, depending on the relative size of the bra cups. If your riser was looped, there was a procedure to unloop it. Another potential problem was twisted risers. You could not steer away from a lake, a power line, or other obstacle if your risers were all twisted together. So you had to scissor your legs to turn yourself around and around to undo the twist.

Suffice it to say, after performing all of these checks and taking any necessary remedial action, you might have ten seconds to enjoy floating through the air before it was time to prepare to land. Now, you might feel differently, and I know that Lieutenant/Captain Menzies did, but getting up at 0300 to get ten seconds of minor enjoyment—looking at the scenery from a bird's eye view—more than eight hours later was not my idea of a good time especially when I could get as good a view from many places with no danger whatsoever.

So one day, I thought I was lucky—a call to get to Kuhberg Hill in 30 minutes to jump with the general. Forty minutes later, I was chuted up and sitting on the floor of the helicopter with my feet hanging out the door. Normally, it would have taken about ten minutes to get over the drop zone and get my “knees in the breeze.” And I could have been back at the Officers’ Club, having a scotch on the rocks, 20 minutes after jumping, secure in the knowledge that I had qualified for another three months of jump pay.

Well, the only problem with my brilliant theory was that it was January in Germany. Everything went like clockwork, and we took off 40 minutes after I had received the call. But the weather had the last laugh. The winds picked up, and the jumpmaster could not let us jump. I’m no longer sure of the exact number, but if the wind was greater than ten miles per hour, it would slam you into the ground so hard that you could not avoid injury even with a perfect PLF.

So we circled the drop zone for more than an hour waiting for the wind to die down. No big deal, you say? Envision sitting on the floor of a helicopter with your feet hanging out the open door, in January, with an air temperature in the 20s, with the wind in the chopper’s 120-knot speed cutting through your fatigues for more than an hour. Because of the last-minute nature of the jump, I had not worn long underwear as I would have if I had known of the jump in advance. I was so cold that all I wanted was to jump even without a chute—I really didn’t care if I died.

Finally, the wind calmed down enough to jump. For the first time, anxious to get to the ground and warm up, I eagerly jumped—using the term “eagerly” loosely because, if you jumped from a helicopter as opposed to just sort of falling forward, the rotor blades would decapitate you. Well, the jump wasn’t bad. Nor was the landing. But the LZ (landing zone) was a muddy field covered with snow. And the wind picked up as soon as I landed. The mud and snow immediately covered me, which wouldn’t have been so bad, because I just would have looked ridiculous. But the mud and snow fouled my quick releases to get rid of the parachute canopy, and the wind started dragging me across the field as I tried to release the chute. After about 50 meters, I gave up and remembered to pull on one of the risers to collapse the chute. It worked, and looking like the abominable snowman, I walked off the LZ toward the jeep that was to take us back. Fortunately, the general was only a little less muddy, so no one gave me a hard time for my unmilitary appearance. Nor did anyone hear me muttering curse words and swearing never to jump again. Of course, I did jump again—three months later—so I could continue to get my jump pay. But I was extremely relieved when I was reassigned to a non-Airborne unit and wouldn't have to jump again.

Lieutenant/Captain Menzies would have thought that I was the wimp of the century for not being thrilled to jump. He had Jump Wings from more countries than you could shake a stick at. Besides Germany, he had Jump Wings from, among others, Thailand, Honduras, Israel, France, Canada, Pakistan, Japan, and Myanmar. And the last pair was what got him in trouble.

His case arrived on my desk as an officer discharge board case. When I first saw it, I groaned, remembering Captain Rockhill—my last officer discharge case client. I hoped that he wasn't being boarded out for larceny—I didn't think that my post-menopausal shoplifter defense would work very well for him. So with trepidation, I opened the file and began reading. Lieutenant (the Captain comes later) Menzies was charged with falsifying the award of Jump Wings from Myanmar to get promoted. I immediately thought that this had to be either the stupidest client that I had ever had or the stupidest case. No one falsifies foreign Jump Wings to get promoted. If anything, foreign Jump Wings would get you non-selected for promotion. Any officer with half a brain knew that the Army, as an institution, didn't like snake-eaters—the Special Forces types. And getting dozens of foreign Jump Wings would cause the vast majority of the officers on promotion boards to question why an officer had nothing better to do to serve his country than collect foreign Jump Wings. So unless my client was an absolute idiot, I saw no way that anyone could prove that he had falsified the award of these Jump Wings *with the intent to get himself promoted.*

Of course, falsifying any document could get one boarded out of the officer corps, so I figured that I'd better find out whether

Lieutenant Menzies had actually earned Myanmar Jump Wings. So I had my trusty paralegal set up an appointment to meet with my client.

Because he was in the National Guard, he had to come see me on Saturday. He worked as an accountant during the week and only became super warrior one weekend a month and two weeks of the summer when he was on active duty. He was already high on my clients-that-I-would-charge-double-my-hourly-rate list if I could have charged clients as a JAGC-Off for making me dress in my uniform and go to work on a Saturday morning. I had this strange theory that I had spent enough Saturdays and Sundays soldiering in Vietnam that I didn't have to do it much now in peacetime. It was damn near 24 hours a day, seven days a week—we didn't have the 24/7 lingo back in the dark ages—for a year in Vietnam. And U.S. Army Europe always seemed to call their alerts on Fridays or the weekend while I was in the 8th Eighth Infantry Division (Airborne)—mustn't forget the Airborne. That way, they could see whether we could get out to our battle positions with enough troops to stop the Soviet Group of Forces Germany from overrunning us. The answer was no—no matter how many troops we managed to drag from their beds or the local Gasthaus—but we had to play the game. Actually, if the Eastern Bloc had come across the boarder and down the Fulda Gap towards us, we would have never been able to get to our fighting positions through the hordes of German civilians fleeing to France. But I digress. Although I might work on an upcoming trial in my quarters over a weekend, I didn't appreciate having to put on my Class A uniform to meet a client on a Saturday morning. And when I saw Lieutenant Menzies with all the badges, tabs, and patches on his fatigues—he couldn't wear his Class A's like a rear echelon type like me, I knew that he wasn't going to make my favorite client list. He had to wear his fatigues as if he were going to do a combat jump into North Vietnam. And even though he did not know what a half-assed paratrooper I was, I could tell that he thought that I wasn't a real soldier. My blouse was hanging up in its usual spot behind my door, so he couldn't see the Combat Infantry Badge and other crap on it that would have served to shut him right the fuck up.

So swallowing my irritation, I went through the normal drill with a new client—getting him to fill out the intake, explaining the attorney-client relationship, and so on. Finally, it was time to find out whether he had actually earned Myanmar Jump Wings—so I asked him.

"Fuck, yes, I earned Myanmar Jump Wings, just like I earned German, French, Italian—"

I cut him off there, not wanting to spend the rest of the day listening to a litany of countries that allowed American officers to earn their Jump Wings. He pulled out a document in what I could only surmise was Burmese—the language of the former Burma, now Myanmar. It did, however, have a pair of ornate Jump Wings pictured in the middle of the certificate. American Jump Wings were pretty basic—silver-gray with a parachute flanked by a pair of wings. The Jump Wings on the certificate were gold and silver with other bright colors for shading. Although I could not read the Burmese, Lieutenant Menzies's name was hand-lettered right under the picture of the wings. It looked pretty authentic, but looking authentic wasn't going to get him off.

So I asked him how he got the wings.

"I signed up for a tour where you went to Thailand and jumped with a group called Friendship Airborne, which got you qualified for Thailand, Cambodia, China, and Myanmar."

"Did you actually go to Cambodia, China, and Myanmar?"

"No, the tour had arranged for officers from those countries to attend so that they could award us the wings. We had to jump once for each country."

Now, this system sounded even less impressive than five jumps for German Jump Wings. One jump for each country? And no member of a promotion board would give any one any credit towards promotion for any foreign Jump Wings, least of all from a country like Myanmar or for only one jump. Once the board looked at your official photograph and saw that you had a military haircut, looked fit and trim, and were not giving the photographer the finger, about the only thing that counted for promotion was your efficiency reports. In a close case, they might give you credit for a medal for heroism, but promotion was 99% about efficiency reports. And he had good—no, make that very good—efficiency reports.

Upon my astute questioning, I ascertained that he knew that foreign Jump Wings were meaningless for promotion purposes, so he certainly didn't have the intent to falsify a foreign certificate for that purpose. And he had a roster of soldiers and former soldiers who had paid several thousand dollars to go to Thailand and get these wings. This scenario was a part of the travel business that I had never heard of, but then again, I wasn't a snake-eater except once when I had to eat a whole bunch of shit in Jungle Warfare School in Panama. Snake isn't bad, but sloth and monkey? Anyway, so we had a list of potential witnesses who could testify that he had actually earned, using the term "earned" loosely, Myanmar Jump Wings.

After I had read the regulation regarding the wearing of foreign badges and decorations, I was satisfied that he could legally earn and wear these wings. So why was the National Guard trying to board him out for falsifying the award of Myanmar Jump Wings for the purpose of getting promoted? Well, after having searched the board packet five times, I finally found the answer—on a buck slip (a form for transmitting another document, known as passing the buck) from a personnel puke who prepared officers' records for promotion boards. The puke (anyone who worked in personnel wherever I had been stationed was automatically labeled a puke) was responsible for going through officer record briefs that were going before a promotion board to make certain that everything was there that was supposed to be there and that nothing was there that wasn't supposed to be there so that everyone had a fair chance for promotion. Well, this buck slip recommended that Lieutenant Menzies's file not go before the board for the following reason: "File contains certificate for Myanmar Jump Wings. Review of the Atlas demonstrates there is no Myanmar. Thus, certificate is fraudulent. Recommend disciplinary action be instituted." It was signed, "Gary Turner, GS-11." So some Department of the Army Civilian, General Schedule Grade 11, had looked at an outdated atlas and hadn't picked up that the Burmese government had renamed itself Myanmar.

Even with this revelation as to how stupid the charge was, I was unable to kill the board. I even wrote the Judge Advocate General of the Army to let him know what miscarriage of justice the National Guard Bureau was inflicting on a fine officer, suggesting that he use his authority to supervise the military justice system to suggest that they dismiss this idiotic proceeding. But to no avail.

So I had to start preparing for the hearing. I had my paralegal contact the other jumpers from the Thailand tour, and several of them remembered Lieutenant Menzies jumping with them. I got an affidavit from a political science professor about the connection between then Burma and now Myanmar. Now, this activity should have been (and was) enough preparation. But Lieutenant Menzies's girlfriend was a graduate of Yale Law School and an associate at a big, national law firm. So naturally, although she specialized in corporate securities—mergers, acquisitions, and initial public offerings—she perceived herself somehow as an expert in military law. I had stupidly agreed to keep her informed on the case if Lieutenant Menzies waived client confidentiality to that extent, which he did. Well, she wore me out. Several times a week, she would call for an update and to make suggestions as to how to defend her true love. Among her suggestions were to move to dismiss the charges because any irregularity in the Myanmar Jump Wings occurred in another country, so the American military had no jurisdiction, and the offense was not service-connected under the U.S. Supreme Court case of *O'Callahan v. Parker.* The only things wrong with her brilliant legal theory were that *O'Callahan* talked about court-martial jurisdiction while this case was before an administrative board, the Supreme Court had overruled *O'Callahan* so that courts-martial had jurisdiction over servicemembers no matter where the offense occurred, and that, if an offense had occurred, it hadn't taken place overseas, but rather when her boyfriend took the document to the personnel office in the United States to be filed in his Official Military Personnel File. Other than that, it was a brilliant legal theory. Later, she instructed me—which instruction I ignored—to seek a temporary restraining order in the federal district court, ordering the military to dismiss the board proceeding. Even if I could have gotten past the federal courts' total lack of interest in involving themselves in discrete military personnel matters (they had this strange belief that the military had more expertise in military matters than they did—strange because it was about the only area of the law that they felt unqualified to decide), the court would have dismissed the case for failure to exhaust available military administrative remedial measures. Every time that I refused to drop all of my other cases and follow her suggestions, she told me that she was going to get Lieutenant Menzies to fire me as his defense counsel. Please do, I thought. Please, please, pretty please.

Although he didn't fire me, he wasn't much better at letting me decide how best to defend him. But at least, his demands made some legal sense. He'd tell me that he had tracked down another witness who just happened to be in Australia and that I could call him at 0300 to interview him. I couldn't even see sticking my paralegal with the job of waking up at 3 A.M. to get yet another witness. We had enough witnesses. Nor did I agree to his demand to challenge all of the board members for cause once we were notified of the date, time, and composition of the board. It seemed to me that on the rare occasions when I had the law and the facts, I didn't need all the procedural mechanisms that I would use to better position the case when my client was as guilty as hell and the government had the evidence to prove it. In this case, I wanted the board to feel sorry for my poor, snake-eater client whose only flaw was that he was too gung-ho Airborne. I didn't want them pissed off at him for challenging them for cause or for wasting their time with a bunch of legal shenanigans.

So finally, it was time for my trusty paralegal and me to drive up to some National Guard Armory in Wisconsin to defend my snake-eater before the board, scheduled to convene at 0900

Saturday morning. We had arranged to meet him the night before to go over his testimony. When we met in the lobby of the Holiday Inn that I was staying at—no Bachelor Officers Quarters in Milwaukee—he was wearing captain's bars. This sight immediately brought three questions to mind. Was the promotion real, or had he forged promotion orders as the admin puke had alleged that he had forged his Myanmar Jump Wings? How did he get promoted when facing administrative discharge for misconduct? And how would I control him at all, now that I no longer outranked him?

Well, the promotion was valid, although it didn't say much for the efficiency of the National Guard Bureau that it would promote an officer that it was trying to discharge for misconduct. And I suppose that it gave me more ammunition to argue that he shouldn't be discharged. After all, he would get a promotion certificate stating that the President of the United States reposed special trust and confidence in him, thereby appointing him a Captain in the U.S. Army National Guard. And because I couldn't really control him anyway—he didn't think that a JAGC captain outranked an Infantry lieutenant—I hadn't lost much. So we went to his room to work up his testimony.

Captain/Lieutenant Menzies, not unsurprisingly, had the typical disease of an officer testifying to save his career—run-off-at-the-mouth-itis. He couldn't just give what I advised—the shortest truthful answer. He had to embellish. I would ask a fairly straightforward question, such as "Did you earn Jump Wings from Burma, now known as Myanmar?"

Instead of replying, "Yes," he would reply, "Yes, just like I earned Jump Wings from Thailand, Cambodia, China, Germany, Italy, Honduras, Israel, France, Canada, Pakistan, Japan, Poland, Kazakhstan, Latvia, the Ukraine—"

I cut him off here, telling him to answer simply, "Yes." I didn't want the board to find him not guilty of misconduct consisting of falsifying Burmese Jump Wings and then vote to discharge him anyway for being so stupid as to collect so many foreign Jump Wings. Yeah, if they found him not guilty of the misconduct, it would be illegal to recommend discharge, but I didn't want him for a client for the extra time that it would take to do an appeal. And his girlfriend would immediately order me to petition the U.S. Supreme Court for a writ of prohibition—prohibiting the military from discharging him.

But the answer to the next question was just as bad. "Captain Menzies, how did you earn these particular Jump Wings?"

"The same way that I earned all of my foreign Jump Wings—by researching what the requirements were, by fulfilling them, and by providing documentation for proper filing in my OMPF."

"No, Captain. What I want is how, as specifically as possible, you earned this pair—not any other pair. Something like, I went to Thailand and jumped with a group called Friendship Airborne, which had arrangements with Myanmar to qualify the members of the group for Myanmar Jump Wings."

"Oky. I went to Thailand and jumped with a group called Friendship Airborne, which had arrangements with Thailand, Cambodia, China, and Myanmar for members of the tour to get jump wings from each of those countries."

I didn't see any need to go into Thailand, Cambodia, and China, but thought that I had better quit while only slightly behind. "Did you do this jump on duty or off duty?"

"Off duty. I always use my vacations from my civilian job to improve my military credentials. I wouldn't use a drill period—my unit needs me too badly."

"Just say, 'Off-duty.'" I was quickly coming to the realization that if I put my innocent client on the stand, he was going to come across as such an arrogant asshole that a real possibility of reverse jury nullification existed. In jury nullification, the defense got the jury to, in essence, decide that the client was guilty of, say, assaulting the trainee, but that they were not going to convict the accused of it because they would have punched the trainee out themselves—and much harder—in similar circumstances. I held the Fort Knox record for an acquittal when I put my drill instructor client on the stand to confess that, yes, he had hit the trainee, but God damn, the trainee needed it, legal or not. The members deliberated for less than two minutes before finding my client not guilty. This win was a particularly satisfying result because the prosecutor held the prior record—four minutes to acquit—in a case in which he had been defense counsel. A military jury couldn't do reverse jury nullification very well, however, because of the requirement for proof beyond a reasonable doubt. But an administrative board might because the standard of proof was only a preponderance of the evidence—51 percent or greater.

So I spent another two hours of wasted time preparing now-Captain/Lieutenant Menzies for his testimony, even though I knew that I couldn't put him on the stand. But for client control purposes—read, "I didn't want to explain either to him or to his girlfriend why he couldn't testify or tell him that I thought he would come across like an asshole and convict himself of conduct unbecoming of a dipshit"—I prepared him to testify, knowing that I couldn't let him. Instead, I'd just rest after the recorder failed to prove his case.

As it happened, the recorder never even got the chance to prove his case. I had to request the President of the Board, a National Guard full colonel, to allow me to call one witness by telephone before the recorder put on his case because my witness was in Australia and that was the only time he was free to testify. The recorder, who had probably figured out that this matter was the bull-shit case of all time, had no objection, so I put on the witness's testimony that, yes, he had jumped with my client in Thailand and that both of them had earned Myanmar Jump Wings. Initially, I had thought that this evidence would take the wind out of the recorder's case, but the witness was so convincing that I had a flash—why allow the recorder to put on a case? So I moved for a finding of not guilty, arguing that there was nothing in the way of evidence that the recorder could put on that would negate the witness's testimony, so why waste the day mucking around with this matter? Besides, I argued, the case was against Lieutenant Menzies, not Captain Menzies. Further, I argued, even assuming that it was the same respondent, the National Guard had enough confidence in him to promote him, so he could not have committed the charged misconduct.

Well, the board members, probably balancing hearing all of the evidence against getting out on the golf course on a weekend that they didn't have drill, were agreeable, and after a short deliberation, they found that my client had not committed any misconduct. The President even apologized to my client on behalf of the National Guard for his being hauled before a board—an apology that pleased Captain Menzies's girlfriend highly—so highly that she even deigned to compliment me on my representation of her true love.

So I returned home, secure in the knowledge that I had established legal precedent—yes, we have Myanmar, we have Myanmar Jump Wings today.

8

How to Lose a Guilty Plea

"If I tell you I'm good, you would probably think I'm boasting. If I tell you I'm no good, you know I'm lying."

—Bruce Lee

I never thought that I would see the day, but I finally got a good officer client! And a female officer at that! Major LeBlanc was a top-flight Medical Service Corps officer—the branch that provided the logistical support to the military's medical components. Her efficiency reports were uniformly perfect—what we called "top blocked" or, in other words, the block by the one officer standing at the top of the pyramid of 100 officers. And she had awards and condemnations up the wahzoo. Well, maybe I shouldn't say up the wahzoo about a female client. I hadn't exactly made a lifelong friend of Captain Rockhill by asking her whether she was post-menopausal.

So, if Major LeBlanc was so perfect, how did she end up facing a general court-martial? She was charged with falsifying her physical training (PT) test. Apparently, she had always maxed her PT tests, just as she had maxed her fitness reports. But one day, she had a cold and was afraid that she might not max it and put the test off. She also put it off for the next couple of scheduled dates, and then, by the time that she felt better, she was past due to take the test, and she was very busy because her unit was facing an Inspector General investigation. Preparing for such an investigation was an around-the-clock activity. So she got into trouble when the training NCO said, "I've got to have your PT test score right now, Ma'am, or the IG is going to ding us. Did you max it as usual?"

Not wanting the Inspector General's team to assign a deficiency for not having 100 percent PT test participation, Major LeBlanc spazzed and said, "Yes."

Unfortunately for the good Major, the IG was particularly anal and checked the reported scores against the score cards. And guess who didn't have one? Rather than keeping her mouth shut, my soon-to-be-client admitted that she hadn't taken the test. So the next thing that she knew, she was facing a general court-martial for falsifying her PT test results and for conduct unbecoming of an officer and a gentlewoman. Because she had admitted to the false official statement, I didn't immediately see a brilliant defense, but what with the success of my earlier post-menopausal shoplifter defense, I seized on the hope of a mental health defense. Why would such a perfect officer spazz unless she had some mental disease or defect?

Major LeBlanc was unlike Captain Rockhill. In fact, she might make my favorite client list because she said, quite simply, "Just keep my commission—I'll do whatever I have to do, and you do whatever you have to do."

So once again, I had my favorite shrink—Doctor (Major) George—evaluate her mental condition. And lo and behold, she had PTSD (Post Traumatic Stress Disorder) from having been abused by her father. So at the Article 32 hearing to determine whether the Convening Authority should send her case to a general court-martial, I departed from my usual practice of not putting on any evidence (the beauty of an Article 32, from a defense standpoint, was that you got to see the government's case but could hide yours until later). But this time, with Doctor George's affidavit, I got the Article 32 Investigating Officer to order a sanity board. With Doctor George's affidavit, the board could not do its usual the-accused-is-just-exhibiting-attention-getting-behavior like my strait jacket masturbator and confirmed the diagnosis although it did not opine that she had such a severe mental defect as to not know right from wrong or to be able to conform to the right. In other words, her PTSD was a mitigating factor, not a defense.

Of course, the Chief Trial Counsel had seen quite enough of my creating a defense out of whole cloth, so to avoid the hassle of a general court-martial, he got the Convening Authority to offer my client a General Officer Article 15 in lieu of a court-martial. Accepting this Article 15 was a no-brainer. It avoided a federal conviction for a crime involving dishonesty, and she could not be dismissed from the service—the officer version of a dishonorable discharge. Yes, she could be administratively boarded out for having nonjudicial punishment under Article 15 on her record, but we'd face that later.

So on the appointed day, we appeared in front of General Wosepka, the Commanding General of the Armor Center and Fort Knox. Although one facing nonjudicial punishment has the right only to consult with a lawyer but not to have one actually appear on her behalf, the CG graciously allowed me to act as Major LeBlanc's spokesman. The spokesman (probably spokesperson now, although I may have mentioned that my memoir is politically incorrect) was typically a military supervisor who would point out why the soldier facing Article 15 punishment should not be punished or that the punishment should be very light. After I had put on evidence of my client's PTSD, the general was so touched that he said that he wished he could award no punishment, but because of the need for integrity in officers under his command, he had to take some disciplinary action. So he imposed a reprimand, considerably lighter than the 60 days' restriction, arrest in quarters for 30 days, and forfeiture of one-half of one month's pay per month for two months that he could have imposed.

He did not order an administrative discharge board, but some personnel puke at the Pentagon did, so I had my third officer discharge board—D^{3}FM, Lieutenant/Captain Menzies of the Myanmar Airborne Corps, and now Major LeBlanc.

And again, I got a recorder from the Reserve components, but this time a National Guard JAGC-Off working for the trial counsel section for his two weeks' annual training. He was a full-time prosecutor for Cook County, Illinois, with hundreds of felony trials under his belt. Major Borich was a slightly overweight individual with a booming voice. I could project my voice with the best of them, but he could compete with the Army drum and bugle corps for volume, if not for melodious sounds. And I quickly found out that (a) he had heard of me and my reputation, and (b) he really wanted to kick my ass. And it shouldn't be hard, with a record of nonjudicial punishment and a reprimand signed by the commanding general to prove that my client had committed forgery, what with my PTSD defense already on the table.

So he quickly found a military shrink hack to evaluate whether my client had PTSD. She hadn't, the psychologist opined. So I wasn't going to have my usual unrebutted psychological defense.

So I requested a continuance, stating that I could not have my expert respond to the recorder's expert in the ten days left before the board hearing. My thought was that the recorder's two week training period would be over, he would go back to Chicago, and some more clueless recorder would take over. Great idea, but I didn't reckon on how bad he wanted to beat me. I got my continuance, but he volunteered to come back to Fort Knox on the next available weekend to have the hearing. And he was really hard to deal with—wouldn't give me copies of documents that he intended to introduce in evidence, wouldn't tell me the name of his shrink until the last minute and other such b.s. tactics. Maybe that's how they do it in Cook County.

So I came up with yet another request for a continuance saying that this last minute production of documents and evidence violated due process, but the president of the board denied it upon the recorder's recommendation. So Major LeBlanc and I reported to the board at 0900 on a Saturday morning.

After the usual preliminaries and the denial of my renewed request for a continuance, Major Borich called his first witness—the sergeant who was the Training NCO that she had told that she had maxed the physical fitness test. I immediately rose to my feet and objected, "Mr. President, I am not prepared to relitigate the facts of this matter. The record of punishment under Article 15 and the letter of reprimand establish the misconduct. If we are starting at square one, that the misconduct has not been established and I'm going to have to litigate whether my client committed the misconduct or not, I need a continuance to prepare. All I prepared for was the ultimate issue, whether she should be discharged as a result of that misconduct."

After listening to Major Borich and me argue back and forth for ten minutes, the President threw up his hands and told us to go outside the hearing room and work it out. He was under a lot of pressure to get the hearing over with because the Adjutant General in the Pentagon had imposed a suspense date which had already been missed and was querying Fort Knox every duty day as to why this matter had not been resolved—questions that got the board president chewed out by the post chief of staff.

"So, Captain Thomas, if I understand you," Major Borich bellowed, "you will not object if I put the record of nonjudicial punishment and the letter of reprimand in evidence and you will not put on any defense but only matters in extenuation and mitigation as to why, notwithstanding her guilt, she should not be discharged."

With much less volume, as if I were cowed, I answered, "Yes, Sir. In effect, it's a guilty plea."

So we went back and informed the board of our agreement. The president ordered us to proceed and damned if Major Borich didn't keep trying to show what my client had done. And I kept objecting, forcefully arguing that he was breaking our agreement and, if allowed to continue, I needed a continuance. Major Borich knew he was getting fucked, but he couldn't figure out how. So he finally gave up and rested with the record of non-judicial punishment and the letter of reprimand as his only evidence.

So then I put on her defense. Every time the recorder objected, I said, "Mr. President, I'm not putting on this evidence of PTSD as a defense, but rather a mitigating factor." And the Board President overruled the recorder and let me prove that she was not guilty by proving that she had a mitigating mental health disorder. I could almost see steam coming out of the recorder's ears, but did I care?

Doctor George did his usual brilliant job at explaining her disorder and how it caused her to lie about her PT test. The recorder didn't dare cross-examine probably because he had not prepared to rebut this defense—I mean this mitigating evidence—and because he didn't want to bring out any more evidence that would help my client.

Then I had Major LeBlanc's entire chain of command testify that, notwithstanding this hiccup, they would absolutely take her back. And, while Major Borich might be brilliant at cross-examining a gang member's thug abili witness, he didn't know how to cross-examine senior Army officers. My star witness was a female brigadier general—how good do you have to be to make general as a woman back in the '70s? But Borich bore in on her like she was a brand-new second lieutenant about how she was condoning lying officers and concluded by asking her whether she had ever lied as an Army officer. She refused to answer and the board president growled, "That's quite enough, Major Borich."

After I rested, Major Borich called his psychologist to counter Doctor George. His shrink, a new captain, testified that Major LeBlanc did not meet the DSM-IV criteria for Post-Traumatic Stress Disorder and that, to the extent that she did, it had nothing to do with her lying about her PT test.

My turn. This cross-examination was not one of the more difficult ones that I had done.

"Doctor, where did you get your Ph.D.?"

"Tulane."

"And isn't it true that a Ph.D. from the University of Chicago is more prestigious than one from Tulane?"

"Probably."

"Have you written anything for publication?"

"No."

"How much time did you spend evaluating Major LeBlanc?'

"A little over an hour."

"Did you take a complete psycho-social history?"

"No."

"Did you interview any of her military superiors or co-workers?"

"No."

"Did you interview any of her family members?"

"No."

"Did you review her school, medical, and military records?"

"No."

"Did you administer any diagnostic tests, such as an MMPI?"

"No."

"Doctor, what are the diagnostic criteria for PTSD?"

"I don't know them off the top of my head."

"Did you review the diagnostic criteria?"

"I don't remember—I may have."

"What is the differential diagnosis for PTSD?"

"I don't remember."

"Or is it that you don't know?"

"I would have to look it up."

"So you reached this conclusion that she did not suffer from PTSD after a one-hour interview of her unaccompanied by any review of records, by any interviews with people who know her, and by any psychological tests—isn't that true?"

"Yes, but I stand by my diagnosis."

In sur-rebuttal, I called Doctor George, who had spent more than 100 hours doing all of those things as testified to in my case-in-chief. I had only one question for him. "Doctor George, you heard Captain Janick testify. How would you characterize his methodology and his diagnosis?"

Now good trial attorneys say that you should never ask the question that you don't know the answer to, but I knew that Doctor George would come through. And he did.

"Malpractice." This terse answer was as coldly effective as a Master An *ippon*—a killing stroke in a karate match.

"No further questions."

Major Borich decided to quit while he was behind, and it was time to argue whether the board should recommend Major LeBlanc for discharge. The arguments were predictable. Major Borich bellowed about how the Army was no place for lying officers. I calmly pointed out that Major LeBlanc's behavior was an aberration, caused by stress and PTSD, and that all of her chain of command wanted her back.

The board members had to make two recommendations to the convening authority. He could, under the regulations, improve the result for my client, but not worsen it. For example, if the board recommended discharge, he could suspend it or disapprove it. But if the board recommended retention, he could not have her discharged. First the board had to decide whether she had committed the misconduct. Second, if she did, the board had to recommend whether to discharge her.

After more than an hour, the board returned. Major LeBlanc and I rose to our feet to hear the findings. The president announced, "It is the unanimous finding of this board, that Major LeBlanc did not commit the misconduct. Further, even if she had, she should not be discharged. This board proceeding is over."

My poor client started to get up and protest—but I pled guilty—but I pulled her back into her seat and said, "Shut up. We won!"

Major Borich really looked pissed. He didn't offer to shake my hand or offer congratulations as I would have done even though I would have hated to lose to him. The practice of law is vicious enough without acting like a jerk, win or lose. But in the face of his discourtesy and after all of the hassle that he had given me in the period leading up to the hearing, I couldn't resist. "Do you often lose guilty pleas, Major?"

He didn't answer. But I smiled at the thought of him going back to the trial counsel section and, upon being asked how it went, having to admit that he had lost a guilty plea. And I later learned that, after the board president had told the staff judge advocate how he had treated the female general, the SJA ordered Major Borich to apologize to her in person. Couldn't happen to a nicer fellow. Major Fred—Loser of Guilty Pleas—Borich.

9

Home Teamed

Or

Yes, We Have No Jurisdiction—We Have No Jurisdiction Today

"Techniques will occur when a void is found."
—Master Gichin Funakoshi, from Karate-do Kyohan

All of the defense counsel at Fort Knox generally dreaded having to go to another installation to defend a soldier. Not only did you miss your own, familiar law library and trusty paralegal—it was hard enough to get travel funds for yourself, much less your paralegal—but also you often didn't know the judge, you didn't know the staff judge advocate, and perhaps no one knew that you were the baddest son of a bitch in the valley, so they had better take your offer to plead your client guilty in return for a sentence of an Army Commendation Medal, a kiss on both cheeks, and a Jamocha milkshake. Now, I have no idea what such a Jamocha milkshake is, but that was the saying for a ridiculously light sentence for a serious crime. Sometimes, the trial counsel at the other base was bright enough to call one of the trial counsel at Fort Knox to find out whether Captain Thomas had his shit together or not, and thus would roll over and play dead when he found out that it wasn't worth World War III to fight me at trial, but sometimes, they didn't make such a call. Because much of my success was bluff, based on my undeserved reputation from the first case that I had had in front of Judge Savage, the case that I had won only because I had had the same combat patch as the court members, I liked it when the other side believed that I was the next thing to Perry Mason and decided that it wasn't worth the hassle to fight me.

But Captain Ferguson, the Chief Trial Counsel of Fort Benjamin Harrison in Indianapolis, Indiana, brilliantly turned my undeserved reputation against me when I was detailed to represent Private Cornwall before a court-martial at Fort Ben. The Judge Advocate General, in his infinite wisdom, had decided that not everyone was qualified to be a defense counsel, so defense counsel had to be certified as competent. Ultimately, this theory led to the establishment of the Trial Defense Service, which removed defense counsel from the supervision of the Staff Judge Advocate—the chief prosecutor. Now, the SJA could no longer (in theory) give defense counsel a bad efficiency report, which would result in their non-selection for promotion. Of course, all that the SJA had to do was bad mouth them enough throughout the JAG Corps so that no one on the promotion board would vote for their promotion, but that's reality, not theory.

Fort Ben had no certified defense counsel, so they had to ask Fort Knox for certified defense counsel, and I got stuck with Private Cornwall, who was facing a general court-martial for rape. The maximum punishment for rape was life imprisonment, a dishonorable discharge, forfeiture of all pay and allowances, and reduction to the lowest enlisted grade. Cornwall was in deep shit.

The prosecution, however, did not have the case of the decade. Tina Bell, the alleged victim, was about as much an ideal virgin rape victim as had been Mrs. Williams, the alleged victim of the alleged indecent assault and indecent exposure by Lieutenant Wyndham. Yeah, Cornwall had screwed Tina, but it was clearly consensual. She cried rape just because her boyfriend had found out that he was sloppy seconds—actually, sloppy fourths because two others had also taken their turn—and following a black man, as well—actually, three black men. So to avoid grievous bodily injury, Tina told her boyfriend that she had been raped by a black soldier.

So the CID—Criminal Investigative Division of the Military Police—responded to the report that Miss Bell had been raped by immediately apprehending Private Cornwall, who fit the general description of the rapist, reading him his Article 32, Uniform Code of Military Justice, rights—similar to a Miranda warning—and interrogating him. The dumbshit waived his Article 32 rights, stated that he wanted to talk, and said that he did not want an attorney. The CID agent told him that it would go better for him if he admitted to sexual intercourse with Miss (they weren't into the more politically correct Ms. back then) Bell. After all, the CID said, voluntary sexual intercourse with an adult when neither was married was not a crime under the Uniform Code or civilian law. To get this admission, they recounted examples of cases in which an admission of voluntary sexual intercourse resulted in the military dropping the charges. They guaranteed that if the intercourse was voluntary, he was off the hook.

So Private Cornwall admitted to voluntary sexual intercourse with Miss Bell, thinking that he was home free. Unfortunately for him, however, Miss Bell could not identify whoever it was who had penetrated her. She failed to pick him out of a lineup. She even said that her assailant had a big dick. Cornwall didn't. Shades of Lieutenant Wyndham. But his admission to voluntary sexual intercourse tied him to the alleged rape as the perpetrator. So he was facing life imprisonment because he had confessed to voluntary sexual intercourse. So I had to defend him—and at another base, at that.

But the case was defensible, I thought. He had not confessed to rape. If the trial counsel put the confession in to prove the identity of the alleged rapist, I would point out that the prosecution couldn't have it both ways—he was truthful when he said he stuck it in and he was lying when he said she spread her legs, inviting it. In addition, the confession clearly wasn't his words. No offense, but Cornwall was a high school dropout from Harlem. I seriously doubt that he told the CID agent, "After I had inserted my penis into her vagina and ejaculated, I performed fellation (apparently an archaic variation of fellatio) on her." He might have said, "I went down on her twat," "I ate her snatch," or "I lapped her pussy," but he wouldn't have said any version of the word fellatio—he had no idea what it meant. Hey, I said that this book was a politically incorrect memoir of the real Judge Advocate General's Corps.

In addition, the prosecution had not referred the other two alleged rapists to a court-martial for some unknown reason. In fact, the Convening Authority had allowed them to resign in lieu of court-martial, so they were civilians, albeit with an other-than-honorable discharge, which denied them all military and veterans' benefits. But at least, I didn't have to worry about the government granting them immunity and ordering them to testify against my client.

I took some heart from the Article 32 Investigation. Miss Bell showed up to testify in the perfect outfit for the defense. She wore a black silk number that I would have expected to see on a Vietnamese prostitute. It looked like sexy pajamas. All that was missing was the slit up the side of the leg. Now I don't know whether the pants were tap pants or culottes. All I knew was that a military jury would consider her a slut, which would be fine with me.

But how could I make sure that she wore it to the trial? When I cross-examined her at the 32, I got her to admit that it was the same outfit that she had worn on the night of the alleged rape, so all I had to do was move Judge Savage—he rode a circuit that included Fort Ben and would preside over my client's court-martial—to order her to wear the outfit on the ground that it was relevant to show why my client had a reasonable belief that Miss Bell had consented. I didn't move for an order that she wear the same tarty make-up, figuring that she would do so anyway.

On my way back to Fort Knox, I was stopped by the MPs for allegedly going two miles over the speed limit and given a ticket—a somewhat surprising ticket because, even though MPs loved to bust officers, they would seldom do so for two miles over the limit.

I didn't think much about it at the time, but later on found out its relevance to my client's case.

Of course, the Article 32 Investigating Officer found that the case should go to a general court-martial, and the Convening Authority—the Major General who was the installation commander—agreed. So after having gone through the normal pretrial drill—interviewing witnesses, getting and reviewing discovery, drafting motions, and the like, I drove up to Fort Benjamin Harrison. Again, I didn't think much of it when the MP at the gate didn't just wave me through. Usually, the MP would see the blue officer registration, waive me through, and salute. This MP, however, omitted the wave-through and required me to stop, asked to see my ID card, and then required me to show him my license, state registration, and proof of insurance—items I had to have to get my up-to-date blue officer registration. Then he kept me sitting there in the heat—my car wasn't air-conditioned—for twenty minutes while he "checked to see whether my documents were in order." He eventually came back and said that I was free to enter Fort Ben. Again, I didn't think much of it other than perhaps some Inspector General investigation had found that Fort Ben was too lax in its traffic control and they were overreacting—which would hardly be a new concept for the Army.

So in blissful ignorance of the fact that Captain Ferguson had made me persona non grata for all of Fort Benjamin Harrison, I checked into the Bachelor Officers Quarters—after having been told repeatedly that I didn't have a reservation and finally having to call the Staff Judge Advocate Office to confirm that they had made a reservation—and spent the evening working on the case. In the morning, I went to the SJA office, only to learn that the spare office usually reserved for visiting defense counsel was being painted and that I wouldn't have a place to work during the trial other than the law library. Once again, I was too stupid to read anything into these hassles because they didn't seem out of the ordinary for the Army. So I went into the courtroom and waited for the trial to start.

Immediately after Judge Savage had called the court-martial to order, Captain Ferguson began reading from the script—accounting for the parties, noting that the charge had properly been referred for trial by Major General Friday, and so forth. But when he got to the part of the script that read "the prosecution has no challenge for cause against the military judge," he departed from the script and instead said, "The prosecution challenges the military judge for cause."

My head jerked up from the witness statement that I had been poring over in hopes of finding some new avenue of cross-examination. The prosecution never challenged Judge Savage. He was too prosecution oriented. As a defense counsel, I routinely challenged Judge Savage for being pro-prosecution—not that he ever granted the challenge. So did many other defense counsel, not out of any real hope that he would ever recuse himself from presiding over the trial but because we wanted him to know that we knew that he was anti-defense for some unknown reason. I have no idea why we cared because challenging him gained us nothing. But trial counsel never challenged him.

"Grounds?" Judge Savage growled, looking at Captain Ferguson from under his bushy white eyebrows as if the trial counsel had suddenly sprouted horns.

"I have several grounds, your honor."

"State them." Judge Savage really looked pissed at having the prosecution question his judicial integrity. He could put up with defense challenges—defense counsel had to appear to be fighting against the might and majesty of the United States government on behalf of their dirtbag clients. Parenthetically, I had a full colonel shit all over me for calling accused servicemembers dirtballs when teaching military justice to student officers, reprimanding me for forgetting that they were soldiers. Sorry, Colonel, but as a former Infantry platoon leader in combat and a company commander in Germany—neither of which you ever were—I knew a dirtbag when I saw one. And I'd never call a real soldier that insulting epithet. And I have no remorse about not being politically correct and calling a dirtbag or a dirtball or a dud or a doofus or a dumbshit what they were, including you, colonel, although perhaps not to your face because that would be the crime of disrespect to a (allegedly) superior officer. If Master An had taught me anything, it was not to start an attack that you couldn't win.

But back to the court-martial in progress, the government ought to be respectful of a full colonel military judge with close to thirty years of service who usually ruled in the government's favor. And although I would challenge him for cause to perform my most vital defense function—to have my client go to the U.S. Disciplinary Barracks somewhat happy that someone had fought for him—I never disrespected Judge Savage. And he knew it. He knew that I was just posturing for my client's benefit. But by challenging him, Captain Ferguson did disrespect him.

On behalf of the United States government—or at least on behalf of this particular prosecution—Captain Ferguson responded to Judge Savage's query as to the grounds for challenge. "First, Your Honor, you are from Fort Knox. So is the defense counsel. And he is one of your favorite trial lawyers. So you will favor him in ruling on motions and evidentiary objections."

This revelation was news to me. I knew that Judge Savage liked the fact that I made a lot of motions because he wanted to log more hours on the bench than any other judge and that dealing with my many and inventive motions helped him do so. Why he wanted more bench time than any other military judge totally escaped me. He was a full colonel. He wasn't going to make general. And he was now within a year of mandatory retirement.

In addition, he ruled against me on the vast majority of my brilliant motions, so much so that I made motions that I didn't care whether I won or not just so that he would have ruled against me a half-dozen times or more before I'd make the motion that I wanted to win. My strategy was to cause him to perhaps worry about looking too prosecution oriented if he didn't grant a defense motion once in a while and thus grant the one that I really wanted to win. I'm not saying that he didn't recognize this strategy, just that it worked often enough for me to continue to use it as the need arose in any particular case.

I always believed in motion practice when defending a probably guilty client. If you have the facts, argue the law. In one case, for example, I could not let my client testify. The prosecution would destroy him on cross-examination and be able to bring out two prior convictions that would otherwise be inadmissible to impeach him. So the only way to get his self-defense defense out was to get the trial counsel to put his statement to the military police into evidence. But the trial counsel wasn't going to. He was going to save it for impeachment if my client testified and said he wasn't even there. How could I cause the trial counsel to admit the statement into evidence in his case-in-chief? I decided to make him think that I didn't want it in evidence.

So I moved to suppress the statement for failure to comply with Article 31—the military version of the Miranda warnings. I submitted a well-researched, twenty-page brief in support of the motion even though I didn't want the statement suppressed and knew that Judge Savage wouldn't suppress it. During the suppression hearing, I fought desperately to keep the statement out of evidence, so desperately that the trial counsel, who was well aware of my reputation, decided that the statement must be devastating to my case and that he had better put it into evidence in his case-in-chief rather than saving it to rebut any case that I might put on.

One thing that I had learned prosecuting and defending soldiers was that confessions were overrated. Why do you need a confession when you have five eyewitnesses and a videotape of the crime? Or evidence that the CID had strip-searched their confidential informant before sending him to buy drugs, given him marked twenty-dollar bills, observed the transaction, searched him when he came back, recovered drugs from his person, arrested the seller, and recovered the marked bills? What could a confession possibly have added to that pile of evidence? What I had learned was that, when military law enforcement got a confession, they quit investigating. Well, what if they had coerced the confession? What if the suspect had had borderline personality disorder and would confess to anything? What if they had put the words in the suspect's mouth so that some sneaky defense lawyer—not that I knew any, of course—could argue to the jury that his client didn't confess? In my opinion confessions were overrated.

So Judge Savage duly ruled against me, the trial counsel put my client's confession into evidence, I rested without putting on any evidence and argued to the jury that the government must have believed that my client acted in self-defense because they had put his statement that it was self-defense into evidence, and the jury duly found my client not guilty.

Anyway, back to Private Cornwall's court-martial, I wasn't too worried about this ground for challenge. Judge Savage ruled against me 90 percent of the time—hardly showing me great favoritism. And I thought that I could use the time that he had thrown his gavel at me as some evidence that he was not biased in my favor. Judge Savage always wanted to waffle you out of your position, so he wouldn't have to rule against you and, consequently, appear anti-defense. But I refused to waffle. I would say, "Your Honor, I have stated the defense position, and I adhere to it. Rule against me if you must, but I adhere to my position." In one case, I did this once too often, and he threw his gavel at me. He apologized, saying that it had slipped when he was trying to gavel me to silence, but it wasn't slipsies. If anything, Judge Savage was pissed at me for getting him reversed on appeal on a jurisdictional issue after he had denied my motion to dismiss for lack of jurisdiction.

"Do you join in this motion, Counselor?" Judge Savage asked me.

In retrospect, maybe I should have, increasing the probability that he would grant it and that we would get a nice delay while the Chief Trial Judge assigned another judge. But if the trial counsel wanted to get rid of him, I thought that I should not help make it happen. As it turned out, the trial counsel was way more devious than I had given him credit for. So I answered, "No, Your Honor."

"Next ground, Trial Counsel."

"Second, the acquittal rate for sex crimes courts-martial that you have presided over is 50 percent lower than that of the Army-wide average, reflecting a bias against rape and other sex-crime victims."

Captain Ferguson then offered a certified record, showing all military judges' conviction rates in sex crimes. Judge Savage had the lowest conviction rate by a considerable margin.

Now, the implication that Judge Savage was biased against sex crime prosecutions or victims was bullshit. What the statistics did not reveal was that defense counsel never waived a military jury to go judge alone in any case, much less a sex case, that Judge Savage presided over. He was too prosecution oriented. And as a gentleman of the old school, he was very solicitous of women, put them on a pedestal, and viewed any form of sexual assault very dimly. So maybe Fort Knox juries were easy on sex crimes—a sort of version of the theory that you can't rape a WAC—what we called the "mere WAC rule" or indecently grope Mrs. Williams—but that jury habit was no reflection on Judge Savage.

But Judge Savage's face turned as white as his hair as he read the statistics.

"Do you join in this ground, Captain Thomas?"

"No, Your Honor."

"Court will be in recess to deliberate on this challenge for cause."

While Judge Savage deliberated—read called the Chief Trial Judge for guidance—I went to the witness waiting room to see whether the alleged victim was properly dressed to convince the court members that she had not been raped. She was. On the way back, I saw Captain Ferguson greeting officers who I could only assume were court members, including a captain wearing military police brass. All of a sudden, the light bulb came on. I put Captain Ferguson's challenge for cause together with the speeding ticket, the hassle at the installation gate, the lost BOQ reservation, and the recently painted visiting defense counsel office and realized that he had set it all up. By challenging Judge Savage for cause, he would get Judge Savage to bend over backward to avoid looking prejudiced against rape victims, and he already had the court members in his pocket, which was clearly apparent from the brotherly greetings that they were giving him. I was going to be home-teamed. I had always kicked Ferguson's ass before, but now he had turned into the Bruce Lee of military prosecutors.

Just as I figured out how Captain Ferguson had brilliantly set me up and before I could figure out any brilliant countermoves, the bailiff called us back into the courtroom. Judge Savage was ready to continue.

I was not surprised when he denied the challenge for cause. He could have saved face by granting it "to avoid the appearance of impropriety," without admitting any prejudice, but I knew that he wouldn't go there. So before I could find a minute to think about how to counter Captain Ferguson's tactics, the trial was proceeding, and we were litigating my motions. But Judge Savage did not grant any of my absolute winner motions. Yes, I made some motions that I expected to lose, but Captain Ferguson brilliantly rolled over and played dead, so I won the motions that I wanted to lose, and by the time we came to the one that I wanted to win—to suppress my client's admission to voluntary sexual intercourse—a clear winner even before a pro-government military judge, I had won six motions in a row, and Judge Savage was in a panic to rule in the government's favor to avoid looking anti-rape-victim. So I lost all of my brilliant winner motions. And the confession to voluntary sexual intercourse—the only evidence that tied my client to the alleged rape—was now in evidence.

After Judge Savage had ruled against me on my last winner motion, I realized that I was going to lose the case. With all of Captain Ferguson's buddies on the court-martial panel, ready to make sure that the gunslinger from Fort Knox did not fuck up Fort Ben military justice, it did not matter what the evidence did or did not show, much like having all of the court members wearing the same combat patch that you were wearing. And winning on appeal wouldn't help my client or me. He might spend two or three years in the Disciplinary Barracks at Fort Leavenworth before the appeal was decided, and if Captain Ferguson beat me, my mystique was gone. Once I lost to a trial counsel who was viewed as mediocre, no one would cave when I made a motion. No one would give me a great plea bargain. And my future clients would suffer. I wasn't that worried about myself. I would probably be more likely to get promoted if I didn't fight so hard for the accused servicemembers. I might even get some free scotch on the rocks at the Officers' Club if I wasn't ruining Fort Knox and Fort Ben military justice. But I needed my undeserved reputation to properly represent my clients who were facing the might and majesty of the United States government.

Ok, so my ego was in it, too. I didn't want to be known as the first defense counsel to lose a rape case in front of Judge Savage. And I was going to. At that point, I thought that I had as much change of getting my client a not guilty finding as I had had of actually beating Master An when we sparred.

I had no idea how to reverse this juggernaut that was about to bury me. I would get no favorable rulings from Judge Savage, the court members would believe anything that Captain Ferguson or his witnesses said, and no evidence that I, the hired gun from Fort Knox, put on was going to be listened to, much less believed.

In a panic, to buy myself some time to come up with some brilliant maneuver to recoup Private Cornwall's defense, I blurted out, "Your Honor, the defense moves to dismiss the charge and specification for failure to plead subject matter jurisdiction under *United States v. Alef.*"

How I came up with this shit on the spur of the moment I have no idea to this day. The famous U.S. Supreme Court case of *O'Callahan v. Parker* had held that the military could not court-martial a servicemember for an off-post civilian type offense, such as rape, as opposed to a uniquely military offense, such as desertion, unless the offense was "service-connected," because trying anyone for an off-post offense by court-martial deprived the accused of his or her constitutional rights to indictment by grand jury and trial by a jury of one's peers. Such a jury, under the U.S. Constitution, had to consist of twelve impartial jurors who had to reach a unanimous verdict. This requirement was a far cry from the hardly impartial minimum of five court members who were the accused's superior officers or, upon request, at least one-third of the accused's superior non-commissioned officers. Later on, as recounted a couple of chapters ago in the tale of Lieutenant/Captain Menzies, the U.S. Supreme Court overruled *O'Callahan*. But at this point, it was still the law of the land.

In *United States v. Alef*, the Court of Military Appeals (later to become the Court of Appeals of the Armed Forces), ruled that the prosecution must plead—that is, spell out in the charges—the basis for jurisdiction. For an off-post drug sale, for example, the prosecution had to allege that the accused servicemember had sold the drugs to an individual who had said that he was going to resell the drugs to servicemembers on post, thereby screwing up good order and discipline.

I previously mentioned that I had gotten Judge Savage pissed off at me for getting him reversed. That case involved an off-post sale of Thai sticks (marijuana wrapped around a skewer dipped in heroin) to an undercover Criminal Investigative Division agent. The prosecution had just pled that my client had sold the drugs to a person whom he believed would resell them on post. After the *Alef* case came out, I decided to actually contest jurisdiction—in other words not just argue that the government did not properly plead it, but also that they didn't prove it. In other words, I argued that, because it was pled in the charge, it had to be proven beyond a reasonable doubt just like everything else in the charge. And I actually put on evidence that, because the alleged sale was to an undercover military policeman, there was no chance that the drugs were going to end up in the hands or lungs or bloodstream of a soldier. I also introduced a letter from the state's attorney of Radcliff County, where the off-post crime had occurred, that he was willing to prosecute the case, which would result in my client being afforded his constitutional rights to indictment by grand jury and trial by a jury of his peers (yes, I had researched that his sentence would have been much less if convicted in a Kentucky state court than by a court-martial). But notwithstanding this aggressive attack on jurisdiction, Judge Savage ruled against me and found jurisdiction, and my client was duly convicted and sentenced to a dishonorable discharge, forfeiture of all pay and allowances, and two years' confinement.

On appeal, however, which I wrote and forwarded to the Appellate Defense Counsel, not trusting him to brief it properly, the Army Court of Military Review agreed with me, found no jurisdiction, reversed the conviction, and dismissed the charges.

On the one hand, having the appellate court, which consisted of his fellow full colonels, reverse him really pissed Judge Savage off. On the other hand, it gained me a certain grudging respect. And that respect caused Judge Savage, out of concern for another possible reversal, to at least listen to my motion to dismiss the rape charge against Private Cornwall for failure to plead jurisdiction. The charge read that my client, "did, at Fort Benjamin Harrison, rape Miss Tina Bell." That should have been enough of a pleading to establish jurisdiction because *Alef* applied to off-post offenses and my client's alleged crime took place on a military post. But I argued that, for all we knew, Fort Benjamin Harrison was, even though we were in the courtroom of that military installation, like Fort Wayne, Indiana, a township with no connection with the military. Further, I argued, the pleading not only did not say that Fort Ben was a military installation, but also that it did not state that it was an exclusive federal jurisdiction and that, for all we knew, it was a propriety use installation where the federal government had ceded jurisdiction to the state of Indiana.

Well, I didn't expect this spur-of-the-moment bullshit to work, but I figured that Judge Savage, who was always mindful of ways to increase his time on the bench, would order us to write trial briefs on the issue and that this development would buy me at least a day to figure out how to avoid losing the first rape case presided over by Judge Savage. And another thing that Master An had taught me was that, if your opponent hurt you, buy time—time to recover and ultimately defeat him.

But Captain Ferguson surprised me again, but in the opposite way. He rolled over and played dead, arguing that he had adequately pled jurisdiction and that was that. Apparently, Captain Ferguson had not studied under Master An. Judge Savage, desperately afraid that dismissing the charge for failure to plead jurisdiction would make it look as if he were anti-rape-victim was practically begging Captain Ferguson to move to amend to add the phrase, "an exclusive federal jurisdiction," after the phrase, "did, at Fort Benjamin Harrison, Indiana," but Captain Ferguson would not do so.

To this day, I don't know why, after all of his brilliant maneuvering to set me up to lose, Captain Ferguson caved. I thought that perhaps he had thought that I had another dozen motions behind this one, that he was ultimately going to lose, and that, this way, he could blame it on Judge Savage. Maybe he thought that it wasn't rape and that this caving was a face-saving way of dropping the case. I don't know. All I do know is that Judge Savage, with tears standing in his eyes, granted my motion and dismissed the case, most likely believing that dismissing the rape charge killed any chance that he had for being allowed to be recalled after retirement to remain a judge. Apparently, he did not want to be remembered as the military judge who had never presided over a rape conviction.

I, on the other hand, viewed this miracle as a gift from God and fled Fort Ben as quickly as I could shake hands with my client, pack up my books and papers, and clear out of the BOQ. The only slight pause in my flight was when I ran into Judge Savage, who was also loading his suitcase into his car so that he could leave the BOQ. He said, "Captain Thomas, why didn't I just grant the challenge for cause and I'd have been out of this dog of a case?"

"Because you weren't biased, Your Honor."

"Maybe so, but the Trial Counsel made it look that way."

"The case isn't necessarily over, Your Honor," I replied. "They can still add the jurisdictional language and re-prefer the charge."

"Yes, they can, but I won't preside over it. I'll assign it to another judge. Have a good trip back, Captain."

"Yes, Sir. You, too."

I never thought that I would feel sorry for Judge Savage, but pro-prosecution as I might perceive him, he was a real JAG—not a JAGC-Off—and I was damn lucky to learn how to try cases in front of him. And later on, he recommended me to be a military judge. Yeah, I might grumble about his rulings, but you'd better not bad-mouth him. And I won't soon forgive Captain Ferguson.

To add insult to injury, I was stopped again for speeding as I left Fort Ben. But I did not tell the MP that he had no jurisdiction to stop me because Judge Savage had not found that Fort Ben was an exclusive federal jurisdiction because I was not interested in spending the night in the military police station lockup. So I just smiled sweetly, took the ticket, decided that paying the fine was worth it to avoid losing the first rape case in front of Judge Savage, and drove south to the friendly confines of Fort Knox, where my undeserved reputation remained intact. And they never did resurrect the charge against my client, but rather resurrected the resignation in lieu of court-martial that he had submitted, which the convening authority had denied, and released him from active duty with a general discharge under honorable conditions, which afforded him his military and veterans' benefits—a result that didn't bother me much, because I wouldn't have to return to Fort Ben for his court-martial for rape on an exclusive federal jurisdiction. So, yes, we had no jurisdiction, we had no jurisdiction that day.

10

What Do You Want, a Court-Martial?

"The balance between victory and defeat often hangs on simple matters."

—*Genshin Hironishi, from* Karate-Do-Nyumon

Sergeant First Class Eugene Russell flunked his piss test. He came up hot for cocaine. Not a wise move for a senior non-commissioned officer. I was next on my list to be defense counsel at the next administrative discharge board, so I assigned myself the case, figuring that he must have some good matters in mitigation that could at least get him an honorable or a general under honorable conditions discharge that would allow him to keep his veterans' benefits. But SFC Russell didn't want even an honorable discharge. He wanted the board to retain him, the way that Major LeBlanc's board had retained her, so that he could retire at half-pay in two more years. Now, it is one thing to get a person who fudged a PT test result under great stress and who could maximize the PT test any day of her life retained and quite another to get a cocaine user retained. The Army takes a dim view of non-commissioned officers who use cocaine. And SFC Russell was a tanker in the 194th Armored Brigade—the largest single combat brigade in the Army. Commanders of tank brigades tend not to like to have their multimillion dollar tanks commanded by cocaine users. Can't image why.

SFC Russell had had a great record. Bronze Star with "V" device for valor, two Purple Hearts, and all of the other basic issue service medals from Vietnam. He also had the rare Soldier's Medal, the only medal for heroism in peacetime, for saving another servicemember from a burning automobile. But even though his chain of command would say that his duty performance had been stellar, they would not go the next step, as Major LeBlanc's commanders had done, and say that they wanted him back. In fact, on cross-examination, they would answer that there was no place in the Army for non-commissioned officers who used cocaine. So I had to somehow find a way to convince the board that he had not used cocaine.

I didn't think that pleading him guilty to get him found not guilty was likely to work again. The word had gotten around about that tactic, and the recorder in this case, an aggressive new captain who wanted nothing more than to make his reputation by kicking my butt, wasn't going to fall for it. No, I needed a real, factual defense.

SFC Russell provided the start of one. To this day, I don't know whether he was lying through his teeth or not, but he swore to me that he had never knowingly ingested cocaine. He believed that he might have unknowingly ingested cocaine at a party where he ate some cookies that might have been spiked with coke—and not the kind that they bottle in Atlanta in both regular and diet cans. Now, if he had tested positive for marijuana, more correctly for 11-nor-delta-9-tetrahydrocannabinol-9-carboxylic acid (9-carboxy-THC), a metabolite of delta-9-THC, which is the primary pharmacologically active component of marijuana, we wouldn't have been able to use the innocent ingestion defense. Scientific tests had conclusively demonstrated that having marijuana smoke blown in your nose for hours in a tiny, airtight closet would not result in a high enough nanogram level of THC to fail a military urinalysis test. Besides, SFC Russell had not spent all night in a small closet, unconscious, with several marijuana smokers blowing smoke in his face.

But one can innocently ingest cocaine. Eat enough poppy seeds, and you may come up positive for cocaine for a relatively short period—about a day and a half. In addition, coke is soluble in

Coke™ and other soft drinks. The most brilliant use of the innocent ingestion defense was the female airman (yeah, a female in the Air Force is an airman—go figure—this memoir is not the only thing politically incorrect about the military) who stated in her court-martial defense that she may have innocently ingested cocaine when she had intercourse with her boyfriend who had been taking a drug containing cocaine for toothache pain. The defense didn't work, but it was novel. Apparently, the only problem with the defense was that, as the laboratory drug expert testified, she would have had to have had intercourse with at least seven different males who had recently used a recreational dose of cocaine just before the urinalysis. Perhaps, the defense would have worked better if it had been oral sex—more cocaine in the bloodstream or something.

I couldn't try that defense for SFC Russell. Not only did I not put on entirely fabricated defenses, but also such a defense might have beaten the cocaine charge but would have resulted in his discharge under other than honorable conditions for homosexuality. But innocent ingestion at a party might work.

So the first thing that I had him do was to go to a civilian laboratory and get another urinalysis. If the test came up hot, then any subsequent urinalysis that his command did would likely also turn up hot, and the innocent ingestion defense doesn't work very well when the alleged cokehead keeps testing positive. But he passed.

I was not confident enough about an innocent ingestion defense, however, to stop looking for something better. So I thought I'd better analyze the test procedures to see whether the chain of custody was defective or the test procedures were improper. The recorder was less than pleased at my request for the so-called "litigation packet" from the Forensic Toxicology Drug Testing Laboratory (U.S. Army). These packets contained all the chain of custody and lab testing documents.

The recorder said that he would provide them, probably believing, with some justification, that I would make some due process argument that would harm his case if he didn't. But then he said, “I don’t know why you want this crap. The only thing that the board has to decide is what type of discharge your client is going to get. The discharge is a done deal.”

Not wanting to give him what my friends called the glazed-eye look, I walked away, mumbling, “Whatever.”

My friends had always told me that when someone challenged me, most often in basketball or racquetball games, my eyes would glaze over, and I would start playing like a madman to avoid losing. I saw no reason to give this young, inexperienced JAGC captain the glazed-eye look because he already wanted to beat me badly enough as it was.

I had first gotten the glazed-eye look in a court-martial before I had even become a JAGC-Off. When law school wasn’t in session, I had to report to Fort Sill, Oklahoma, for on-the-job training. I had prosecuted a few simple cases, such as AWOL, because trial counsel (prosecutors) did not have to be lawyers at that time the way that defense counsel did. But one poor soul had waived his right to a qualified attorney defense counsel out of some strange belief that my medals, Combat Infantry Badge, and Jump Wings were worth something in the courtroom. They were, but I really didn’t know it until the “It Don’t Mean Nothing” case after I had become a JAGC-Off. My client was charged with fraternizing with the Vietnamese refugees at Fort Chaffee, Arkansas. He had talked with two young Vietnamese women for about ten minutes one evening and had turned down nonjudicial punishment by exercising his right to demand trial by court-martial and wanted me to defend him.

I got the glazed-eye look when I went to the trial counsel, Captain Huffman, to ask him whether he needed a formal, written request for defense witnesses. He took one look at me, wearing Military Intelligence branch insignia instead of JAGC brass, and walked away without answering, apparently believing that he was above talking to non-JAGC defense counsel. This treatment pissed me off. Where was his Combat Infantry Badge? So I got the glazed-eye look. As a result, I spent the next week in the Oklahoma City University School of Law library and, once the court-martial had started—a judge-alone trial because I thought that my defenses were more likely to appeal to a lawyer than to a court-martial panel—moved to dismiss the charge because the order, not to fraternize with the Vietnamese refugees, was unconstitutional and, hence, illegal. I submitted a twenty-page legal brief arguing that the order had no valid military purpose because you had to "fraternize with the Vietnamese refugees" to properly take care of them, because "fraternize" was not defined and could constitute nothing more than a simple exchange of pleasantries, and because the order violated both my client's and the refugees' First Amendment right of freedom of association, citing cases that this freedom was not limited to citizens. The trial counsel wasn't even ready for this tirade from some dumb law student. The military judge, however, deferred ruling on the motion until the conclusion of the case.

Then, after having cross-examined the prosecution witnesses to bring out that they didn't know what the order prohibited, that they knew of no reason why they couldn't socialize with the refugees so long as they didn't have sexual relations with them, and that they didn't remember my client being at the formation where the Sergeant Major put out the Commanding General's order not to fraternize, I moved for a finding of not guilty on alternate grounds—that my client had never received the order and that, assuming arguendo that he had received it, he could not possibility have disobeyed it because there were no Vietnamese refugees at Fort Chaffee with whom to fraternize. I supported this second ground with Immigration and Naturalization Service regulations and United Nations documents to show that, once the "refugees" had been admitted into the United States, they had become "parolees." So there were no refugees at Fort Chaffee with whom my client could have fraternized. By this time, Captain Huffman was as shell-shocked as if he had taken on Master An in a bar fight and didn't even ask for a recess to try to find some authority to the contrary. And he wouldn't have.

So I perhaps ended up with a first—a concurrent dismissal because the order was unconstitutional because the government had not offered any proper military purpose for the overbroad order and a finding of not guilty because the government had not introduced any evidence that my client had heard the order and because he could not have disobeyed it because there were no Vietnamese refugees to fraternize with anyway.

"Don't speak to me, motherfucker," I thought to myself as I passed Captain Huffman on the way out of the courtroom, only to be yanked up by the military judge's order, "Captain Thomas."

"Yes, Your Honor."

"You just killed an ant with an atomic bomb. Any one of those defenses was enough."

"Couldn't take that chance, Your Honor, not having defended anyone before" seemed like a better response than "Had to, Your Honor. I had gotten the glazed-eye look."

So that experience left me with the strong belief that I didn't want the young recorder to get the glazed-eye look and go to ridiculous lengths to beat me. So I nicely asked, pretty please, for the litigation packet and some other discovery documents, including the military records of the board members.

The day of the hearing arrived, and I had received everything but the board members' 201 files. I wanted these military records so that I could determine whether any challenge for cause existed against any board member. Administrative board procedures did not afford the respondent any preemptory challenges. So I asked my opponent, "Where are the board members' 201s?"

"Why do you need them?'

"To see whether any grounds for challenge exist."

"You can question them—you don't need their 201s."

"Looking at their records helps me figure out what questions to ask."

"Look," the young captain replied snidely, "I don't know why you are going through all this drill. I already told you that the discharge is a done deal—all the board members are going to decide is whether it is honorable, general, or other-than-honorable."

"Well, if the board members are predisposed to discharge my client, that predisposition in itself is a ground for challenge."

Exasperated at my stubborn refusal to roll over and play dead, the young trial counsel blurted out, "What do you want—a court-martial?"

Good idea. Why hadn't I thought of it? A court-martial was exactly what I wanted. The trial counsel would have to prove that my client had knowingly ingested cocaine beyond a reasonable doubt at a court-martial as opposed to the lower standard of preponderance of the evidence at an administrative board. In addition, I would be able to get every bit of the discovery that I was due. But I wasn't certain that my client wanted to risk the possibility of jail time just to get a better chance at saving his pension.

"Let me check with my client."

Once I had told SFC Russell that the recorder had told me that the only issue at the board was what type of discharge he would get, thereby forfeiting his pension, and that the government would have to prove knowing ingestion beyond a reasonable doubt at a court-martial, he jumped at the chance.

"Ok, hotshot," I said to the recorder. "You've got your wish. We want a court-martial." At this point, I was beyond worrying whether my opposing counsel got the glazed-eye look. In fact, I wasn't so sure that I didn't want him to get it because he was inexperienced enough that, if he went for overkill, he might screw up.

Because the board members were waiting, the illustrious recorder had to immediately contact the convening authority for authority to dismiss the board and begin court-martial proceedings. The gung-ho captain even managed to contact the general while he was flying around in his helicopter observing training maneuvers. After about forty minutes, he returned to the corridor outside the conference room where the board was to be held.

"Ok, here's the deal. Your client can have a court-martial under one condition. It must be a judge alone trial. The convening authority doesn't want a panel of his officers tied up for a couple of days. That's it. Take it or leave it."

I privately thought that this deal was as illegal as hell. Although a servicemember could waive his right to a trial composed of officer members and elect trial by military judge alone, he couldn't do so as a condition of a guilty plea. So how could it be a condition of getting oneself court-martialed? Not that the issue had ever been raised before to become an appellate ruling. But if the board members were already prejudiced in favor of a discharge, those same members might be on the court-martial panel. So we might get a fairer shake from the military judge. "Ok, captain, you're on."

Sure enough, a few days later, SFC Russell's charge sheet appeared in my inbox. It charged him as follows: "In that Sergeant First Class Eugene H. Russell, United States Army, C Company, 6th Battalion, 32d Armor, 194th Armored Brigade, did on or about July 6, 1975, at Radcliff, Kentucky, wrongfully use a controlled substance, to wit cocaine."

So this alleged wrongful use took place on Saturday night of the 4th of July weekend. The urinalysis was quite sneakily held the following Monday morning at 0800 hours so that the command could catch anyone who had let down his hair and partied with the wrong substances over the long holiday weekend. As I looked at the litigation packet and thought about the time frame, another approach to the case suggested itself.

The government's theory was that SFC Russell had used cocaine at a party the evening of Saturday, July 6. The trial counsel had found two witnesses who were at the party and would testify that cocaine was available. They had seen lines of cocaine on a mirror on a table in one of the bedrooms. They had not, however, seen my client snort or ingest cocaine, although they did see him drinking mixed drinks. The party had started at about 2000 hours (8 P.M.) and lasted until about 0200 hours (2 A.M.). With the positive urinalysis, the government didn't need a witness who actually saw SFC Russell use cocaine, but the trial counsel apparently had gotten the glazed-eye look after all and was trying to add this circumstantial evidence to the direct evidence of the urinalysis. Big mistake. Charging my client with using cocaine at the party instead of just using it sometime within the two or three days just before the urinalysis gave me a defense.

So we started out our judge-alone trial. The prosecution called the two party-goers who testified that my client was at the party, along with cocaine. On cross-examination, I brought out that they had not seen my client use cocaine, had not seen him in the same room with the cocaine, had not heard him talk about using cocaine, and had not seen him act under the influence of any illegal substance. On re-direct, the trial counsel brought out that the witnesses had not observed him the entire evening and that he could have been in the room with the cocaine while they weren't looking.

Then the trial counsel called the forensic toxicologist from the drug-testing laboratory. I had stipulated to the chain of custody because there was nothing wrong with it that I could make anything out of. The toxicologist looked like a scientific expert, dressed in a sports coat with corduroy patches on the sleeves and a string tie. He wore wire-rimmed glasses and sported a wispy beard. The trial counsel did a competent job of establishing his credentials as an expert in drug testing. Again, I stipulated to his credentials, because I wanted him to testify as an expert when I cross-examined him. So the military judge duly allowed him to testify as such. Military law is similar to civilian law regarding expert testimony. An expert may give an opinion on the basis of scientific, technical, or other specialized knowledge.

So the expert confidently testified to the testing procedures and that SFC Russell's sample had been properly collected, transported, maintained, and tested under the relevant Department of Defense ("DOD") instruction. He testified that the sample had come up positive for cocaine under the initial immunoassay test and that the confirmatory test by mass spectrometer was also positive for cocaine. The trial counsel made him recount all this boring scientific crap about how the two tests had been conducted and how they identified the illegal substance. Sounded like trying to kill an ant with an atomic bomb to me, but who was I to talk?

Finally, it was my turn. I asked some fairly innocuous questions about the percentage of false positives and about the problems at some military laboratories that had made them lose their accreditation so that I could sneak in a few points that I wanted to rely on later.

"Doctor, the use of cocaine can be fatal, can't it?"

The trial counsel got up to object, but then sat down, believing that I had really stepped in it. Why would the defense want to show the military judge how serious cocaine use was? Why bring out evidence that would get your client hammered on sentencing?

"Yes."

"Doctor, the medical literature makes a distinction between a fatal dose and a lethal dose of cocaine or any similar dangerous drug, does it not?

"Yes."

"Would it be correct to say that a fatal dose is fatal in 100 percent of cases and that a lethal dose is fatal only approximately 50 percent of the time?"

"Correct."

"And a fatal dose is approximately 750 to 800 nanograms?"

"Yes."

Then, I went back to a line of innocent questions about quality control—questions that made the trial counsel smile, believing that I was committing the common cross-examination faux pas of asking questions that just set the direct examination in stone. After a few of these questions, I slipped in another series of more critical questions.

"As I understand your testimony, you test for benzoylecgonine—BZ—to determine cocaine use?"

"Yes."

"Doctor, the half-life of benzoylecgonine is between seven and nine hours, isn't it?"

"Yes."

"So if we used eight hours as an average, every eight hours or so the nanogram level in urine would be 50 percent less."

"Correct."

After a few more innocuous questions, I asked, "Doctor, the cut-off level under the DOD instruction to report a sample as positive for BZ is 100 nanograms, correct?"

"That is correct."

"What was SFC Russell's nanogram level?"

"As I recall, it was 375 nanograms. If I may look at the lab report?"

"Be my guest."

"Yes, 375."

"And he provided the sample as of 0800 8 July?"

"That's what the chain of custody document said."

"So if we use an 8-hour half-life for benzoylecgonine, eight hours earlier at midnight—2400 hours on 7 July—the nanogram level would have been 750 nanograms, right?"

"More or less."

"And if we back off another 8 hours, to 1600 hours 7 July, the nanogram level would have been 1500 nanograms, correct?"

"That seems correct."

"And if we back off another 8 hours, to 0800 7 July, the nanogram level would have been approximately 3000 nanograms, right?"

"Approximately."

All of a sudden, the prosecutor didn't look so smug. In fact, he was frowning as he tried to digest where this line of questioning was taking his carefully crafted case.

"And if we go back another 8 hours, to 2400 hours 6 July, the nanogram level would have been approximately 6000 nanograms, correct?"

"That seems correct."

"So, doctor, let me see whether I got this math straight. If my client had used cocaine as charged on or about 6 July—any use earlier than 2400—assuming an 8-hour half-life, the nanogram level would have been even higher?"

"That seems correct."

"Let's be more charitable. Let's give the government the benefit of the doubt and say that the half-life of BZ is nine hours rather than eight. By my calculation, the nanogram level would have been 6000 at 2100 hours, just after the start of the party?"

The witness sat there a few minutes, apparently trying to do the math in his head. Finally, he responded, "I can't be sure without pencil and paper, but that calculation seems right."

"Now, Doctor, you previously testified that a fatal dose was approximately 750 to 800 nanograms?"

"Yes."

"So wouldn't enough cocaine to give one a 6000 nanogram level in the urine kill you deader than a doornail immediately after ingesting it—regardless of the manner of ingestion?"

"Yes, it would."

"Doctor, do you see the Sergeant First Class sitting at the defense table?"

"Yes, Sir."

I was finally getting a little respect from the government's expert.

"Does he appear dead to you?"

"Objection!" Trial counsel finally figured out how his case was going down the tubes.

"Grounds?" was the terse response of the military judge.

"The expert is not a coroner, medical examiner, or even a medical doctor and is not qualified to give an opinion on this point."

"Your Honor," I responded, "you qualified the witness as an expert in forensic toxicology. Unless I'm sadly mistaken, toxicology is the study of the adverse effects of substances on living organisms. Dr. Whittaker testified without objection as to the lethal levels of cocaine. He must be qualified to testify as to whether one is dead or not. And even if I am wrong, I believe that he can give a lay opinion on whether the accused is alive or not. Or I expect that you could take judicial notice that the accused is not dead."

"Objection overruled. You may answer the question, Doctor."

"He certainly appears alive to me."

"But he would have been dead if he had consumed enough cocaine to have a 6000 nanogram level on Saturday night, July 6, that would have been down to 350 nanograms at the time of the test Monday morning at 0800 hours on July 8?"

The witness looked at the trial counsel for help, but getting none, muttered, "Yes."

"I couldn't hear you, Doctor. Was that answer a 'Yes?'"

"Yes."

"So it seems to me, Doctor, that we must have one of three explanations for my client not being as dead as a doornail. One, that wasn't his urine that was tested, chain-of-custody notwithstanding. Two, the test was defective. Or, three, he used cocaine only a few hours before the test on the 8th and not on July 6th."

"If that is a question, that would seem right."

"Would it be correct to say, with a reasonable degree of scientific certainty, that my client could not have ingested enough cocaine between 2100 and 2400 hours, or indeed at anytime on July 6,th to have had a 350 nanogram level at 0800 on July 8th and survived?"

"Yes."

"Sorry, Doctor, but I lost some hearing in Vietnam. Again, was that answer a 'Yes?'"

"Yes, Sir."

"Your witness, trial counsel."

"Doctor, the accused could have used cocaine on the evening of July 7th to where the 350 nanogram level the next morning would not indicate the ingestion of so much cocaine as to kill him?"

"Objection, Your Honor. Irrelevant."

The trial counsel quickly responded to my objection. "It is highly relevant, Your Honor. You could find the accused guilty by exceptions and substitutions, excepting the words "on or about 6 July" and substituting the words "on or about 7 or 8 July."

I responded. "Your Honor, although I will concede that the phrase "on or about" ordinarily gives the government some latitude and that in some cases the trier of fact could substitute one date for another, such is not the case here. I had requested a bill of particulars from the trial counsel, and in it, he said that the cocaine use in question occurred at the party between the hours of 2200 and 2400 hours on 6 July. So that was what we prepared to defend. We didn't prepare to defend cocaine use on any other date as the bill of particulars limited it to that date."

"Trial counsel, what say you?"

"We did so state in our response to the defense request for a bill of particulars that the use took place on 6 July as Captain Thomas said, but the government should not be precluded from trying to show use a mere day later by his slick tactics."

"Well, Counsel," the judge fixed the trial counsel with a cool stare, "you could have plead on or about 6 July to 8 July, but you chose to try to prove that it had occurred at this party, and you even brought witnesses in, quite unnecessarily in my opinion, to show that there was cocaine at the party and that the accused was there. So I'm going to limit the evidence to evidence that the accused may have used cocaine during the period charged. Does the government have any more evidence?"

"No, Your Honor."

"Captain Thomas, do you have any motions?"

I can't say that I had ever had such a gold-plated invitation to make a motion for a finding of not guilty. So I didn't waste much time doing so.

"Your Honor, the defense moves for a finding of not guilty. The evidence is clearly insufficient to sustain a conviction for cocaine use on 6 July. The government's own expert said that, if the accused had used cocaine on that date, then he would be dead. He's not dead. But the government's case is." Well, that last comment was uncalled for, but I couldn't resist.

"Government, do you oppose?"

"Yes, Your Honor. The accused was at a party where cocaine was present and turned up positive for cocaine a couple of days later. All this nanogram level nonsense is nothing more than a clever defense smokescreen. On a motion for a finding of not guilty, you must view all of the evidence in the light most favorable to the government. You should deny the motion."

"The defense motion for a finding of not guilty is granted. Sergeant First Class Russell, you'd better thank your lawyer for doing a good job. But I would admonish you that, if you ever use cocaine again, I'll put you under the jail. Court is dismissed."

The military judge could not have much more clearly told us that he believed that my client had used cocaine, but could not convict him of use on July 6, as charged.

I turned to SFC Russell, expecting to see a big smile. Instead, he grabbed me by the arm and asked, "What does that mean? What does admonish mean? Am I going to be executed and buried under the jail?"

I would have laughed, but my client looked so pathetic that I just patted him on the arm and said, "He found you not guilty. Admonish means 'to warn.' He warned you not to use cocaine or you'd go to jail next time."

Now, he smiled.

But the trial counsel didn't. You've got to know when to get the glazed-eye look and when not to. Or at least not to let it blind you as to how the other side could use your over-proving your case against you.

11

“You Got to Know When to Hold ‘Em, Know When to Fold ‘Em, Know When to Walk Away, Know When to Run”[1]

or

You’re Supposed to Pee *in* the Bottle

“To win one hundred victories in one hundred battles is not the highest skill. To subdue the enemy without fighting is the highest skill.”

—*Sun Tsu, from* The Art of War

After the Vietnam War was over, the Army started cutting its size. They had RIFs—reductions in force—in which they got rid of many officers, regardless of how good their military records were. The Army also cut the size of the branches that were not, perhaps, as essential to fighting as the Infantry, Artillery, or Armor branches. So some staff wienies at the Pentagon considered whether we needed so many lawyers.

Actually, the U.S. Army’s Judge Advocate General’s Corps was the largest law firm in the United States. Eighteen hundred officers wore the JAGC insignia on their uniforms—more than

---

[1] From the song “The Gambler,” written by Don Schlitz and made popular by Kenny Rogers.

wore the suits, Armani or otherwise, of the biggest civilian law firms. The JAGC insignia consists of a sword and a quill pen superimposed over a wreath. The quill pen is appropriate—JAGCs do enough writing—but I've never quite figured out the sword. My attorney/editor/writer friend sees it as a reference to either the sword that Lady Justice wields along with her scales or the thought that the pen is mightier than the sword. Be that as it may, back to RIFs.

So the bean-counters in the Pentagon were taking a hard look at why the Army needed 1,800 lawyers. Actually, some Army officers wondered why the Army needed any lawyers at all. The Army Judge Advocate General, known as TJAG, was trying everything possible to keep all of us so busy that retaining, so to speak, 1,800 lawyers was a no-brainer. If our strength were cut in half, the bean-counters might also decide that the JAG Corps didn't need a two-star general, that a one-star general would be enough. TJAG didn't want to lose a star. And one of the ways to keep us busy to show why we needed so many lawyers was to try more cases by court-martial.

Now this plan wasn't easy to carry out. With the Vietnam War over and no more draft, all of the soldiers were volunteers. Any draftees left in the Army had reenlisted, so they were also volunteers at this point. And volunteers did not commit so many crimes as reluctant-to-serve draftees had. In addition, mandatory urinalysis cut way back on drug usage and the crimes associated therewith. So how would the Army keep the court-martial rate up? Well, one way was by taking what we called mox nix offenses, from the German phrase *"es macht nichts"* meaning that it makes no difference, and making those offenses war crimes. I don't know how the staff judge advocates decided to start advising the convening authority that, for example, a Command Master Sergeant, the highest ranking enlisted man, should face a general court-martial for being caught with an adult porn magazine rather than chewing him out and ordering him to submit his retirement papers by the close of business. Maybe at the annual Worldwide JAGC Conference, which all of the JAGC big shots went to, TJAG said, "We need more courts-martial, guys, or you can forget making general because the Corps won't have any." But as a defense counsel, I do know that we started seeing more chicken shit cases going to court-martial.

Perhaps the worst example of this trend was the case of Master Sergeant Nutter. MSG Nutter was the highest ranking non-commissioned officer in the Provost Marshal's office. The Provost Marshal, a full colonel, was the highest-ranking law enforcement officer on Fort Knox, equivalent to a sheriff. And MSG Nutter was his operations NCO. He decided what Military Police ("MP") personnel went on what patrols, and so forth.

Well, MSG Nutter got into trouble at a unit party. Whenever anyone left a military unit under favorable terms, as opposed to being discharged with a bad conduct discharge, he or she would be feted at a hail-and-farewell party. All of the departing soldiers would receive presents of little value because the regulations limited the amount that could be spent on such gifts. The "hailed" newcomers would be introduced and welcomed into the unit. Although these parties may have toned down lately, before the activities of Mothers Against Drunk Driving ("MADD"), another name for hail-and-farewell might have been "hoist (your drink) and fall over." As long as you avoided the MP checkpoint, drinking was not only permissible but also encouraged. And an MP ought to be able to avoid the MP checkpoint, particularly one like MSG Nutter, who assigned his subordinate MPs to the checkpoints.

But notwithstanding that he knew where the checkpoints would be and could easily avoid them, MSG Nutter had tried to do the right thing. He had his 19-year old daughter drive him to the party at the Non-Commissioned Officers' Club and told her to return a couple of hours later to pick him up so that he wouldn't have to drive under the influence. So he thought that he could have all of the Jack on the rocks that he wanted. Jack Daniels was the macho drink of choice for many senior non-commissioned officers. After all, what would ordering a pina colada, a chi chi, or a glass of chardonnay do to their tough guy images? A Scottish sergeant major could get away with drinking single malt scotch (actually a Scottish sergeant major could get away with drinking anything that he wanted), and who cared whether a French sergeant drank wine? But an American non-commissioned officer had to drink beer or Jack.

Well, maybe he could have all of the Jack that he wanted at some unit parties, but it wasn't a very good idea at this one because his ex-wife showed up on another sergeant's arm. They had had a particularly nasty divorce and custody fight over their now 19-year old daughter, and MSG Nutter was less than thrilled at having the Uniformed Services Former Spouses' Protection Act specify that his wife would get half of his pension when he retired—whether she hooked up with another servicemember or not. As one might expect, one's ex and her new boyfriend amounted to a recipe for trouble. After heated words, MSG Nutter allegedly shoved new boyfriend. Some nearby women started screaming, and the room full of MPs who should have been used to drunken brawls did nothing to defuse the situation. One of the MP wives screamed, "He's got a gun!"

Although he didn't have a gun, MSG Nutter sobered up quickly at the thought of a bunch of trigger-happy, inebriated MPs deciding to shoot him in the belief that he was armed and ran out of the club. Maybe he, too, had studied under Master An, who had taught me that just because you can inflict considerable damage on your opponent does not mean that you have to prove it and that many times you are better off just walking away. Fortunately, his daughter was just pulling into the parking lot to pick him up, and he flagged her down and jumped in. She took off.

Unfortunately for MSG Nutter, however, he was now a suspect for assault and battery, possession of an unregistered firearm, and carrying a concealed weapon. So the Provost Marshal, who took a dim view of drunken fights at his MP parties, called the MP desk sergeant to put out an all-points bulletin for MSG Nutter, warning any MPs who responded that the suspect was armed and dangerous.

The next thing that MSG Nutter knew, he was lying facedown and spread-eagle on the road with two MPs pointing their pistols at him. Nor did things improve. Next, he found himself with his hands cuffed behind him and being transported to the MP station having been apprehended for assault and the two firearms charges. No plastic ties—they didn't have them back then—but rather double-locking steel handcuffs ratcheted tight. A search of MSG Nutter and his car and the streets where his daughter had driven him from the club to where he was stopped failed to turn up any weapons, unless you count his daughter's nail file.

At the MP station, the MPs ordered MSG Nutter to "hand over your I.D. card." He responded by saying, "Why do you need my identification card? You know who I am. I work here with you."

Then, the arresting officers ordered him to pee in a bottle, apparently to gather evidence of his blood-alcohol level. He was so drunk that, when he tried to comply, he couldn't hit the specimen bottle and peed all over himself and the floor. Irritated at the mess that he made, the MPs locked him up in the drunk tank to await his commander's decision as to how to handle the case.

Apparently, the SJA or the Chief Trial Counsel got to the commander of the Military Police Company and the convening authority because SFC Nutter found himself facing a general court-martial for assault consummated by battery, carrying a maximum penalty of six months' confinement; disorderly conduct, carrying a maximum penalty of 4 months' confinement; carrying a concealed weapon, which had a one-year confinement maximum; and two specifications of disobeying a lawful order by refusing to surrender his ID card and by refusing to pee in the bottle, each carrying a one-year sentence. With other authorized punishments, he faced a dishonorable or bad conduct discharge, forfeiture of all pay and allowances, reduction to the lowest enlisted grade, and confinement for three years and ten months. Bad as it was, the confinement wasn't the problem—a dishonorable discharge or bad conduct discharge would lose him the 75 percent of base pay retirement that he was only months away from at more than twenty-nine years of service.

After the charge sheet and supporting documents recommending trial by general court-martial had come across my desk, I asked myself why the fuck this case was a court-martial. Why didn't the Provost Marshal call him into his office, chew him a new asshole, give him a reprimand, and order him to submit his retirement papers by the end of the day? That's what I would have advised if I had been the Staff Judge Advocate, especially because I wasn't going to make general in the JAG Corps even if they quadrupled the size of the corps. MSG Nutter had a perfect record, for God's sakes, up to this point.

But I couldn't convince anyone that they should drop the court-martial in return for my client submitting his retirement papers and accepting a nonjudicial punishment, punishment could consist of a one-grade reduction, forfeiture of half of his pay for two months, extra duties for forty-five days, and restriction for sixty days. So we went to trial. My opponent was Captain Ross, a pretty decent trial counsel who fought hard but fair.

My client bought my suggestion that we request a panel of one-third enlisted members. A military accused has an absolute right to a court-martial composed of officers and/or not less than one-third enlisted members. My theory, based on my experience, was that when you had a senior non-commissioned officer like my client charged with minor shit, other senior non-commissioned officers would protect him. And they would be less likely to feel pressured to hammer my client than young lieutenants and captains who would be more concerned with what the president of the court, a full colonel, thought of their performance as court members. If, however, the accused senior NCO was charged with a drug crime or other serious charge, the last thing that you wanted was other senior sergeants on the panel who would hammer one of their own who violated the code of the senior NCO. But my client's charges were mox nix, so we had another master sergeant and two sergeants major on the panel.

Captain Ross called as a witness my client's ex-wife's boyfriend, who testified that my client had shoved him during an argument about why my client should have to pay his ex half of his pension when she was going to marry the boyfriend and divorce him and have two half-pensions. Seemed like a good question to me, but not one that formed a valid defense. But I brought out on cross-examination that the boyfriend had not suffered any injuries, except perhaps to his pride, and that he was actually sorry for getting into a confrontation with a brother MP. I also brought out that he believed that my client was as drunk as a skunk. Lay witness testimony is admissible as to whether one is intoxicated and does not need the scientific purity of a medical expert's opinion. Drunk as a skunk was just fine.

Then, the trial counsel called the woman who had allegedly seen the pistol that my client allegedly had concealed on his person. I managed to elicit from her that she had imbibed something more than six glasses of wine before the altercation between MSG Nutter and his ex-wife's date, that she couldn't describe the alleged pistol other than it was small, that she supposed it could have been one of those cigarette lighters that is shaped like a small pistol, and that she had panicked when the shoving started, especially knowing that MPs often carried firearms. She added, when asked, that my client "was as drunk as a lord." A little more high-class than drunk as a skunk but equally helpful.

Next, the trial counsel called one of the two MPs who had arrested MSG Nutter. He testified that he had given my client a lawful order to surrender his ID card and to pee in a bottle and that my client had disobeyed both orders. My turn.

"Sergeant, you have had considerable experience with intoxicated soldiers, haven't you?"

"Yes, Sir."

"Would it be correct to say that you have arrested more than a hundred individuals for driving under the influence?"

"Yes, Sir."

"And your conviction rate for those arrests approaches 100 percent, does it not?"

The witness positively beamed. He couldn't believe a cross-examination was making him look so good. "Yes, Sir."

"Using your vast experience as a Military Police officer, how would you characterize the intoxication level of my client?"

"He was way past DUI, Sir. He was falling down drunk."

"Now, Sergeant, would it be correct to say that you followed proper MP procedures in how you handled this case?"

"Absolutely, Sir."

"Sergeant, you knew who my client was, didn't you?'

"Yes, Sir."

"You didn't need to see his identification card to determine who he was, did you?"

"No, Sir."

"In fact, you saw him on every duty day, did you not?"

"Yes, Sir."

"He assigned you your duties, didn't he?'

"Yes, Sir, most of the time."

"Was there any doubt in your military mind whom you had apprehended?"

"No, Sir."

"So why did you order him to surrender his ID card?"

"I don't know, Sir."

"Wasn't it because you wanted to stack a few more charges on him?"

"No, Sir."

"Hadn't he pissed you off by assigning you to patrol the tank gunnery ranges from 2400 hours to 0700 hours the week before because your uniform was not up to MP standards?"

"That didn't piss me off, Sir."

"Isn't that assignment about the most boring, cold, wet, and miserable duty a Fort Knox MP can get?"

"Yes, Sir."

"But you weren't pissed at him sticking you with it?"

"No, Sir."

"Isn't it true that you were going to do whatever you could to get him to screw up so that he would get slammed by the MP commander?"

"Objection," the trial counsel interposed, "the defense is badgering the witness."

"Withdraw the question, Your Honor. Sergeant, when my client responded to your order to surrender his ID card by asking why because you knew who he was, did you say anything else?"

"No, Sir."

"Did you say words to the effect of it doesn't matter whether I know you or not, I'm ordering you to surrender your ID card?"

"No, Sir."

"Now, let's turn to this alleged disobedience of the order to provide a urine sample. Did you perform a field sobriety test?"

"No, Sir."

"Did you conduct a breath-analysis test?"

"No, Sir."

"Did you apply for a search warrant to take a blood sample?"

"No, Sir."

"So instead, you ordered him to piss in a bottle."

"Yes, Sir."

"Is it standard MP procedure to take urine samples, as opposed to blood samples or breath-analysis, in DUI cases?"

"Not to my knowledge, Sir."

"Have you ever required a urine sample in a DUI case before?"

"No, Sir."

"But you testified that you followed proper MP procedures in this case, didn't you?"

"That's what I said."

"Did MSG Nutter tell you that he was not going to provide a urine sample?"

"No, Sir."

"In fact, he tried to do so, didn't he?"

"Yes, but sort of half-assed. Sorry, Your Honor."

Because it wasn't Judge Savage, but rather a reserve judge performing his two-week annual duty, he wasn't all that bothered by the soldierly language. He just nodded pleasantly at the witness and said, "Continue."

"Now, you already testified that my client was falling down drunk?'

"Yes, Sir."

"And he tried to comply, didn't he?"

"Perhaps. But maybe he pissed all over the floor and his pants to avoid providing evidence about how intoxicated he was."

"So let me see if I understand your testimony. My client was falling down drunk, but he was astute enough to deduce that a urinalysis might provide evidence against him and that if he appeared to try to piss in the bottle but instead sprayed his urine over the whole area so as not to supply a testable sample, he would magically be found not guilty if tried. Is that your testimony?"

"Something like that."

"No further questions."

The direct and cross-examination of the other arresting officer went about the same way. MSG Nutter was not beloved of the MPs that he supervised, and I managed to show that they enjoyed both arresting and humiliating him.

The trial counsel rested. After asking for a 39a session so that the court members were not present, I made my usual motion for a finding of not guilty. A defense counsel didn't want to have the judge deny a motion for a finding of not guilty in front of the members because that would imply that the judge had found at least some evidence against the accused. The trial counsel made the standard argument that viewing the evidence in the light most favorable to the prosecution, he had presented sufficient evidence for the jury to convict. I thought the judge might throw the failure to hit the specimen bottle out, but he denied all of my motions. I asked for a recess before putting on my case. As I sat in my office, pondering what to do, it dawned on me that I had to fold 'em. I had to rest without putting on any evidence. I could call some witnesses to say that they never saw my client with a gun that night. I could call my medical expert to testify that my client was too intoxicated to willfully disobey either of the orders, and I could call my client to testify that he didn't have a gun and that he didn't willfully disobey any orders. But if I did that, the prosecution was going to bolster his weak case on my case through cross-examination of my witnesses.

Well, MSG Nutter wasn't wild about this tactic. He wanted to tell his side of it. But even though I had prepared him to testify in the days leading up to the trial, I knew that he would run off at the mouth and convict himself of something that he might avoid a conviction for if we rested. So even though the decision whether to testify or not is the accused's decision, I told him that he wasn't going to testify. He'd just have to trust me.

After we had returned to the courtroom and the judge had called the court to order, I rested. The crestfallen look on the trial counsel's face told me that I had been right to fold 'em. So the puzzled court members were excused again—less than a minute after they had all trooped in and sat down—and we had a 39a session to hammer out what instructions the military judge would give the members.

After the 39a session, the court members returned to hear arguments and the judge's instructions. The trial counsel got to go first. He did a decent job of reminding the court members of what the witnesses had testified to and pointing out which testimony proved which element of each offense. Then, it was my turn.

"Mr. President, members of the court, thank you for your attention in this trial in which the government has taken a minor incident at a party and turned it into a general court-martial which could not only send my client to jail but also award a punitive discharge so that he would lose all of his retirement pay."

"Objection, Your Honor," the trial counsel practically shouted, "the collateral consequences of a sentence are not relevant and are not in evidence."

"Objection sustained. The court members will ignore any reference to whether the accused will lose his military pension."

Thank you, trial counsel and Your Honor, I thought, for hammering the point home in the court members' minds. "Let's look at the more serious charges first. Carrying a concealed weapon. Where's the weapon? MSG Nutter was quickly apprehended. A search of his person and the vehicle that he was riding in produced no weapon. A search of the streets that his daughter had driven him down produced no weapon. No one saw it except an intoxicated woman who admitted that she had panicked when the shoving started. And she admitted that, if she had seen anything, it could have been one of those cigarette lighters that look like small pistols. The prosecution has not proven this charge by anything more than mere speculation, much less met its burden of proof beyond a reasonable doubt. This party was an MP party. Don't you think that, if there had been a gun, they would have found it? They didn't because there wasn't one.

"Let's take the disobedience of the first order—the order to produce his ID card. His Honor, the military judge, will instruct you that, to be lawful, an order must have a valid military purpose and not be given merely to enhance an accused's punishment. An example of that would be if a sergeant gives an order that a private disobeys and a captain repeats the order solely because the punishment for disobeying an officer is more severe than that for disobedience of a non-commissioned officer. Well, there was no valid military purpose for giving this order. The arresting officers knew full well who MSG Nutter, their military superior in their unit, was. Rather, they gave this unnecessary order just to be able to charge him with something else. Further, the military judge will instruct you that voluntary intoxication is a defense to disobedience of an order if one is too intoxicated to willfully disobey the order. The government's own witnesses described MSG Nutter as 'drunk as a skunk,' 'drunk as a lord,' 'falling down drunk,' and 'totally blitzed.' And let's not hold it against him that, although he had perhaps drunk way too much, he had a designated driver. Remember the arresting officer's testimony that, when they stopped him, his daughter was driving. He didn't say that he wouldn't do it—he asked why did he needed to produce his identification card because they knew who he was.

"And this charge of disobeying a lawful order to provide a urine sample is the stupidest of all. It was not a lawful order for the same reasons that I outlined concerning the order to produce his ID card. And he clearly tried to comply. In fact, I'd argue that he did provide the sample, even if most of it ended up on his pants and the floor instead of the sample jar. Remember, he's falling down drunk, totally blitzed. It was physically impossible for him to hit the specimen bottle. His Honor will instruct you that physical impossibility is a defense to disobedience of a lawful order.

"Now, maybe the trial counsel has put on some evidence of disorderly conduct and/or that MSG Nutter shoved his ex-wife's date. So what? No one was hurt, and this whole event should have been a hiccup that should have been smoothed over instead of turning it into the crime of the decade. An all-points bulletin for MSG Nutter—one of their own—who was armed and dangerous, for God's sake! Well, he wasn't armed, and he walked away from the incident at the club and was going home with his designated driver. That's not Bonnie and Clyde. But maybe, the MPs don't have enough to do, or maybe, as I brought out on cross-examination of the arresting officers, they just don't like a master sergeant who enforces discipline, so he ends up spread-eagled on his face on the street."

"Objection, Your Honor," the trial counsel interposed, "the arresting officers are not on trial here."

Wanna bet? And thanks for making that point clearer to the court members. I knew that most military members did not particularly like MPs. So I hoped to play to that bias to help my client. Yes, he was an MP also, but now he was the victim of MP arrogance—something that the court members could relate to.

"Objection overruled," His Honor responded.

"No, court members, at most, my client was drunk and disorderly. Convict him of that if you have to convict him of something. But he clearly is not guilty of carrying a concealed weapon or disobeying an order to produce his ID card or to piss in a bottle. Please don't compound the chain of events that took this minor incident and made it the Fort Knox crime of the decade by buying the trial counsel's ridiculous arguments suggesting that he has proven disobedience of these two orders and carrying a concealed weapon beyond a reasonable doubt. Now, the trial counsel gets to argue first and last, so this speech is my only shot at it. I would merely ask that, after you have heard the trial counsel's rebuttal argument, you analyze it in light of what I've argued. Again, thank you for your attention. MSG Nutter and I fully expect that you will do your duty and fairly and justly decide this overblown case."

The trail counsel got up to object, but the military judge gestured for him to sit down and *sua sponte*—on his on motion—instructed the court members to disregard my argument about an overblown case. Thank you again, Your Honor, I thought.

I felt pretty good about our chances after the trial counsel's rebuttal argument, which did little but repeat his initial argument. He didn't really address the intoxication issue or whether the orders had had a valid military purpose. He just kept ranting about how I was blowing a smoke screen at the members to confuse them. Well, I had learned a long time ago that blowing a smoke screen at military juries wasn't likely to work. Unlike 99 percent of JAGC-Offs, I had been a military court member. In fact, I had been the president of a general court-martial, so I knew from first-hand experience how they thought. Military juries were not likely to fall for any JAGC bullshit because they were either all officer juries that had more than 50 percent master's degrees and all bachelor's degrees or officer and one-third enlisted member juries in which the enlisted members were senior non-commissioned officers, with some of them having college degrees and all of them having more than a decade of military experience. No, military juries were blue-ribbon juries, and they weren't going to fall for a smoke-screen defense. And this one wasn't going to buy trial counsel's argument that my defense was a smoke screen. In fact, those who had sat on a number of court-martial jury panels would recognize the argument that the defense was blowing a smoke screen as the desperate argument of a losing government case.

The military judge instructed the jury, including all of the instructions that I had requested on the lawfulness of orders, on the defense of voluntary intoxication negating the ability to willfully disobey an order, and the defense of physical impossibility to obey an order. I had always believed that, when the military judge instructed as you said that he would in your argument, it gave your entire argument credibility. And because instructions were agreed to before argument, one knew what the judge would say.

So the jury went off to deliberate, and MSG Nutter and I went back to my office to wait. One might wonder why I had conceded drunk and disorderly. I didn't really have a defense to it or to assault and battery. But I hoped that if I suggested to the jury that, if they had to find my client guilty of something, it was drunk and disorderly, they would do so and not convict him of assault and battery, which, again, we had no defense to. A drunk and disorderly conviction carried only a four-month sentence to confinement with no punitive discharge included. So it would give the jury something to convict my client of that would not endanger his retirement. The assault and battery charge did carry with it a possible sentence of a bad conduct discharge—a discharge that would have lost my client his retirement. In addition, I had always believed that the most important asset that I had as a lawyer was my credibility. So if I had made some bullshit argument about how he was not guilty of any of the charges, it would have seriously undermined my arguments about the serious charges—the concealed weapon and the two disobedience charges.

We didn't have to wait long. About twenty minutes later, the bailiff came to my door and announced that the members had reached a verdict. After everyone had returned to the courtroom and the judge had accounted for the parties, he asked the president of the court whether they had reached a verdict.

Now, the last few seconds before the military jury announces its verdict are the worst, tough on the defense counsel and tougher on the accused. The problem is that the suspense kills you because the judge goes through this protracted drill, starting with this instruction: "Bailiff, would you retrieve the findings worksheet from the President and give it to me." So the bailiff saunters over to the President, retrieves the findings worksheet, walks up to the bench, and hands it to the judge. The judge then looks it over to make sure that it is in proper form. If the panel has not filled it out properly, it is a lot easier to fix before the findings are announced, so the judge always makes certain that it is in proper form before allowing the President to announce the findings.

"I have examined the findings worksheet, Appellate Exhibit V, and it appears to be in order," the judge announced. "Please return the findings worksheet to the President," the military judge instructed the bailiff. Again, the bailiff sauntered up to the bench, took the worksheet from the judge's hand, and meandered over to the President to give him the worksheet back. Ok, maybe he walked quickly, but when you are on pins and needles awaiting the verdict, it seems like forever.

"Will the accused and counsel please rise. Mr. President, you may announce the findings," the judge officiously intoned.

MSG Nutter and I stood up and faced the President, who had also risen for this important announcement. Reading from the findings worksheet, as if he didn't know what they had decided, he said, "MSG Nutter it is my duty to inform you—"

Right there, I knew that they had convicted him of something. The way the findings worksheet read, the language for a guilty finding was "inform you," and the language for a not guilty finding was "advise you."

The President continued, "—that this court finds you, of the specification of Charge One and Charge One, not guilty."

Great! I thought—that was the assault and battery.

"Of the specification of Charge Two and Charge Two, guilty."

That was the drunk and disorderly charge. Ok, that's not bad, depending on the other findings.

"Of the specification Charge Three and Charge Three, not guilty."

That was the concealed weapon charge.

"Of specification one of Charge Four, not guilty."

That was the disobedience of a lawful order to surrender his ID card charge.

"Of specification two of Charge Four and of Charge Four, not guilty."

That was the disobedience of a lawful order to provide a urine sample charge. So all that they had convicted him of was being drunk and disorderly. Hooray! My client, while not doing cartwheels, looked relieved because I had told him that, if all that they convicted him of was being drunk and disorderly, he would get to retire although perhaps not as an E-8.

The military judge asked us to please be seated and told the trial counsel that the court-martial would now hear the personal data concerning the accused shown on the charge sheet.

Although he didn't look too happy, Captain Ross followed the script and read such things as the accused's date of entry, rank, unit, and so forth. When he had finished, the judge asked the prosecution whether it had other matters to present.

If the prosecution had evidence in aggravation, why the sentence should be more severe, such as prior convictions, records of punishment under Article 15, Uniform Code of Military Justice, and the like, this part of the court-martial would be the time to introduce them. But my client had had a spotless record, so there was nothing for the trial counsel to present. And because my client had been convicted of only the minor offense of being drunk and disorderly and because a punitive discharge was not an authorized punishment for that offense, he could not call a witness to say that, because my client had no rehabilitative potential, he should receive a punitive discharge—that is, a bad conduct or dishonorable discharge. So trial counsel mumbled that the prosecution had nothing further to present.

The military judge had previously advised MSG Nutter of his right to present matters in extenuation and mitigation, so he merely asked me whether we had any matters to present. We did.

Even though we didn't face a punitive discharge and even though we really didn't care about the possible four months' confinement—the court members weren't going to sentence MSG Nutter to confinement for this offense—we did care about trying to head off a possible reduction in rank, which could cost him tens of thousands of dollars in retirement pay. So we had to put on evidence that the sentence should be very light. It wasn't hard to do.

I put into evidence all of MSG Nutter's letters of commendation, certificates for the medals that he had been awarded, including combat awards, such as a Bronze Star with "V" device for valor, a Purple Heart for a wound sustained in Vietnam, certificates of graduation from military schools, and efficiency reports that showed that he had always been given the maximum ratings for his duty performance.

Now that he had been convicted only of being drunk and disorderly, I was able to call the deputy provost marshal to testify that, notwithstanding one incident at a party that might have been, in part, the unit's fault for condoning excessive alcohol use, his duty performance had been exemplary and that he would be willing to serve with my client anytime as a master sergeant or even as a sergeant major.

Finally, I had my client give an unsworn statement. A convicted accused servicemember had three choices: to remain silent, to testify under oath, or to give an unsworn statement. The difference was that one could be cross-examined if one testified under oath during the sentencing phase. But one could not be cross-examined on an unsworn statement although the prosecution could offer evidence to rebut any untrue statement of fact in an unsworn statement. So I had my client give a carefully prepared unsworn statement that he was sorry for drinking too much and losing control, that he had tried to do the right thing by having his daughter as his designated driver, and that having his ex-wife flaunt her new boyfriend in his face had led to his drinking too much and acting stupid. He recounted his financial situation, which was quite tight with paying alimony to his ex-wife and supporting his daughter. He also said that he had submitted his retirement papers.

On my guidance, he had submitted his retirement papers so that, if the court members thought that he was a loose cannon or otherwise wasn't suitable to stay in the Army as a master sergeant, they would believe that they didn't have to reduce him in rank or discharge him because he had already voluntarily retired. Now, the punitive discharge was no longer possible, but I wanted to keep his

E-8 rank, and his having bowed out of the Army gracefully after this hassle would likely cause the court members to believe that they didn't need to reduce him in rank when he would no longer be on active duty anyway. Of course, the command had not acted on his request to retire because he was "flagged." A "flag" was a suspension of favorable personnel action while one was being investigated or prosecuted so that one couldn't be promoted, discharged, or retired while pending disciplinary action for misconduct. It was sort of like what happened to Lieutenant/ Captain Menzies when he was promoted to captain a day or so before appearing before a discharge board for allegedly falsifying foreign jump wings to get promoted. They had forgotten to flag his records. But they had flagged MSG Nutter's records. Because he said that he had submitted his retirement papers, however, I offered a true copy of his retirement request into evidence so that the court members would see that, unsworn statement or not, he had asked to retire.

The trial counsel had no rebuttal, so after hammering out the instructions on sentencing drill, it was time to argue. As many military judges did, this one gave each side but one argument and let the defense go first or last as it saw fit. No one ever chose to go first because, if you did, you couldn't try to knock out any good points that the other side made.

The trial counsel argued that, because MSG Nutter was a military policeperson, his drunk and disorderly conduct was far more serious than if some tanker non-commissioned officer had had a little too much to drink. After all, MPs were supposed to enforce the law, not break it. He also did a good job of using the possibility of a concealed weapon and the all-points bulletin to demonstrate how this simple on-its-face drunk and disorderly charge could have caused a lot more damage. What if, he argued, it had ended up with a high-speed chase after the accused fled the club? He concluded by asking for the maximum sentence: four months' confinement, forfeiture of two-thirds pay per month for four months, and reduction to the lowest enlisted grade—Private E-1. Well, the confinement, he could do on his head. The problem was that any reduction would cost him thousands of dollars in retirement pay and that a reduction all the way down from E-8 to E-1 could cost him hundreds of thousands of dollars in retirement pay.

Once I had basically got a client off without any punishment by entering into a plea bargain in which the convening authority agreed to disapprove any confinement adjudged by the court members. What the convening authority was really interested in was a bad conduct discharge. So during the sentencing phase of the trial, I argued that that court should give my client the maximum period of confinement, but not a punitive discharge. The court members bought this argument and sentenced my client to the maximum period of confinement but no Big Chicken Dinner. Because the plea bargain required the convening authority to disapprove any confinement, my client effectively ended up with no punishment other than having a court-martial conviction on his record. Of course, I had chosen to argue last so that the trial counsel couldn't persuade the court members that, if they didn't confine my client, they should at least discharge him. Neither the court members nor the military judge knows the terms of the plea bargain when deliberating on a sentence.

But I couldn't use that argument because confinement was still a possible punishment because we had no pretrial agreement. So I thought that my best argument was to ridicule the trial counsel's desire to confine my master sergeant with more than twenty-nine years of service who had gotten drunk and disorderly and who had submitted his retirement papers.

"Mr. President, members of the court, thank you again for your attention. A good argument exists that sentencing decisions are tougher than deciding guilt or innocence. In the findings stage of a court-martial, the trial counsel has either proven his case beyond a reasonable doubt or not. But sentencing is often nowhere near as clear-cut.

"First, you cannot sentence MSG Nutter for what he might have done or for what might have happened as the trial counsel wants you to do. He's bringing up these possible results of being drunk and disorderly because he doesn't really have any evidence that anything significant resulted from this incident.

"Second, His Honor will instruct you that you may consider, along with the needs of good order and discipline, factors in extenuation and mitigation. Factors in extenuation are nothing more than extenuating circumstances—things that make the offense less severe. Here, a number of factors make the drunk and disorderly charge less severe. It was a unit party, and perhaps, the unit bears some responsibility for having the alcohol flow so freely. And MSG Nutter tried to do the responsible thing—he had a designated driver.

"Yeah, he drank too much, but consider the circumstances—after a very acrimonious divorce that had included a custody battle, his ex-wife appears on the arm of another member of the unit, and they have words. And notwithstanding the way some others at the party—who may have had a few too many themselves—overreacted, no one was hurt. MSG Nutter could well have gotten nasty and tried to beat up his ex-wife's date. But he didn't. And when people started overreacting, he left the scene. No, as drunk and disorderly goes, this situation was a mild one.

"Mitigation, on the other hand, consists of all of the other reasons that a court-martial might award a very lenient punishment. In this case, matters in mitigation include MSG Nutter's spotless record—no courts-martial and not even a nonjudicial punishment when he was just a young soldier. Twenty-nine years of unblemished service.

"And his service was far from mediocre. You have before you his efficiency reports, letters of commendation, and award citations, including combat awards. His service has been exemplary. And remember the Deputy Provost Marshal's unrebutted testimony that MSG Nutter's duty performance was exemplary and that he would be willing to serve with him again in grade, or indeed, in the higher grade of sergeant major.

"As far as his financial situation, consider that half of his pay goes to his ex-wife and that he is supporting his daughter. The forfeiture of two-thirds pay that the trial counsel argued for would clearly work a severe financial hardship on him because he will have to pay his wife's support whether he is earning any money or not.

"Now, I'm not even going to respond to the trial counsel's ludicrous argument that you should sentence MSG Nutter to the maximum four months' confinement. What would that sentence accomplish?

"Nor is his argument that you should reduce him to Private E-1 any the less ludicrous. Does this one minor incident mean that he should retire as an E-1? Not hardly. The Deputy Provost Marshal suggested that he should, not withstanding this minor incident, be promoted. And reducing him to E-1 would cost his ex-wife the one-half of his retirement pay that she would otherwise get. I don't know about you, but I'd rather get one-half of E-8 pay than one-half of E-1 pay.

"The defense would ask you to view MSG Nutter's military service as a bank account. He has been making deposits for more than twenty-nine years. He's made thousands of small deposits consisting of days of outstanding duty performance in a high pressure job as a military policeman. He's made large deposits as evidenced by a Bronze Star, two Meritorious Service Medals, six Army Commendation Medals, and all of the other awards and commendations. He's even deposited his blood as evidenced by his Purple Heart from Vietnam. Now, I submit that this one minor withdrawal hardly wipes out more than twenty-nine years of valiant and dedicated service. If you have to award some punishment, forfeiture of $200 is sufficient. Thank you."

The military jury deliberated for only about 15 minutes, returned to the courtroom, and sentenced my client to forfeit $100 a month for two months.

Captain Ross had the good grace to come up and congratulate me, although he did manage to call me an asshole for resting without putting on any evidence. "I was going to make my case cross-examining your client."

"And you don't think that I knew that?"

"I was hoping."

"Well, Dennis, you've got to know when to hold 'em and know when to fold 'em when you become a defense counsel. And my advice, which I'm sure you don't want, is the same for the government—you've got to know when to walk away from a case and when to run. And I know it wasn't your decision to try the case, but really, arguing for the maximum sentence?"

"Yeah, I know. I should have just said, 'The government expects that you will arrive at an appropriate sentence' and sat my ass down."

"Well, if you'll sit your ass down at the bar at the Officers' Club, I'll by you a beer. And I'll even get my client to tell us where the MP checkpoints will be tonight so you won't have to pee in a bottle!"

And we did. You've got to know when to hold that cold, frosty mug.

12

Coming Aboard, Lieutenant Colonel James Thomas, U.S. Army Retired

"They don't let you stop in the street."

—Master An

Ok, so I'm no longer a JAGC-Off. I'm a retired JAGC-Off. I topped out as a lieutenant colonel and retired at twenty years because it was abundantly clear that I wasn't going to make full colonel. I had stayed in the courtroom as long as I could—even asking to be a military judge when I made major because that was the only way that I could remain in the courtroom. And I was a pretty good military judge, but perhaps that achievement was my undoing. First, being a military judge, while arguably prestigious, was not the way to make high rank. Finding the correctional custody facility of the major general who commanded Fort Campbell, which is in both Tennessee and Kentucky, to be unconstitutional and illegal punishment when I was a mere major was not the way to get him to approve my promotion if he turned out to be one of the line officers chosen to sit on the JAG promotion board with the JAGC general officer. No sane JAGC-Off who wanted to make full colonel or higher ever sought out a military judgeship. Second, being a military judge as a major kept me from getting my ticket punched properly. As a major, you were supposed to be a deputy staff judge advocate, preferably for a combat division.

The Army is all about ticket punching. If I had stayed in the Infantry, I would have had the right start—Infantry platoon leader in combat in Vietnam. An Infantry officer who had sense enough to stay in the Infantry would have followed that start with Infantry company commander, preferably in combat, but, if not, then overseas in Korea or Germany. Such an Infantry officer would then have attended the Infantry Officer Advanced Course at Fort Benning, Georgia, followed by a tour in the officer's secondary military occupational specialty, which could be something as noncombatlike as public affairs. After having gotten the secondary MOS assignment out of the way, such an Infantry officer would go back to the Infantry to be a battalion assistant G-3, operations officer. At that point, the Infantry officer was supposed to be in the top 40 to 50 percent of majors and thereby selected to attend the U.S. Army Command and General Staff College at Fort Leavenworth, Kansas, followed by an assignment as a brigade G-3, operations officer, or battalion executive officer. An Infantry officer that punched all of these tickets, with max officer efficiency reports, would be a lock for lieutenant colonel and, with any luck, the pre-command course and one's own battalion command. With punching all of these tickets and perhaps with an instructorship at the Infantry School or the Command and General Staff College somewhere in the middle, the Infantry officer would be in good shape for the U.S. Army War College at Carlisle Barracks, Pennsylvania, brigade command, and full colonel.

The JAG Corps also had ticket punching. After the JAGC basic course, you wanted to be assigned as a trial counsel, preferably at an Infantry or Armor division or, at least, at an installation that supported that type of unit, such as Fort Bragg, North Carolina, with its 82d Airborne Division. You damn sure, if you wanted a JAGC career, didn't want to bounce between legal assistance and claims. Then, you wanted to attend the JAGC Advanced Course and be assigned as a deputy staff judge advocate, again preferably at a combat division or at an installation supporting such a unit. For your other tour, visions of sugar-plums dancing in your head meant getting assigned as an instructor at the JAGC School in

Charlottesville, Virginia, or serving at the Office of The Judge Advocate General in the Pentagon, where you could brown-nose The Judge Advocate General ("TJAG") and the three other general officers stationed there, as well as the colonel who was the head of PP&TO, the Personnel, Plans and Training Office, which recommended future assignments to TJAG. Sufficient perfect efficiency reports and brown-nosing would get you selected for the next level of schooling. Selection for the Command and General Staff College or the Joint Forces Staff College ("JFSC"), in Norfolk, Virginia, which had been established as the Armed Forces Staff College in 1946 and incorporated into the National Defense University in August 1981, then put you in good shape for lieutenant colonel and a staff judge advocate job. Good efficiency reports as an SJA and perhaps another Pentagon tour (again, with sufficient brown-nosing) would get you your full colonel eagles.

Well, between coming into the JAGC late and trying to stay in the field so that I could try cases, I missed getting most of the tickets punched. I had been a trial counsel, but had spent more time as a defense counsel, God forbid, and was too senior to go to the JAGC Advanced Course. Not only did taking it by correspondence, as I did, raise the red flag that I was some kind of weirdo, but also I didn't get the year of hobnobbing with my fellow students, the instructors, and all of the JACG brass that found reasons to visit the JAGC school to get properly brown-nosed. Then, instead of punching the deputy staff judge advocate ticket, I went off into the hinterland of the military judiciary. By some absolute fluke, I was selected to attend the U.S. Army Command and General Staff College, at Fort Leavenworth, Kansas, which punched that ticket and could have resurrected my career. The colonel from PP&TO told me that I was the exception that proved the rule—you had to be politically connected to be selected. He said that no one on the selection board had ever heard of me, but that I had the best record of all.

So how is that assignment the kiss of death? Well, stupid me—I used my knowledge of the real Army and experience in real live combat and graduated as an honor graduate of CGSC. And consequently, they kept me on the faculty to teach military law, leadership, stress on the battlefield, and other nonlegal topics, as well as being the academic counselor to a staff group of the Army's best and brightest when I should have been a deputy staff judge advocate or a staff judge advocate to punch the proper tickets.

PP&TO told me that no one else could do this tough job and refused to move me to punch my ticket. They even kept me an extra year—a four-year tour when it was supposed to be only a three-year tour. So after four years of being rated the best instructor, the best academic counselor, the best foreign officer sponsor, and so forth on the faculty, I lost it and was no longer perfect.

So I was reassigned to a job that wasn't a staff judge advocate position, and I knew that it was over. No full colonel, just a succession of boring administrative jobs far away from the courtroom. So I retired at twenty years.

The only trouble with this abrupt career change was that I was basically unemployable. In my mid-forties, with my only legal expertise and experience being in military law, and having no client base did not make me attractive to big law firms. Can't image why. I had not been bright enough to get training and experience with government procurement law so that I'd have had specialized knowledge that a law firm or a defense contractor could use. And I had no real family left who could help me open a law office in some small town and refer me enough business to survive. After having received many rejections saying "thank-you-for-your-resume-but-we-have-no-position-for-someone-with-your-unique-qualifications-but-feel-free-to-contact-us-when-you-can-bring-in-a-half-million-a-year-in-billables," I managed to get a job teaching legal writing at a law school in Chicago. Legal writing instructors are at the low end of the faculty totem pole, ranking just slightly higher than a faculty secretary, but lower than the dean's secretary. The position did, however, provide me a modest income while I developed a civilian practice. I thought that spending two years studying civilian law might give me something more marketable than trying to defend servicemembers as a civilian counsel when they got a free military lawyer and didn't have much money to hire a civilian attorney anyway.

Fortunately for me, because I was never going to become a tenure track member of the facility with a degree from a "non-producer" school, one of the members of the faculty was a full colonel in the U.S. Army JAGC Reserves and decided to help me out. Producer schools were Harvard, Yale, Michigan, and the like, the prestigious schools from which 90 percent of law school faculties were recruited. And to top it off, I was a white, Anglo-Saxon, male baby-killer from the Vietnam War, even though I had seen no babies out in the jungle where I was, much less killed them. But I was hardly politically correct in the law school even though I was perhaps the most anti-war member of the faculty, what with being the only one who had actually seen it up close and personal. But I digress. Professor/Colonel Gibson both helped me get the legal writing appointment and, as a famous member of the Chicago legal community and as one known as the expert on military law, referred all of the cases that he did not want to be bothered with to me.

The first such case occurred as follows. Professor/Colonel Gibson poked his head into my office—using the term office loosely because it was little more than a closet—and announced that he had a military appeal that he wanted my help on. I quickly agreed, not out of any hope of financial reward, but because the good Professor/Colonel was one of the few on the faculty that acknowledged my existence in a positive manner and I wanted to say thanks.

A couple of weeks later, he stuck his head into my office again and said, "Come on. The client is in my office and you need to meet him." Grateful for any excuse to stop grading legal writing assignments, I practically jumped up and followed him to his large, sumptuously appointed tenured professor office. On the way, he said, "What's your fee for doing the appeal? You are going to do all the work, so you get all the money."

I had never charged a fee for my legal work in my life and didn't have the faintest clue. If pressed, I would have probably said $500. But for once in my life, I kept my mouth shut other than to tell him to set the fee because I had no idea what to charge.

The "client" turned out to be the real client's father. The client had pled guilty to some military delicts, and his father, praise be, was willing to pay for a civilian lawyer to do the appeal rather than relying on the free military appellate lawyer. After a few minutes, Professor/Colonel Gibson started explaining legal fees to the client's father. He started out by saying that this case would not be appropriate for a contingency fee in which the lawyer gets a cut, often one-third, if he wins because there was no pot of money to get a third of at stake. This case was not a wrongful death case in which the newly deceased was earning $250,000 a year and had a 35-year work life expectancy. One-third of an Army captain's back pay for the time that he had lost it because of his court-martial sentence wasn't much, and his lawyer wasn't likely to get it anyway because winning an appeal in a guilty plea case was only a little more likely than the law school promoting me to full professor and giving me tenure. Then, the good Professor/Colonel contrasted hourly rate fee arrangements with flat fees, outlining the pros and cons of each.

"The good thing about the hourly rate is that you can say stop at any time and not owe any more. The bad thing is that the other side can do all sorts of things to make your lawyer have to spend a lot more money than anticipated. With a flat fee, you know what it's going to cost you up front. It is a little bit of a gamble—you win if the attorney prices it too low and has to spend a lot more hours than anticipated, and he wins if he somehow magically gets a good result with little effort. But if you price it right, you may be happy getting that good result even if you might have had to pay less on an hourly."

When asked which he preferred, the client's father, a successful businessman in Chicago, immediately said, "A flat fee."

Professor/Colonel Gibson said, "Fine. That will be $15,000."

I almost fell off of my chair. I had been hoping for $1,000, maybe $1,500, and I would have done it for $500. But I recovered quickly and managed to look like getting more money at one time than I ever had in my life was no big deal. The businessman pulled out his checkbook, asked whom to make the check out to, and handed me the check. I told him that I would review the record of trial and contact his son and, with his son's permission (the actual client), get his dad's approval of what issues to brief on appeal. We shook hands all around, with the check clutched in my free hand, and then, I went back to my office, which all of a sudden didn't look so shabby. And the check didn't even bounce.

Well, as expected, there was not much to appeal, but both the captain and his father wanted me to proceed. I think that the father wanted to support his son even if there was little point to it. I had cashed the check, but not spent the money in the event that I couldn't find anything to appeal and had to return the money. I did a world-class brief, but ultimately lost the appeal.

Before the appeal had run its course, however, the good Professor/Colonel struck again. The parents of a marine stationed in Japan had contacted him. Their son was facing an Article 32 investigation at the Marine Corps Air Station in Iwakuni, Japan, for having killed another marine, and they did not trust his military lawyer to zealously represent him. Now, I didn't have the faintest clue what the case might turn into—anything from the charges dismissed because the Article 32 would show that, for example, the killing was justifiable, to a capital murder trial. So a flat fee would have had to be extremely high to cover that much lawyering—and in Japan, no less. So now being adept at setting legal fees (yeah, right), I told the distraught parents that I would represent their son at the Article 32 for $250 an hour plus $100 an hour for travel time and all expenses. They agreed and wrote me out a nice $20,000 check to get started.

The only problem was that the Article 32 was in three days and I had no passport. Back then, active duty servicemembers did not need passports, just their official orders to travel for a permanent change of station (PCS) or temporary duty (TDY) abroad. I had so recently been an active duty servicemember and had had no plans to go overseas that I had no passport. As a matter of fact, I had never had a passport. But by invoking the 6th Amendment's right to counsel for this poor marine facing a potential death sentence overseas, I went to the federal building in Chicago and got an emergency passport in a day from the State Department's Passport Agency. The only available seat going to Tokyo was business class on Northwest Airlines, so with the parent's permission, I booked the seat.

The travel agent, however, had no idea how to get from Tokyo to Iwakuni. Fortunately, one of my law students was Japanese, and I had helped him with a minor problem, so the "Giri/On" (the Japanese concept of who owes whom), was flowing my way. Not only did he provide me detailed instructions as to how to get to Iwakuni, but also he took me to see the President of the Chicago branch of Sumitomo Mitsui Bank to exchange my dollars for yen traveler's checks. Have you ever tried to make exchanging $1,000 for yen traveler's checks appear to be worth the time of said President who personally came out of his office, which took up half a floor of the Sears Tower, to greet you, had some Geisha-type secretary pour tea in an elaborate ceremony, and treated you like a billion dollar investor? I actually thought that the porcelain tea service was worth more than my transaction if not my entire net worth. After having had Judge Savage throw his gavel at me, I was able to act like this service was the only proper way to treat me, but was cowed enough to up the $1,000 to $2,000 to make the transaction appear a little less low-level. Of course, comparing one or two thousand dollars to the deals that he normally dealt with was somewhat like comparing a minnow to a whale or a karate white belt to Master An, but perhaps because I was some kind of professor or the other and had helped a Japanese student whose father was probably somebody known to the bank president, he treated me as if I were MacArthur appearing before the Emperor just after the surrender of Japan in World War II. And I got my traveler's checks.

Next thing I knew, I was sitting in business class on Northwest, drinking a Chivas on the rocks and wiping my brow with the steaming hot towel so nicely provided by the attractive flight attendant in a kimono while the poor souls in tourist filed aboard. Every so often during the flight, I would take a short break from the first-run movie, sip my second (third, fourth) scotch and check my watch. Ah, another $100. Let's see, an 18-hour flight—that's decent money.

It was late at night when I arrived at Narita International Airport in Tokyo. I didn't think that I could get to Iwakuni that night, so I stayed in a hotel by the airport. I had thought that my office at the law school was a closet, but my first Japanese hotel room made my office look spacious. The room was not designed for a 6-foot tall *gaijin,* Japanese for foreigner. But I got a couple of hours of sleep. I had largely avoided sleeping during the flight—helped by the scotch. And it's a lot easier to travel west than east because you can stay awake as the time zones get earlier and earlier so you can sleep when you get to your destination, as I had learned in my Army days.

The next day, I took a train to Haneda, the domestic airport, which was on the other side of Tokyo, and flew to Hiroshima, from which, according to my student's instructions, I could catch a train to Iwakuni.

From the Hiroshima airport, I took a bus to the train station. I felt very strange as the only *gaijin* on the bus, towering over the Japanese and riding past the Hiroshima Peace Memorial, marking ground zero for the first atomic bomb. But the people couldn't have been nicer, and one gentleman, seeing me standing in the train station like a total moron, took me to the ticket window, helped me buy my ticket, and took me to the correct platform to catch the train to Iwakuni.

Once there, I met with military counsel and my client, attended the 32, and acted like the typical clueless civilian defense counsel. I saw no reason to alert them that I did have a clue—not wanting them to assign their best prosecutor to combat me if acting dumb could avoid it. My client was charged with manslaughter—

shooting another marine in the neck while horsing around on guard duty.

Now, I saw several ways in which the trial counsel could get a homicide conviction rather than one for mere manslaughter, so I downplayed the 32 so that no more damaging information came out than what they already had and beat feet back to Dodge—or in this case, Chicago. The military defense counsel, whom I had kept on the case so that I wouldn't bankrupt my client's parents by having to fly back to Japan every time that the judge wanted to have a court session on some scheduling issue, put me on the bullet train to Tokyo. This time, I avoided the Japanese hotel, stayed at the Holiday Inn at Narita for very little extra money, and had a room that I could turn around in before I flew back.

The wheels of military justice ground on, and I found myself flying back to Japan for the trial. My client's parents had mortgaged their home to give their son the best defense possible. But this trip had a different final destination from my first trip because the Marines were going to try the case at Osan Air Base in the Republic of Korea, where the killing had occurred while my client's unit was on temporary duty there for some military reason or the other. So I flew out of Narita and landed in Seoul before making my way by car to Osan Air Base south of Seoul. I had always wanted to visit Korea because of the respect that Master An had developed in me for Korean culture.

The case against my client was really strange. The maximum penalty for the killing—so long as it remained manslaughter—was fifteen years for voluntary manslaughter and ten years for involuntary manslaughter, but he was also facing 16 years for two assaults on Koreans in which no harm was done. In addition, his chances of getting a lesser sentence to confinement were greatly reduced by having the evidence for those charges convince the jury that my client was a loose cannon who liked to play with loaded firearms—especially because after the two assaults with a dangerous weapon he had been warned not to play fast and loose. In fact, his command had not even disciplined him for those two assaults, only adding the charges after the killing.

That sequence of events gave me an idea. Because I had attended the Article 32 investigation and these charges against the Koreans had hardly been mentioned and definitely not preferred, I moved for a new Article 32 on the ground that the referral to a general court-martial was improper because the additional charges had not had a proper Article 32 investigation. The military judge, a Navy captain, said that he tended to agree but wanted some time to research the issue.

The next thing I knew, the charges were withdrawn from the court-martial, thereby depriving the military judge of authority to rule on the motion, and the case was referred to a new court-martial presided over by a Marine Corps military judge. Further, the best Marine prosecutor in the Pacific theater was magically appointed as trial counsel, and the original trial counsel was demoted to assistant trial counsel. Apparently, my dud impersonation at the Article 32 hearing was no longer operative.

Well, I raised all sorts of holy hell, contending that the withdrawal and re-referral were improper because the discussion of Rule for Courts-Martial 604, permitting withdrawal, notes that charges should not be withdrawn from a court-martial arbitrarily or unfairly to an accused and that such an action was unfair when the prior judge had indicated that he was going to rule in the accused's favor on a motion. Further, the convening authority had not included any reasons for the withdrawal, as required.

But the Marine judge ruled against me with the help of some brilliant, although legally incorrect, argument by the trial counsel. I understood why he was the best trial counsel in the Pacific theater. He was good.

But I was better. After all, I had been trained by Master An, and we were in Korea. When I returned to Osan several weeks later for the actual trial, I had not given up on getting rid of the two assault charges. So, consistent with my old active-duty reputation as Mister Jurisdiction, I moved to dismiss the additional charges for failure to comport with the notice and waiver provisions of the Korean Status of Forces Agreement (SOFA).

I must admit that I enjoyed the dead silence as the trial counsel and military judge digested this level of motion practice. After a suitable interlude, I marched on.

"Your Honor, the Status of Forces Agreement classifies crimes committed by servicemembers of signatories to the Agreement into three classes: exclusive host nation, here Korea, jurisdiction, under which Korea has exclusive jurisdiction over crimes that violate Korean law, but not the visiting country's laws; exclusive jurisdiction in the visiting forces for cases in which the offense violates the visiting force's laws but not the host nation's; and concurrent jurisdiction for cases in which the offense violates both nations' laws, such as the charges in this case. In such cases, the nationality of the victim is key—the country of the victim's nationality has primary concurrent jurisdiction but should give 'sympathetic consideration' to a request for waiver of the primary concurrent jurisdiction. And no such request was made."

Well, the way that this thing happened, with the charges against the Korean nationals thrown in as an afterthought without even an Article 32 investigation, I surmised that the command had failed to get such a waiver of Korea's primary concurrent jurisdiction. And upon checking, I was right. My client's command and the prosecutors had failed to seek this waiver from the sovereign state of Korea.

Well, the best trial counsel in the Pacific theater was indeed good. He almost fought me off, arguing that this portion of the Status of Forces Agreement was not for the benefit of the accused, so he could not invoke it to avoid prosecution. And the judge, who had replaced the judge who appeared willing to grant a defense motion, did not want to throw out these additional charges. But ultimately, he had to, so he dismissed them.

But as I said, Captain Lane, the trial counsel, was good. He immediately moved to adduce evidence of the two assaults under Military Rule of Evidence 404(b) to show lack of mistake or accident. The general rule is that evidence of a person's bad character is not admissible to show that the person had committed a crime, but under 404(b), evidence of uncharged misconduct, although inadmissible to prove character and that a person acted in conformity with that bad character, was admissible to prove motive, opportunity, intent, preparation, plan, knowledge, identity, or absence of mistake or accident. This savvy bit of lawyering was an unwelcome development. Even though my client did not face the additional sixteen years of imprisonment for the two assaults, having them come into evidence would ensure that he got the maximum imprisonment for the killing, whether voluntary or involuntary manslaughter. But I convinced the military judge that the trial counsel could put on evidence of the unrelated assaults only if I raised the defense of accident or mistake—which I had no intention of doing. And I didn't. I rested—you've got to know when to fold them—without putting on any evidence and argued to the jury that the prosecution's case did not rule out accident or mistake.

Well, this tactic worked better than I had hoped. After all, the trial counsel had eyewitnesses to the shooting and a confession of sorts. But the jury came back with the best result possible other than an impossible acquittal, a finding of guilty to the lesser charge of involuntary manslaughter. And after the sentencing portion of the trial, the jury sentenced him to only one year's confinement and a bad conduct discharge. One year was a gift from God. His military counsel had been prepared to plead him guilty to all of the charges for a plea bargain that the convening authority would not approve any sentence in excess of ten years. And because he had been kept in pretrial confinement, he was already almost one-third of the way through the ten months that one serves with time off for good behavior on a one-year sentence.

So I went back to Seoul to catch my flight back to Chicago. After this win, I thought that I deserved the Hyatt Regency Seoul. It was not the worst evening of my life sitting in the restaurant on the top floor, sipping Chivas, eating bulgogi—Korean beef barbeque—and looking out at the Han River. At the Command and General Staff College, we had war gamed the North Koreans attacking across the Han River Estuary, which would have conquered Seoul in little more than a day before we (hopefully) repulsed them with our superior air power. It was kind of nice to see the Han River after having fought off the best Marine prosecutor in the Pacific and having saved my client almost a decade of jail time. I felt especially good because I had earned my legal fees and then some.

Unfortunately, I got only one more court-martial defense in the Orient, but it was a doozy. You've no doubt heard the old saying that no good deed goes unpunished. Well, I did a good deed and got rewarded. A former Navy master chief called me up from Japan. He had somehow heard about my performance in the Marine Corps court-martial in Korea and wanted me to appeal his conviction. He sent me his record of trial, and he had very good grounds for appeal. But he couldn't meet my price from the brig, especially because the court-martial had busted him to E-1 and ordered forfeiture of all pay and allowances. But he seemed like a nice guy, and his conviction, for sexual abuse of his minor stepdaughter, appeared bogus. The prosecution witnesses were so contradictory as to what had allegedly happened, and the defense had impeached them so thoroughly that I could not image how he had been convicted. So I told him exactly how to frame the appellate issues to make certain that his free military appellate attorney got them right. More than a year later, I got a call from him. The appeal had worked, and he was a master chief again. He was very grateful—although I note that he did not forward any part of his back pay to me in gratitude—and I congratulated him and wished him well in the short time that he had before happily retiring.

I didn't think about the matter again until I got a phone call from Yokosuka, Japan, from one Master Chief Noma as follows:

"Sir, Master Chief Martinez told me how you had helped him on his appeal and recommended you as the best person to represent me. I'm facing sixty-five years and a dishonorable discharge, and my military lawyer just wants to plead me guilty for a ten-year sentence, which would lose me my retirement if they give me a dishonorable or bad-conduct discharge."

"Ok, Master Chief, can you fax me the charge sheet? Have you had an Article 32 hearing yet?"

"Yes, give me your fax number, and, no, we haven't had the Article 32. My defense counsel said that, if we waived the 32, we might get a better plea bargain."

I gave him my fax number and asked him to fax me the charge sheet and any supporting documents that he had and call me back in an hour. Upon reviewing the documents, it did not take a genius in military law to see that Master Chief Noma was in deep kimchee—Navy bastardized Asian speak for "deep shit." He was facing a general court-martial for larceny, internet child pornography, indecent language communicated by email both to an adult and to a minor, and other related charges, including conduct to the prejudice of good order and discipline by doing the aforesaid acts.

It seemed that the master chief had recently decided that he was close enough to retirement that he had better get computer-literate. So he bought one and freaked out when he found the internet. Noma was a bachelor and had lived in Japan for the past nine years. So in his lonely bachelor non-commissioned officer's quarters or whatever the Navy called his on-base housing, he managed to get into some chat room and make friends with a woman in North Carolina. They got friendlier and friendlier and began discussing what they were going to do when they got together. And I don't mean what restaurant they were going to go to. The only problem with this correspondence was that the woman was some kind of religious freako who got her kicks suckering men into such conversations and then turning them in. I would not have thought it too bad if she had been entrapping pedophiles who were trying to lure children via the internet, but some lonely sailor who was talking sex with an adult? And it didn't really seem like his fault that she had had her minor daughter do some of the email replies so that she could turn him in for communicating sexual language to a minor. But it wasn't entrapment because only the government can entrap a person in such a way that it amounts to a legal defense. If a private citizen, not acting as a government agent, entraps you, you are SOL—a nonmilitary acronym for shit outta luck.

This chatty woman notified the Naval Investigative Service, who got a search authorization from Noma's commander, broke down his door, and found him surfing for porn. They apprehended him and seized his computer.

Unfortunately, although the internet history showed that he had visited hundreds of adult porn sites, the Naval forensic computer expert found three pictures in his cache memory depicting child pornography. Eventually, he told me that he had not been surfing for child porn and, when the pictures came up, he immediately hit the "X" in the upper right hand corner of the screen to flush them. He didn't know about cache memory. So perhaps the most serious charge was possession of child pornography.

When he called back, I said that under legal ethics I could not guarantee any results but that I was quite confident that I could do better for him than his military defense counsel, who wanted to plead him guilty in such a manner that he would receive a punitive discharge—whether dishonorable or bad conduct didn't make much difference—and lose his pension—75 percent of his pay because he had thirty years of service. Then, I outlined my fees, $250 an hour plus $150 an hour travel time. I had finally figured out that, although travel time might be pleasant drinking Chivas in business class, it still was time that I couldn't earn money working on other cases. So I had raised my travel time fee. I finished by saying that I wanted to use another lawyer to assist because to save his pension we were going to need what I called the full-court press. We were going to have to blow away the prosecution, who had the might and majesty of the U.S. government and its deep pockets. As it turned out, not so deep as the trial counsel would have liked. I told Master Chief Noma that I wanted $10,000 in my trust account to cover travel expenses and legal fees for the Article 32, which we could not, under any circumstances, waive. I wanted to do the opposite of what I had done in my last trip to Japan. Rather than appearing meek, mild, shy, backward, old-fashioned, quaint, and conservative—that is, a typical clueless civilian defense counsel—I wanted to nuke them at the 32. Oops. Saying "nuke them" probably wasn't politically correct for a hearing in Japan. But after all, this book is a politically incorrect memoir.

But Master Chief Noma wasn't ready to pull the trigger. He kept asking, "How do I know that you will be worth the money?"

I kept answering, "Other than Master Chief Martinez's recommendation, you don't. And I can't guarantee any results. If you want phone numbers of other satisfied military clients, I can provide them. But you already know that your military counsel isn't aggressive enough. I am. I'm retired. I can piss off the admiral without worrying about whether it is going to keep me from being promoted. And I'm more than willing to discuss my qualifications and early strategy with the caveat that it may change as things develop. But you are going to have to make up your mind whether $20,000 to $50,000 in legal fees and expenses is a sound investment to save your approximately half million dollar retirement."

Well, Master Chief Noma didn't sound very happy, but he ultimately agreed. I started making the travel arrangements for the Article 32 hearing and called up my former student, P.D. Dixon, a former Marine drill instructor, who had helped me on several of my military cases while he was still a student and who now had a successful law practice in Kansas City, to see whether he was willing to go to Japan to second chair me in a court-martial. Not surprisingly, he was.

We roughed it business class to Tokyo, where our client picked us up at Narita International Airport for the several-hour drive to Yokosuka Navy Base on Tokyo Bay on the other side of the city from the airport. On the trip, we learned that our client was the second senior E-9 in the Navy. In other words, only one enlisted sailor outranked him. He had been, until being reassigned to bullshit duties pending court-martial, a harbor pilot. So he had the apparently easily replaceable assignment of piloting a U.S. nuclear carrier up Tokyo Bay, the busiest harbor in the world, avoiding the outgoing oil supertankers. Can you imagine such a collision in Japan, where our nuclear history is suspect, at best? But once he was charged, his command relieved him of his duties and assigned him to sit in a warehouse and keep it cleaned up. Honestly, I do believe that the military eats its young.

Safely ensconced in the Bachelor Officers Quarters—the defense was going to be expensive enough without charging him for staying in a Japanese hotel—we met with Lieutenant Carter, the detailed defense counsel, and went over all of the documents that the trial counsel had provided in the case to get ready to cross-examine the government's witnesses at the Article 32. Then, we walked over to the Staff Judge Advocate's office to pay a courtesy call on the trial counsel. And guess what? He was sitting there chatting with the Article 32 Investigating Officer, Lieutenant Commander Sharon Pennell. After we had exchanged handshakes all around and verified the time and location for the hearing, she excused herself. We made nice with the trial counsel and then left to go find the gym for a workout. As we left the building, we ran into LCMDR Pennell, who we learned was actually stationed in Okinawa. She added that she liked doing Article 32 investigations because the shopping was much better in the Yokosuka Navy Base Exchange than on Okinawa. Thinking that she was from out of town, as well, we asked her to dinner and told her to bring along the trial counsel so that there would be no appearance of impropriety—as if a dinner were going to cause an Article 32 investigating officer to do anything but recommend a trial by general court-martial. She declined. So we went to get our workout in and go to dinner by ourselves at the Officers' Club. We had already had some great Japanese food, thanks to our client, who, having served in Japan for almost a decade as the harbor pilot for Yokosuka Navy Base, spoke Japanese. He had taken us where no tourist had ever been, where the food was fantastic and the sashimi must have been alive in the sea about an hour before we ate it. But this evening, after our workout, we were in the mood for a good old American steak and some cheap scotch on the rocks.

But lo and behold! Who was sitting across the dining room at the O Club eating dinner with the prosecutor? LCMDR Pennell. Now, we had our first tactical nuke.

So when the Article 32 hearing started, I immediately challenged LCMDR Pennell for cause, stating that she was biased in favor of the prosecution because she would eat dinner with the trial counsel, but not the defense, and would therefore always find for the prosecution so she could continue to get her shopping trips to the base.

I almost felt sorry for her, but she could have invited us to join her and the trial counsel at the O Club. She turned a deep red and immediately recessed the hearing. Then, we twiddled our thumbs for several hours while she apparently read every case on challenges for cause in the entire law library and made numerous phone calls. Finally, I walked into the library and said, "Commander, just say that you are not predisposed, rule against the challenge, and let's get going. We have made our record for appeal."

Believe it or not, she actually gave me a grateful smile and complied. We actually could have cared less whether she presided over the Article 32 or someone else did. No Article 32 Investigating Officer was going to do anything but recommend a general court-martial with these charges.

Between challenging the investigating officer for cause and aggressively cross-examining the government's witnesses, we at least got our client's confidence. P.D. did a particularly brutal cross of the Navy's forensic computer expert. I tore up their Tanner staging expert—a physician who can give an expert opinion as to the age of a child based on physical characteristics. Because the child porn website was out of Sweden, the prosecution could not prove that the three images were of a minor in the usual way—by putting the birth certificate into evidence. My cross examination focused on the question of how, because the doctor had not actually seen the alleged child—just a digital image—the doctor knew that it had not been morphed back from an image of a ninety-year-old? He didn't know.

This cross-examination was a little bit of a gamble. Alerting the prosecution to the morphing idea would allow them to try to get a forensic computer expert to testify that the images had not been morphed. But then I would get to move for the government to fund two defense experts—a Tanner staging expert and a computer morphing expert. And I wanted to use tons of motions to pressure the government and reassure my client.

This aggressive stance made our client very happy. At least, he felt that, if he was going to go down, he was going to go down fighting. But we knew that, challenged for cause or not, the investigating officer was going to recommend trial by general court-martial and that the convening authority, the Commander, U.S. Naval Forces, Japan, was going to follow that recommendation. So we returned home and started preparing. P.D. started outlining the cross-examination of the government's witnesses from the notes that we had taken during their Article 32 testimony, and I started preparing motions. Unfortunately, there was no Status of Forces Agreement jurisdictional issue because all of the alleged victims were U.S. citizens.

Sure enough, a couple of weeks later, we got a phone call from the Chief Trial Counsel, who told us that the Convening Authority had referred the case to a general court-martial and that he was going to conference the military judge in to set a trial date. He did, however, screw up. When I asked why the trial counsel had not made the call, the Chief Trial Counsel, a lieutenant commander, said, "Because he left this morning to go get married in Florida. So I'm handling the case until he gets back from his honeymoon." Then, he conferenced in the military judge.

Well, this news was like feeding chum to a shark. The illustrious Chief Trial Counsel made the usual bullshit statement, "Your Honor, the government is ready for trial," believing that civilian counsel would request at least a two- or three-month continuance.

But I responded, "So are we. We will be there in two days—the quickest we can get to Japan."

Now, the government always says that it is ready, whether it is or not. And no one ever calls them on it—at least up to now. Well, with the trial counsel on his honeymoon and with the G-2 (intelligence) that we had developed during the Article 32, we knew that an immediate trial fucked the prosecution—even before the honeymoon leave. P.D. and I had made friends with all of the worker bees—the court reporters, the paralegals, and so forth—and had learned that the command had almost no budget left for courts-martial and had a major rape case coming up involving witnesses from all over the Pacific—all of whose travel expenses and TDY (temporary duty) pay would have to come from the court-martial budget. That case involved the rape of a Japanese girl, no less. Consequently, for good relations with the host country, they had to prosecute the case vigorously.

But my client's case was going to be very expensive. The government had to bring the alleged victim of lewd and lascivious language and her mother to Yokosuka, as well as a half dozen other witnesses who were scattered across the Pacific and the continental United States. Their Tanner staging expert, for example, had just been transferred to a Naval hospital in the Philippines. We had learned that the child victim of the lewd and lascivious language and her mother did not even have passports. And I had some pretty good ideas about how to get the prosecution to have to spend big bucks to assist the defense.

I would have liked to be clairvoyant so as to read the Chief Trial Counsel's mind as he thought about getting ready for trial in two days without his prosecutor being present and not only having to get passports for his witnesses, but also having to get them from the East Coast of the United States to Yokosuka. But he could hardly tell the judge, "Your Honor, I lied when I said the government was ready to proceed."

And before he could come up with anything, I said, "Thank you, Your Honor. We have to cut this off and make some quick travel arrangements. Our staff will notify you of our arrival time. We can start the trial the next morning."

A little over 24 hours later, we were back in Japan. Our client picked us up at Narita airport to drive us to the naval base. Master Chief Noma looked worried. The first words out of his mouth were, "I'm fucked. They called Lieutenant Ryan back from his honeymoon leave to try the case. You said that his boss would probably have to try it and that he hadn't been in a courtroom for years."

"Don't worry about it," I responded. "I doubt that Lieutenant Ryan is going to be all that motivated after missing his wedding night. And although he seems to be a decent prosecutor, you've got the dream team. And we've got some ideas about how to de-motivate him even more."

So we checked into the BOQ for the second time, and I got out my trusty laptop and fired it up. I had done the research for the motions back in the States, where I had access to computerized legal research. P.D. went on his mission to mess with the trial counsel's mind while I started cranking out motions. Master Chief Noma stood by my desk, alert to satisfy any need that I might have—after all, the trial was scheduled to start the next day.

So I cranked out a few motions. I had taken typing in high school—the only boy in the class. I took a lot of grief from the guys, but since I was a 110-pound nerd with thick glasses back then, it didn't make me that much more of a wimp. But taking typing was the smartest thing that I had ever done because I can type fast and I can compose as fast as I type. I had won an essay contest my junior year in high school, so the local paper hired me as a reporter for my high school's sports during my senior year. Talk about going from a nonentity to a big man on campus. The jocks quickly figured out that, if they were not nice to me, they didn't get their names in the paper or they didn't get much of a write-up. A big difference exists between "Tim Crook scored a crucial 15 points" and "Tim Crook padded his statistics by scoring 15 meaningless points after the game had already been decided." And between the star athletes fawning over me and walking through the gate with my date without paying by flashing my press pass, my status with the better looking girls improved drastically. Well, ok, at least I was up to the mid-level girls that were not embarrassing to date and occasionally a very good looking one. Yes, I know. Looks shouldn't be the only thing that matters. But I'm a guy, and this book is a politically incorrect memoir. Anyway, the next thing that I knew, three major newspapers hired me to write high school sports for them. So I had to call in the story of the football or basketball game right after it was over—changing it for four different papers—so that they could have the story for the morning edition. So I learned how to compose very fast—from my handwritten notes taken during the game and the stat sheets handed out to the press. As far as legal motions and the like, I might not be good, but I'm fast. I'm as fast at cranking out motions as Master An is at seizing a nanosecond's opening in your defensive stance.

So while P.D. got the trial counsel drunk and worked on destroying any slight motivation that he might have had to aggressively try the case, by commiserating as to how his boss had fucked him over by calling him back from his honeymoon—before he could even consummate the marriage for God's sake—I cranked out the motions. They included these:

- Motion to dismiss for illegal prior punishment—making the second senior enlisted man in the Navy sit in a warehouse all day doing nothing but sweeping the floor and taking out the garbage. This motion wouldn't win, but if we went down the tubes, it might mitigate the punishment because he had been "punished" in some sense already.
- Due process violation in nine-month delay before preferring charges. I couldn't bring an actual speedy trial motion because the government had not violated the time limits specified in the Uniform Code of Military Justice. They had not violated them because they had waited so long to prefer charges. This motion was a loser, but trial counsel would have to spend a fair amount of time to respond to it.
- Motion for a new Article 32 investigation because the Investigating Officer was biased in favor of the government. Again, probably a loser, but who knows?
- Motion to disqualify the admiral as the Convening Authority because of personal interest and bias. One of the paralegals had told us that the admiral had gone ballistic when he heard that his only harbor pilot was a pedophile and vowed to put him "under the jail." Military law specifies that the Convening Authority—the officer who creates the court-martial and refers the case to

it—is a quasi-judicial officer who must be impartial, much like a judge. This motion was unlikely to win, but the client loved it. He was later heard to boast, "My lawyers tried to fire the admiral."

- Illegal search and seizure of my client's computer. Again, unlikely to win, but colorable enough to require many more hours for the trial counsel to research and write his opposition brief than it took me to write it.
- Motion to suppress certain statements that my client made during the search and subsequent apprehension—the military term for "arrest." Actually, the statements were exculpatory—they didn't hurt us any—but, again, the trial counsel probably wasn't slick enough to simply say, "Fine. I won't admit them." Instead, he would have to research and write another brief in opposition to our motion.
- Motion to fund a Tanner staging expert at government expense. This one was a winner and would delay the trial for a month or more—when the prosecution had already blown their budget by starting to fly the witnesses to Japan. The motion was a winner because the age of the alleged child porn victim was the heart of that charge and there was no way the military judge would not allow us to challenge the government expert through an expert of our own.
- Motion to fund a computer morphing expert. Ditto. Regardless of whether the government adduced an expert to testify that the pictures had not been morphed, we could adduce evidence that they had been or could have been.
- Multiplicity. This motion challenges whether the prosecution unreasonably multiplied one offense into many.
- Motion in limine to exclude tapes and other evidence seized during the search and not the basis of charges as being overly prejudicial under Military Rule of Evidence 403. MRE 403 permits the judge to exclude evidence when its prejudicial effect substantially outweighs its probative value.

Several hours later, I had these and several other, less critical, motions done and printed out on my handy-dandy portable printer.

Our illustrious client went to P.D.'s room and gave him the signal that I was done—almost as important a duty as plying me with Chivas to keep my creative juices flowing while I cranked out the motions. My client later told P.D. that he had kept the fire extinguisher handy in case the combination of my typing speed and the alcohol had set the computer on fire.

A few minutes later, P.D. brought Lieutenant Ryan by my room under the pretext of saying "goodnight." P.D. had gotten the good lieutenant into a reasonable facsimile of a drunken sailor who could say little more than, "My boss fucked me. Fuck this case." A position we could deal with.

So I greeted him and commiserated as to how his boss had fucked him by saying, "When I was the Chief of Criminal Law, I would have tried the case myself before pulling one of my trial counsel off of his honeymoon leave." Then, evil as I am, I said, "But, before you go, here are 17 motions. I didn't want to wait until tomorrow morning because you might not have enough time to respond properly."

I almost felt bad when he was pathetically grateful for my dumping these motions on him at midnight when the trial was the next morning. But P.D. had done a great job of messing with his mind, and the scotch hadn't hurt.

Lieutenant Ryan was a trooper, however—or whatever word the Navy would use for a servicemember who did his duty when the chips were down. As he walked back to his quarters, he read the motions and apparently thought, "Oh fuck." He sobered up rapidly. Instead of going to his quarters, he went to his office and called the trial counsel assistance office in Washington, D.C. With the time change almost halfway around the world, they were ready to assist. They told him that several of the motions, most notably the motions to produce experts at government expense, were winners and they couldn't help him. Knowing of the lack of funds and even if they were able to call the witnesses off before all of the travel costs were expended, Lieutenant Ryan knew that the case was fucked. So he called his boss, the Chief Trial Counsel, at 0500 hours (5 a.m.) and told him that they had to enter into a plea bargain if they wanted any type of conviction. The Chief Trial Counsel was not sympathetic and said that he would not recommend any plea bargain that did not allow for the accused to receive a punitive discharge and at least five years' confinement. Now, Lieutenant Ryan knew that we weren't going to enter into any such plea bargain.

So he woke me up at 0515. "Sorry to wake you, Sir." (Now, I was "Sir.") "I know it is last minute, but would you consider a plea—and, if so, on what terms?"

Well, I knew that, even with the lack of funds and the couple of sure winner motions, a punitive discharge and jail time were far from impossible. If the court members saw the child porn pictures, they could put Master Chief Noma under the jail, regardless of his great record and regardless of whether he knowingly possessed them or not. And I knew that if I came up with an absolutely ridiculous plea bargain, Lieutenant Ryan could never sell it to the Convening Authority. So I had to carefully craft a plea bargain that would protect my client's retirement. So I offered to plead my client guilty to several of the charges if the Convening Authority would agree to disapprove any punitive discharge, suspend any confinement in excess of three months, and disapprove any reduction below the grade of E-7 whether adjudged by the court or imposed by operation of law (any sentence of confinement or punitive discharge of an enlisted man automatically reduced the accused to the lowest enlisted grade, E-1, by operation of law).

If the Convening Authority accepted this plea bargain, the worst my client could get was three months' confinement, reduction from E-9 to E-7, and forfeiture of two-thirds of his pay for three months. Restriction to limits, extra duty, and/or a reprimand were also possible, but unlikely. Thus, after three months of confinement, he could retire as an E-7 at three-fourths of E-7 pay. Not as good as three-fourths of E-9 pay, but far better than nothing if he got a punitive discharge and no retirement or next-to-nothing if he was not awarded a punitive discharge but reduced all the way down to E-1.

I also sweetened the pot by saying that, if we got the plea bargain, we would go judge alone, so that the Convening Authority did not have to take his senior officers away from their important duties to sit as court members. Military law disfavored putting waivers of one's right to trial by court members in plea bargains, which only resulted in informal agreements to do so. And P.D. and I had researched the military judge and wanted him to do the sentencing anyway, for reasons that I will detail when we get to that point.

Lieutenant Ryan seized on this like a gift from God. Jail time was possible! He said that he would recommend the plea bargain and get back to me.

I later learned that the Chief Trial Counsel said that he would not recommend the plea bargain to the staff judge advocate and that the latter said that he would not recommend it to the admiral.

Now, the good trial counsel was between a rock and a hard place. The witnesses were on their way from the States, and if they got here and if the judge granted the motion for funding defense witnesses, the trial would have to be continued for a month or more, they would have to be sent home at government expense and there was no money to bring them back again. And he knew that the mother was already pissed at having to yank her daughter out of school and would really be pissed when she learned that it was for nothing—that the trial had been continued. So Lieutenant Ryan did the unthinkable for a military officer. He went not only over his boss's head but also over the head of his boss's boss—the SJA. He went to the admiral's quarters, barged in on him at breakfast, and sold the deal. Although going over his boss's head was a career killer, the trial counsel had the consolation of thinking, "That will teach them to call me back from my honeymoon." And because he had asked me whether I might have an opening for a young associate while we had been at the base for the Article 32 hearing, I didn't think that he was planning on a long Navy career anyway.

Our client wasn't thrilled at pleading to anything, but ultimately agreed that the risk reward ratio favored pleading guilty to communicating lewd and lascivious language to another (not necessarily to a child because we convinced the trial counsel that one has no way of knowing whether the party on the other end of an internet conversation is who they say they are; men pass themselves off as women on the internet and vice versa; children pass themselves off as adults). And the deal preserved most of his pension. I had offered to plead to this charge because I didn't think that the military judge was too likely to get that upset about a bachelor talking dirty in emails—especially when he was also presiding over a court-martial involving a brutal rape of young girl in Okinawa. The email paled in comparison.

So instead of pursing all of my motions, we pled Master Chief Noma guilty to one specification of communicating lewd and lascivious language to another. Under the plea bargain, the government had to dismiss the other charges if the military judge accepted the plea. We had filed the motions even though we knew that we were going to plead guilty because we wanted the military judge to see how hairy the case would be if he didn't accept the plea. The military judge appeared somewhat confused as to how two pages of charges ended up being a guilty plea to just one charge—and far from the most serious—charge. But he didn't seem all that upset as he contemplated having the week he had blocked out for the trial free and not having to rule on all of the motions. Maybe he could go shopping with the Article 32 Investigating Officer.

Lieutenant Ryan was still so pissed at being hauled away from his bride before consummating the marriage that he did not put on any evidence in aggravation—why our client should get a punitive discharge or some jail time. But we put on great evidence in mitigation—why our client shouldn't really be punished at all. First, we put on his boss, a lieutenant commander, who testified that he would immediately take him back in grade—in other words, no jail time, no reduction in rank, no discharge. He also pointed out that the duty assignment that Master Chief Noma had had for a year while awaiting trial was punishment in and of itself—the second senior enlisted man in the Navy being reduced to sweeping floors and hauling out garbage. Two other witnesses testified the same way. Lieutenant Ryan didn't even bother to cross-examine them.

We also introduced Master Chief Noma's retirement papers, which I had had him submit even though the Navy would not process them while he was pending charges. Shades of Master Sergeant Nutter, whom I had also caused to submit retirement papers. I wanted the judge to know that, if he didn't slam-dunk my Master Chief Noma, he was going to be out of the Navy anyway and that it would be civilian authorities who had to worry about whether he talked about what experimental positions he would like to try with (hopefully) an adult woman over the internet—which communications (and positions) were probably not even illegal under civilian law.

Finally, we put our client on for a sworn statement. In one sense, this tactic was defense counsel heresy. You didn't put your client on for a sworn statement because that exposed him to cross-examination and, if he said anything untrue, the trial counsel who didn't get as severe a conviction and sentence as he wanted could then get payback by charging the accused with perjury. In this case, he wasn't going to say anything that would perjure him, and I didn't think that the trial counsel was motivated enough to cross-examine him. And the judge might be more impressed by a sworn statement than an unsworn one.

As I said, we had wanted to go judge alone rather than have a military jury sentence our client. Why? We had researched the judge and found that he was a frustrated Admiral Nimitz or Spruance. He loved naval operational matters. So we planned to have our client testify about his career—entirely proper and admissible on sentencing—so that the judge would be sitting there masturbating at all the operational details. Under my respectful questioning, Master Chief Noma recounted such highlights of his career as taking the first nuclear carrier into Subic Bay in the Philippines. This feat had required months of planning and work, including dredging the harbor to make it deep enough that the pride of the Navy's carrier fleet did not run aground. Running aground might ruin the welcoming ceremony in which the President of the Philippines would be piped aboard and given the VIP tour.

Then, I had him recount how he would be helicoptered to a nuclear carrier that was about to enter Tokyo Bay and go to the bridge, relieve the captain of his command, and take the carrier up the bay, dodging the outgoing oil supertankers, and make a hard a-port to dock in Yokosuka, timing his turn so that the carrier was not cut in two by an outgoing oil supertanker. He brooked no argument from the crew—if he said, "Hard a-port," they'd better damn well start spinning the steering wheel or however one turned a nuclear carrier. Probably with a computer joystick or mouse nowadays or, God forbid, some kind of iPod. We could believe that he took no shit even though he was not a commissioned officer and as many as a dozen officers might be on the bridge at the time by the way he back seat drove when P.D. was driving. P.D. had an international driver's license, so Master Chief Noma would let him drive at times when we were going out to dinner. When P.D. would hesitate, Noma would bark out, "Stick your prow out there, P.D."

The military judge was entranced by this testimony and other stories about our harbor pilot's career. I had him conclude by asking him how he felt about ending his career in this manner.

"Sir, when I was a mere seaman, scraping rust off of the hull of a carrier, I never thought that I would have the honor of piloting one. I wish that the last days of my career would have involved taking a ship up Tokyo Bay one last time rather than sitting in a warehouse and sweeping its floors because I thought with my dick instead of with my head. I apologize to the Navy and the command for my actions. I assure Your Honor that I will bring no more discredit on the Naval Service."

After we had rested, the trial counsel did not put on any rebuttal evidence. So the only evidence that the military judge had to help him arrive at an appropriate sentence was that in the last few months of 30 years of perfect service, he, a bachelor, told an apparently willing female email correspondent what activities they might engage in when they got together after she had initiated that line of chat. The only Naval officer witnesses testified that they would take him back in grade, admissible evidence for "don't give him a dishonorable or bad conduct discharge."

And when it came for argument on an appropriate sentence, the trial counsel merely said, "The government is certain that the military judge will arrive at an appropriate sentence"—an absolute license to impose a very lenient sentence.

Because my bank account sentencing argument had worked very well in the past, I saw no reason to depart from it in this case. It boiled down to recounting all of the deposits that Master Chief Noma had made into the account over a thirty-year career in the Naval Service and argued that the one minor withdrawal hardly wiped out all of the deposits. Oops, maybe I shouldn't have talked about deposits and withdrawals in a case in which the conviction was for lewd and lascivious language communicated to another, but the judge didn't seem to pick up on the innuendo. And if he did, it hardly affected the sentence adversely. He sentenced my client to a reprimand. The only lighter sentences would have been "no sentence" or a sentence "to be admonished" (warned not to do it again). So my quite happy client would retire as a Master Chief E-9 with his pension intact and no troublesome confinement to serve. Not a bad result when he had started out facing a dishonorable discharge and sixty-five years of confinement.

Our client was so happy that the next morning he got P.D. and me a tour of the USS John S. McCain (DDG56), an Arleigh Burke Class, Aegis guided missile destroyer that was home ported at Yokosuka Navy Base. As we arrived at the ship, which was docked for repairs, I was surprised to see an honor guard of sailors by the gangplank or whatever you called the thing that you walked up to get from the dock aboard the ship. As Master Chief Noma led us past the honor guard, I heard a whistle—apparently, from the bosun, if I remembered my favorite naval movies correctly—followed by the announcement, "Lieutenant Colonel James Thomas, U.S. Army Retired, arriving." All of the sailors saluted, and I strode up the plank as if I were Admiral Nimitz arriving to take command of the Pacific Fleet. I remembered, again prompted by Hollywood, to salute the quarterdeck and ask permission to come aboard.

One of our client's friends was a master chief on the ship—at least I hope that it was a ship and not a boat—and he gave us the VIP tour. I used to have every security clearance known to man, including security clearances whose very name was secret, but having been retired for a decade, they were no longer good. But my lack of a security clearance didn't seem to stop our tour guide from showing us the Combat Information Center (CIC) and the Fire Direction Center (FDC) and explaining how they could track 200 aircraft simultaneously, tell friend from foe, and target the foe. I won't go into any more detail even though you can probably read how they do so in *Popular Mechanics*. Anyway, I was impressed.

As we left the ship, we proudly wore the blue and gold hats with the scrambled eggs on the brim, presented to us on board. Mine read "USS John S. McCain DDG-56" on the front, "James A-Team" on the back, and "Motion Master" on the side. P.D.'s was the same, except for his name above "A-Team" and "Pimp Master" on the side for his brilliant job of pimping the trial counsel while I cranked out the motions.

And so I've at least temporarily departed my career as a JAGC-Off—at least until some other accused service member with a little bit of money wants to hire a real JAGC-Off, retired or not.

About the Author

Jonathan P. Tomes is a retired U.S. Army JAG Corps officer. Before he was a JAGC-Off, however, he was an Infantry platoon leader in Vietnam and then a Military Intelligence officer in West Germany. He received the Silver Star, the Combat Infantry Badge, and the Legion of Merit, among other awards. He was also a military prosecutor, a military defense counsel, and a military judge. He is the author of *Servicemember's Legal Guide,* now in its 5th edition, published by Stackpole Books, Harrisburg, PA, and *Lawful Orders,* published by Veterans Press. While he was still on active duty, he taught military law at the U.S. Army Command & General Staff College at Fort Leavenworth, Kansas.

Jon is now a civilian attorney practicing in the greater Kansas City area in the law firm of TOMES & DVORAK, CHARTERED. Jon is a skilled attorney, having litigated hundreds of cases, including courts-martial, civilian federal and state cases, administrative board hearings, medical malpractice cases, Public Health Service disciplinary actions, Merit Systems Protection Board cases, physician discipline, and criminal cases. He is a member of the Illinois, Oklahoma, Kansas, and Missouri bars and the federal district courts for the Northern District of Illinois (Trial Bar), the District of Kansas, and the Western District of Missouri, U.S. Court of Appeals for the 5th, 7th, 8th, 10th, and Federal Circuits, and the U.S. Supreme Court.

Jon is also President of EMR Legal, Inc., which provides HIPAA consulting nationwide, and of Veterans Press, which publishes HIPAA compliance materials, including books, training videos, and the *HIPAA Documents Resource Center CD* (now in its 4th edition). He is also a nationally recognized authority and an expert witness on the legal requirements for health information, having written the following books, among others: *The Compliance Guide to HIPAA and the HHS Regulations* (now in its 4th edition) and *Electronic Health Records: A Practical Compliance Guide* (now in its 2d edition), both for Veterans press.

Email him at jon@tomesdvorak.com or call him at 913-385-7990, ext. 306.